THE PERFECT STORM

BOOK ONE:
THE PERFECT STORM

Legacy

*Mothers of Gifted Daughters
Share Their Wisdom*

Lea Stublarec

MSW, Certified Parent Coach

LUMINARE PRESS
WWW.LUMINAREPRESS.COM

Legacy: The Perfect Storm
Copyright © 2024 by Lea Stublarec

All rights reserved. This book or any portion thereof may not be reproduced or used in any manner whatsoever without the express written permission of the author, except for the use of brief quotations in a book review.

Printed in the United States of America

Luminare Press
442 Charnelton St.
Eugene, OR 97401
www.luminarepress.com

LCCN: 2024917135
ISBN: 979-8-88679-673-5

*To my gifted mother and my hero,
Ann M. Stublarec, and to all the gifted women
who gave so generously of their time and wisdom*

Contents

Preface 3
Introduction 33

PART 1: GENDER
Historical Perspective on Gender 37
The Role of Gender in the Perfect Storm 50

PART 2: FEMALE GIFTEDNESS
Historical Overview 63
The Role of Female Giftedness in the Perfect Storm . . . 74

PART 3: MOTHERHOOD AND GIFTED WOMEN
Historical Overview 141
Gifted Motherhood's Role in the Perfect Storm 213
Challenges within the Family 250
Challenges outside the Family 272
Challenges Finding Professional Support 304
Self-Actualizing for Gifted Mothers in
the Perfect Storm 320

Conclusion 353
Bibliography 357
Acknowledgments 377

"And once the storm is over, you won't remember how you made it through, how you managed to survive. You won't even be sure whether the storm is really over. But one thing is certain. When you come out of the storm, you won't be the same person who walked in."

—HARUKI MURAKAMI, *Kafka on the Shore*

PREFACE

RAISING GIFTED DAUGHTERS IS AN ADVENTURE. AFTER raising my two daughters (one highly gifted and one twice exceptional—gifted and dyslexic) and experiencing all the agony, ecstasy, and thrills that entails, I decided to coach parents of gifted daughters. I wanted to share in the excitement of their experience, collaborate with them on learning more about bright females, maximize the joy in their parenting journey, and work together to figure out how to best disrupt the system so both their own and their daughter's giftedness could thrive—something my girls and I would have benefited from when they were growing up.

But first, I thought it best to venture outside my personal experience to learn how others had nurtured their gifted girls in a culture not conducive to fostering bright females. My hope by doing this was to enhance my coaching practice and to share the insights of veteran gifted mothers of gifted girls with those currently raising gifted daughters (and, honestly, to return to research, my comfort zone).

Through in-depth interviews, I had the pleasure of hearing about the triumphs, challenges, and joys of raising a successful gifted daughter in a society that too often ignores the insights of mothers. And I quickly realized that like their daughters, these women were also gifted. The resulting trilogy of books offers a chance to learn about the hopes, dreams, and day-to-day reality of these forty-three women and how they parented. The trilogy highlights a key theme common to all these mothers' stories: the women were heroes who rose to the challenge of effectively nurturing female genius by "poking" the patriarchal, anti-intellectual society in which they lived. In the process, they were transformed, enabling not only their daughters but also themselves to thrive.

VOICELESS

Mothers represent a silent subculture in the world of giftedness and society in general. For the most part, they have neither a voice nor an arena in which to share their perspective, or if they do, their opinions are often ignored or unheard. Raising a successful gifted daughter in our anti-intellectual, misogynistic culture is a huge achievement. Despite this, the wisdom of women who have done so is often lost.

Learning what mothers do to nurture female intellectual potential is critical to building a more highly functional and inclusive society that maximizes the historically untapped resource of female genius. The wisdom of these experienced mothers is invaluable to younger parents of gifted children, especially given today's lack of the extended family ties in which elders could share what they'd learned through the years. Mothers of gifted offspring who have gone before can demystify the process and highlight the joys for women currently raising gifted children. They can prepare them for possible minefields as well as help them find solid ground on their parenting journey, and they can offer much-needed hope to younger mothers going through tough times.

As we know, those who sit at the tables of power are typically white, male, and middle and upper class. They are not mothers. These individuals make decisions that affect the lives of those without a place at the table, defining "reality" for all. They determine whose needs are legitimate and where resources should be allocated. The insights and learnings of those most directly involved in maximizing the potential of gifted girls on a 24-7 basis—their mothers—are largely absent from these discussions.

DOCUMENTING AND SHARING THE STORIES OF MOTHERS who have successfully nurtured gifted daughters is critical for future gifted female offspring and society in general. Doing so helps us understand gifted females more fully, which fosters their well-being and makes it possible for them to contribute to and change society. Beyond this, the mothers themselves benefit from having their stories heard and their personal sense of well-being and fulfillment validated. Psychologist Daphne de Marneffe stresses in her book *Maternal Desire* that there is something unvoiced about the experience of motherhood itself, and she believes that this never raises the possibility that mothers experience themselves vividly and as makers of meaning, sometimes more in their mothering than in any other part of their lives.

AN UNSPEAKABLE LOSS

Even though sharing the narratives of parenting journeys would contribute to maximizing the quality of life for gifted girls, for society as a whole, and for the mothers themselves, their stories often go untold, and this invaluable resource remains untapped. As Annemarie Roeper, a pioneer in the gifted world, put it in her book *The "I" of the Beholder,* "What opportunities do we miss by not hearing our elders and what heightened experiences do they miss by us not allowing them to play their appropriate role in society? How much wisdom goes down the drain unused?"

BY DISREGARDING HOW MOTHERS NURTURE GIFTED daughters and failing to remove societal obstacles to maximizing female giftedness, our society historically has squandered half of its intellectual and creative potential. Looking back over the lives of our female ancestors (many of whom were gifted), how much do we know about them as individuals or how they felt about motherhood? How few of our intergenerational family narratives consider how these women felt about their lives or whether their perspectives were ever taken into account? How much do we know about the struggles they faced being gifted in a society that provided little opportunity to women with high potential? Most likely, the majority suffered the injustice of having their personal experiences denied and hidden from communal understanding. As a result, the wealth of knowledge about the benefits and challenges related to being female, gifted, and raising gifted children has gone undocumented.

Often, the life experiences of gifted mothers who have raised gifted daughters are minimized or ignored. As a result, they have no framework for understanding the uniqueness of their lives as well as their daughters as neurodivergent females. When a society refuses to acknowledge the voices of gifted females in the public arena, it fails to develop language to enable them to describe the reality of their outside-the-box parenting situation. It is therefore nearly impossible for them to communicate, or to prepare proactively for, the challenges many gifted females face.

This situation can lead a gifted individual to feel isolated and like a failure as she struggles to adjust in a more neurotypical world. It can create the context for "gaslighting" (where one's sense of reality is twisted to the point of confusion and self-doubt). Rather than a gifted mother believing in herself, trusting her intuition, and claiming her truth, she is led to believe what others (often more neurotypical individuals with no experience raising a gifted daughter) claim "should" be her reality—causing her to feel confused, unsure of herself, and too ashamed to speak up.

Unfortunately, as women age, they are increasingly disempowered and often made to feel invisible, which makes it even more difficult for them to feel valued and respected. The belief that elders can enlighten and guide younger generations has gone by the wayside (exacerbated in recent years by younger generations relying more and more on social media for news, companionship, entertainment, solace, and "wisdom"). As a result, many senior parents have lost the wise elder status within the family and are no longer viewed as a valuable resource in transmitting life skills, expertise, or social connection. Although there are exceptions, like a number of cases within my sample, typically older mothers and grandmothers have become dispensable in a society increasingly focused on electronic communication, mass media, materialism, and acquisition.

A lack of communal understanding about the reality of the lives of gifted mothers and their gifted offspring limits society's awareness of their challenges and needs. Not surprisingly, this lack of understanding also diminishes society's willingness to distribute resources that might address these concerns. Realizing that our silence as gifted mothers negatively impacts getting the community support that we so desperately need to help ourselves and our gifted daughters is a big motivator to encourage us to find our voice. There is no guarantee that the powers that be will listen, but anything has to be better than suffering in silence and hoping the challenges of nurturing female potential will resolve themselves. Staying quiet continues to oppress all of us as gifted females and squashes our high potential.

WHY?

Gifted mothers inhabit three categories of identity that are generally not granted power: femaleness, giftedness, and motherhood. Cultural attitudes toward these key attributes comprise a perfect storm that negatively impacts the ability of these mothers and, as a result, their daughters to flourish. Under these adverse conditions, gifted females in our society struggle to maximize their potential.

Sadly, gifted mothers often attribute our inability to be heard and thrive to our own weaknesses when the root of the problem typically stems from our culture. The insidious and pervasive discrimination against females, the stifling of female giftedness, and the low status assigned to motherhood in our society means that many gifted mothers come to think that their lack of voice, power, and significance is the result of their isolated choices and personal limitations rather than the perfect storm in which they must try to function. Furthermore, because this socialization has been so effective, we often keep ourselves in check in order to fit constraining cultural norms and tend to judge most harshly other females (often including our own gifted daughters) who don't hold back.

THE POWER OF OUR STORIES

As mothers of gifted daughters, we plumb the depths of the female gifted experience (to paraphrase Dr. Linda Silverman) not only from our own experiences growing up gifted but also from our parenting. As mothers, we are typically given primary responsibility for raising our gifted girls, which includes the challenge of nurturing their high potential. Given the special needs of many gifted children, this is no small task! As a result, mothers hold a unique and holistic view of what it's like to be female and gifted, which frequently takes into painful account the reality that these attributes can positively and negatively impact all aspects of life for our gifted daughters and ourselves.

The value of this perspective is demonstrated by the Indian fable about the blind men and the elephant. (I appreciate that this analogy has been overused in various contexts, but please bear with me, as I think it may be most applicable to this one!) In this parable, the men touch the elephant to learn what it is like. Each man feels a different part and only that one part. When asked to describe what an elephant looks like, the one who felt the leg says the animal is like a pillar, the one who felt the ear describes the elephant as being like a fan, and the one who felt the trunk says the elephant is like a rope. Many professionals who focus on gifted typically base their notion of giftedness on "the particular part of the elephant" that they've experienced (i.e., as an educator, academic, counselor, therapist, psychologist, or researcher). Unlike these individuals, parents, especially mothers, "feel the whole elephant" (literally, many having carried their baby in utero) and care for the whole child's wide range of needs day in and day out. As the primary caregiver in most cases, they have a deep emotional, physiological/hormonal connection to the child via a relationship that lasts a lifetime. Not to minimize the value of professionals working with gifted individuals and appreciating the fact that we are all members of the same tribe—sharing a passion to nurture the needs of gifted—I believe it's critically important to encourage and empower those who have the primary responsibility for raising gifted children, especially gifted daughters, and to welcome their insights into the giftedness arena. This view was echoed by a mother in the study who has two adult gifted daughters and is also a teacher of gifted: "I really listen to parents [of the gifted students I teach], because the teachers I talked to would never believe that my twice-exceptional daughter came home and cried every day after school, because she was always upbeat at school and very cooperative. Starting in the third grade, she would sit on my lap and cry every day—she hated school and begged me to stay home and teach her."

Being empowered to share our personal experiences and insights as gifted mothers with professionals working with gifted children has great potential to enhance the outcomes of their efforts. Perhaps even more important, it demonstrates to our daughters that our ideas as gifted women and mothers have value despite being devalued by society at large. As one mother stated, finding our voice, and embracing our wisdom gives "our gifted girls permission to know their own power, outside of any cultural or societal constraints that are designed to control the masses, so that individual gifted female leaders can emerge." As author Ursula K. Le Guin stated in a commencement address at Bryn Mawr College in 1986, "We [women] are volcanoes. When we offer our experience as our truth, the human truth, all the maps change."

THE GOALS OF THIS STUDY

I began this study to learn how other mothers like myself had raised their gifted girls. I wanted to learn what parenting strategies they found most helpful and what they would do differently in hindsight. I sought to get below the surface of small talk by having long, deep, intimate discussions over two to three weeks to uncover the key details of what this journey involved for each mother. I hoped to be able to share their stories about what mothering successful gifted daughters in our culture involved. (A successful gifted daughter was defined as having graduated from college and currently pursuing her passion—more about these criteria later.)

Not only do these stories provide hope, given that their gifted adult daughters are thriving, they also provide a connection across the generations to let younger mothers know they're not alone. They are part of a larger community of gifted women who've gone before them and who are driven to lighten the load of mothers currently raising gifted girls by sharing what they learned. The mothers in this study provide a sense of the big picture in terms of what raising a gifted female involves. Their stories emphasize what is important over the long haul, serving as reminders that life is long and that our daughters are in our care for only a short part of it. Being able to look back on their parenting journey enabled these women to judge what truly mattered. David Foster Wallace, in his 2005 commencement address at Kenyon College, touched on the importance of this larger perspective by sharing an amusing anecdote: "There are these two young fish swimming along and they happen to meet an older fish swimming the other way, who nods at them and says, 'Morning, boys. How's the water?' And the two young fish swim on for a bit, and then eventually one of them looks over at the other and goes 'What the hell is water?'"

Wallace went on to say that important realities are often the ones hardest to see. To paraphrase Janet Penley, author of *MotherStyles*, the perspectives of these veteran mothers, having come through it all, offer a better sense of what matters in mothering gifted daughters when the cheerios are swept from the floor and the last high school sweatshirt is sent off to Goodwill.

My primary goal for this study is to help younger women raising gifted daughters, but in the course of the interviews, the fascinating personal stories of the gifted mothers themselves emerged. Therefore, a secondary goal of the study became discovering their salient childhood experiences and how they attempted to meet their special needs for self-actualization while raising their daughters at the same time. As a result, these data provide a rich description of how gifted female potential has been nurtured (and in a few sad cases, stifled) across generations.

Finally, these in-depth interviews offered the mothers a rare chance to tell their stories. Each was invited to tell, in its entirety, the story of how she raised her gifted girl or girls (the highs and lows, successes and failures). Their audience was an interested, objective listener (me!) with no agenda other than to document their experiences, greatest learnings, and wisdom.

Parents of gifted children frequently struggle with challenges outside the norm, but they often find it difficult to discuss these struggles, as well as instances when their gifted child shines, with parents of more neurotypical children and friends or relatives unfamiliar with giftedness. Again, our culture's anti-intellectual message—to not brag about your child's intellectual accomplishments—often permeates social interactions. As a result, many mothers learn to suppress their enthusiasm and downplay their gifted daughter's accomplishments in these settings. In many instances, the amazing accomplishments of their gifted daughters remain well-guarded secrets. Sadly, this results in these mothers feeling isolated and repressed, unable to connect with the sources of support available to other parents in their community.

Fortunately, during the interviews, the gifted mothers were able to "brag" freely about their amazing gifted daughters, share their parenting joys, and authentically present all their daughters' brilliant achievements to someone in awe (again, me) of what they and their daughters had accomplished. Maybe even more important, the interviews provided a number of mothers an opportunity to process some difficult experiences they encountered when their girls went through extremely tough times growing up. Some of these included bouts of depression, anxiety attacks, anorexia, overeating, underachievement, dropping out of school, self-injury, trichotillomania, seizures, running away from home, chronic allergic reactions, vitiligo, assuming false identities, and substance abuse. Given that the mothers and daughters overcame these challenges and went on to thrive offers hope to women currently raising gifted daughters. Even though the parenting journey presented challenging bumps, it was possible to overcome them and, for both mothers and daughters, to grow stronger in the process.

Although the women in this study hoped to help mothers raising gifted girls by sharing their parenting journey, they strongly believed that younger mothers should trust their inner wisdom and take from their stories only what's universal and true for them. Paraphrasing Gloria Steinem in *Revolution from Within*, these stories were shared in much the same spirit that explorers share maps to demystify the terrain and inform others about possible minefields as well as solid ground (knowing that the journey each mother of a gifted daughter makes will be uniquely her own). Ideally, this book provides the opportunity for younger mothers of gifted daughters to explore the challenges and choices of gifted mothers who went before them, learn from them, value them, and then venture off to make their own parenting decisions, surrendering any cultural notions of how parenting "should" be in order to appreciate and celebrate how perfectly imperfect and wonderful things really are. I think I speak for the women who participated in this study, giving so generously of their time, and opening their hearts during our interviews, by sharing the words of Karen Maezen Miller in *Momma Zen*: "These words thus flow from my heart to yours, from one other mother to one other mother. I know. I understand. Me too…Learn nothing from this story except to see how things go for you. Do not expect them to go the way they did for me. Do not have any expectations about how things will go. Simply look, listen, wait and trust. Then, just in time and right on schedule, you'll know for yourself."

OVERVIEW OF THE WOMEN IN THE STUDY

The mothers interviewed for this study ranged in age from forty-six to seventy-five (most were in their fifties and sixties) and were highly educated—93 percent had bachelor's degrees, and 70 percent had graduate degrees. Thirty-eight of the mothers were engaged in income-producing work during some period while their daughters were growing up. The five women who were not were actively involved in volunteer work, and two of them homeschooled their daughters. However, as De Marneffe points out in *Maternal Desire*, the mainstream notion about dichotomies between "working" and "stay-at-home" mothers often don't ring true, as shown in this sample. Many of the women seemed to continually evaluate the economic, practical, and emotional needs of their family as well as their own need to self-actualize. They went in and out of the workforce depending upon access to job opportunities, resources, and sources of support. These rigid role classifications often didn't prove applicable to the realities of their lives.

Specifically, for those who did income-producing work (including those who worked only before and after their children were raised), nearly 70 percent were involved in education, and half of these women were involved in the gifted and talented field. Many of those in education were teachers, while the remaining women included two college professors, five college administrators, and six in administration at the kindergarten through grade 12 level. Ten of the mothers had been involved in business, including five who were in science, technology, engineering, and mathematics (STEM) positions, and four of the women were authors. Ten mothers were retired at the time of the interviews. A majority had held a variety of positions over the course of their work history, with one mother listing more than a dozen different career "lives" and still counting!

About one in five of the mothers had one child, nearly half had two, and a third had three or more children. Of these, fifty-eight were included in the study sample of adult gifted daughters. One surprisingly still energetic woman raised seven gifted children ("the last batch a blessed accident") and was providing care for her many gifted grandchildren. Along these lines, nearly half of the forty-three women interviewed were grandmothers.

The fifty-eight gifted daughters ranged in age from twenty-one to fifty (most were in their late twenties to early forties). They were slightly more educated than their mothers (100 percent were college graduates, and 75 percent had, or were pursuing, graduate degrees), and almost half had children themselves. Five of the daughters had two graduate degrees: one had an MD/PhD, one had an MA/MBA, one had a PhD and was currently in law school, and two had a JD/MA). Seven of the daughters had a PhD, five had MDs, one had a JD, one was a DVM candidate, and ten were pursuing a PhD. This level of education seemed notably high, especially given the daughters' relatively young age.

Research conducted by the Gifted Development Center and described in Silverman's article, "What We Have Learned About Gifted Children," found that parents' IQ scores are usually within ten points of their children's. Therefore, not surprisingly, nearly all (if not all) of the sampled mothers were also gifted. Like their daughters, this was supported by IQ scores, enrollment in gifted education classes and/or outstanding academic accolades, and professional achievements. Combining the pool of forty-three mothers with their fifty-eight gifted adult daughters resulted in rich data on 101 successful gifted females.

Unfortunately, the study sample was not diverse in terms of race and ethnicity. Nearly all the mothers and forty-nine of the fifty-eight daughters were white. There was more geographic diversity across the cases. While three of the mothers lived outside the United States, the remaining forty mothers were scattered across the country. Seven raised their families in rural areas. A majority of the daughters grew up in suburban communities or urban centers, and a few spent part of their childhoods living outside the country. While 93 percent of the mothers were married at the time of the interviews, more than half mentioned experiencing marital problems while their children were growing up. In fact, one mother in four was single at some point while raising her daughter. Half of this subset of mothers mentioned experiencing serious financial stress during this period. Conversely, nearly 20 percent were in upper-middle or upper-class income brackets. This economic diversity seemed to confirm the theory that giftedness crosses all income levels.

Another limitation with the sample related to the fact that the internet was not around, for the most part, when the sampled daughters were growing up, so the influence of social networks on gifted girls was not an issue that these mothers needed to address. However, this represents both a positive and a negative factor given that a number of interviewed mothers mentioned their ongoing struggle to access information that their curious daughters craved.

The fifty-eight daughters had careers that were more diverse than the sample of mothers. This is most likely due to the way the sample was collected (more about this in the next section) but also to the greater career opportunities available to females born after the second wave of feminism in the late sixties and seventies. Twenty-six of the fifty-eight daughters were involved in STEM-related fields. Specifically, six were doctors, one was completing her DVM residency, one was a marine biologist, two were engineers, one was a college professor in biology/genetics, one was completing a postdoctoral degree in bioinformatics, two were computer specialists, one was a web designer, two were nurse practitioners, two were radiology/MRI specialists, and one was a high school calculus teacher. The remaining daughters were currently in STEM-related fields in graduate school.

For those in fields not related to STEM, three of the daughters were college professors, two were attorneys, three were corporate executives, one was a financial consultant, one was a high school English teacher and gifted education coordinator, one was an attorney teaching high school English, three worked for nonprofit organizations, and one was conducting graduate-funded research in Asia. There was one journalist, one playwright, one graphic artist, one real estate broker, one director of a national law enforcement agency, and one working for an insurance company. Six of the daughters were in school full time (one was in law school, three were PhD candidates, and two were master's candidates).

Twenty-five of the daughters were themselves mothers. Only four of these were not engaged in income-producing work or in school at the time of data collection. For each of these daughters, it seems this was a proactive choice, as one of the interviewees stated, because their primary passion was caring for their children (several of whom were profoundly gifted). Only one daughter was not employed and did not have children at the time of the interviews. Her mother shared that after getting two master's degrees and being successful in three different professional careers, this highly gifted daughter was struggling with multipotentiality—in other words, the paradox of choice. As a result, she was unclear about her next best choice of career. Five of the daughters with children were single; thirteen were single and didn't have children at the time of the interviews. Ten of the daughters were divorced, and four of these were remarried. More than half of the daughters were married (twenty-one) or living with a partner (nine).

Turning to the issue of whether the daughters were, in fact, pursuing their passion, for nearly 70 percent, this was clearly the case, according to their mothers. For the remaining eighteen daughters, the degree to which they were pursuing their passion seemed to fall along a spectrum and was influenced by a number of different factors. In other words, not too surprisingly, like most things in life, it was complicated, and following one's dream was often a process, not easy to accurately describe with a yes/no response.

The 30 percent of daughters struggling to pursue their dream had myriad reasons for working in jobs not related to what they loved most. Many were employed in jobs that offered a better quality of life in terms of salary, hours, and/or location than jobs in their preferred career. These jobs helped to pay bills, were a better fit with the needs of their families, or allowed them to evaluate career options more aligned with their calling while still being productive. These gifted daughters' professional struggles are typical of the challenges many gifted women face. Documenting these struggles is critical to ensuring that we don't "airbrush reality" for this demographic; this will be explored in more detail throughout the trilogy.

Some daughters in this group faced career limitations because they prioritized the needs of their partners or offspring. One of these young women attended graduate school abroad, fell in love with someone from the country where she studied, and found herself without a green card that would allow her to be employed in her field. She earned money by working at a bike shop (she did, in fact, love cycling) and volunteered as a community organizer (her primary passion). Another daughter was a single mother of a toddler in a high-cost urban area, working full time as a successful sales representative for a global corporation and trying to save money to attend school to become a nurse practitioner. One of the daughters was pregnant with a second child and caring for her profoundly gifted son. She shared that she wanted to quit her flexible nursing job to study psychology related to giftedness, but money and childcare constraints made this impossible. Another daughter worked at home but struggled to find time for her career because she was homeschooling her profoundly gifted son and caring for two other gifted children. One daughter with a PhD didn't earn tenure at the small college in her rural area but couldn't move because her ex-husband (the father of her teen) would not allow it. This young woman hoped to leave the area to follow her passion when her daughter went to college. A final example was a daughter whose husband was in the military. After moving often with a small child, they lived overseas on a military base in a country with limited childcare options and job opportunities.

Financial constraints were another common reason for the subset of daughters struggling to pursue their passions. One example was the daughter working as a highly paid web designer; she wanted to pay off her undergraduate and graduate school loans after she was forced to leave a nonprofit job she loved that didn't pay enough. Another daughter graduated from law school, was on the partner track at a law firm, and was earning a good salary. She was struggling to follow her passion by doing as much pro bono work as possible with the hope of eventually getting the firm to fund a full-time pro bono position.

Several of the eighteen daughters not pursuing their passion suffered from physical limitations or health issues that thwarted their dreams. For example, several mothers cited their daughters' severe allergies as a chronic challenge that forced them to focus more on self-care than their career. One mother described her older daughter's health history, stating that "she had chronic sinus infections that never got resolved until she was…in college, where a new doctor decided to take a CT scan and found that her whole maxillary sinus was still infected after months of treatment and immediately scheduled surgery. To be in chronic pain was just horrid and interfered a lot with her dreams." This daughter suffered from another difficult health concern that was kept off the record, and her mother believed that if her daughter's health had been more stable, she could have done everything that she wanted to do. As it was, she needed to rest a lot and maintain a strict, healthy diet. A second mother pointed out that her daughter's passion was to be a vet because of her love for animals, but her many serious allergies made this impossible.

Another daughter was gifted athletically and intellectually but was unable to follow her dream given the limited opportunities available for women in professional sports. Although she earned a PhD in engineering and was employed by a bioengineering firm, she shared that she would quit in a minute if the opportunity to play professional sports was available. She had been a star at a Division 1 college, but there was no professional women's team in her chosen sport when she graduated. Another daughter worked in the sexist culture on Wall Street; in part because she was paid less than her male peers, she quit to be a full-time mother to her three small children. At the time of the interviews, she was debating whether to return to her job on Wall Street, which she loved despite the macho environment, or to have a fourth child like her mother.

Finally, a musically gifted daughter, who had recently graduated from college, hoped to pursue her dream of singing in the opera but "clutched" (according to her mother) during several auditions for the extremely competitive positions. At the time of the interviews, she was working for an insurance company to pay her bills, doing part-time singing gigs, and continuing to take voice lessons.

NITTY GRITTY ABOUT THE STUDY

I was fortunate to have the help of two experts in giftedness on the study team. Dr. Carol Dweck, an internationally renowned professor of psychology at Stanford University, served as a scholarly eye during the design phase of the study, provided guidance regarding topics to address, suggested a subsample of daughters be interviewed, and shared her wisdom on documenting the study results. The second expert, Dr. Paula Wilkes, was a public school teacher for twenty-five years and a college professor in gifted education. Wilkes is currently in private practice and a specialist with Summit Center-Los Angeles, which provides assessment and support for gifted children. Wilkes provided ongoing support by analyzing the data along with me to ensure inter-rater reliability. She helped to enhance the study by encouraging me to incorporate the latest research and thinking in the gifted field.

I was fortunate to have the support of several organizations that serve gifted families (specifically Supporting the Emotional Needs of the Gifted, National Association for Gifted Children, California Association for the Gifted, and Gifted Homeschoolers Forum) that kindly publicized a request for study participants. The majority of women (twenty-nine) who made up the study sample responded to this plea for mothers of adult, college-educated, gifted daughters currently pursuing their passions. It should be noted that this resulted in sampling bias. As Andrew Solomon points out in his brilliant book *Far from the Tree*, "Parents willing to be interviewed are a self-selecting group; those who are bitter are less likely to tell their stories than those who have found value in their experience and want to help others in similar circumstances to do the same."

In addition to these self-selected participants, I personally solicited mothers who met the sampling criteria, having crossed paths with them professionally (in "gifted world") or while raising our daughters together. This was a group of thirteen women. Because I wanted to experience what it was like being on the other side of the table to improve my interviewing technique, one of the sampled mothers kindly offered to interview me early in the data collection process. I have included my responses in the sample, resulting in a total sample of forty-three mothers. About 25 percent of the mothers had more than one daughter who met the study criteria, so the sampled mothers described their experiences raising a total of fifty-eight gifted girls.

The selection criteria for the study participants were chosen in hopes of coming up with proxy measures for identifying mothers of "successful" adult gifted daughters. However, as we know, defining success for gifted adults, especially females, is a daunting and controversial topic. (Defining "success" for anyone leads one into very subjective territory!) Briefly, the study criteria included a proxy indicator of success, at least in academia (i.e., having a bachelor's degree), as well as a more subjective marker (targeting daughters pursuing their passion). As luck would have it, nearly all fifty-eight gifted adult daughters in the sample were highly functional members of society. These young women were out in the fray, taking risks, being productive, challenging themselves, learning, and struggling to reach their potential and find the best fit for their gifts in the world.

To avoid imposing the limits of my own notion of what qualified one as gifted, a wide net was used to define this term. Participants themselves shared the criteria used to identify giftedness in their daughters. In *Smart Girls: A New Psychology of Girls, Women and Giftedness*, psychologist Dr. Barbara Kerr validates using parental assessments of a child's giftedness, stating: "In fact, my experience has been that parents who suspect their child is gifted are correct 99 percent of the time, making parental judgment one of the best assessments around."

Virtually every mother interviewed offered overwhelming evidence of her daughter's high intellectual ability, often beginning early in the girl's life. This seemed to support what the Gifted Development Center learned over the past thirty years: parents are excellent identifiers of giftedness in their children. For 77 percent (forty-five) of the fifty-eight daughters in the sample, IQ scores were known, with a range from moderately to profoundly gifted, and/or the daughters had been involved in gifted programs at their public schools. (According to NAGC, a gifted child's IQ will fall within these ranges: mildly gifted is 115 to 130; moderately gifted is 130 to 145; highly gifted is 145 to 160; and profoundly gifted is 160 or higher.) In seven of the remaining thirteen cases, the daughters had attended highly competitive private or parochial schools or were homeschooled because their exceptional educational needs were not met by the school system. The final six cases represented those who were twice exceptional, though, unfortunately, their giftedness was unidentified in their early school years. The reality that these six young women were in fact gifted became strikingly apparent as they progressed academically through college and beyond.

Each of the forty-three mothers participated in two one- to two-hour telephone interviews scheduled one to three weeks apart. The interviews were semistructured so the women could describe their parenting experiences in their own words while addressing key issues relevant to raising gifted girls. This enabled them to describe the uniqueness of their parenting journey, allowing new ideas and insights to emerge. In a few cases, the mothers preferred to share their narratives using their own framework with follow-up questions to ensure that targeted items were addressed at the end. This approach encouraged the active participation of the participants in the research process.

The general focus of each interview was based on a method called appreciative inquiry that I learned about from Gloria DeGaetano, CEO of the Parent Coaching Institute (PCI). The approach structures dialogue around discovering strengths and effective strategies (in other words, what works) rather than concentrating on weaknesses or diagnosing pathology. As a result, the interviews were, for the most part, positive, dynamic, powerful, and emotionally intense conversations with passionate, sensitive, caring, complex, thoughtful, and intentional individuals. These discussions were uplifting and inspiring and highlighted many participants' experiences of overcoming obstacles to nurture their gifted daughters. Many respondents shared the pride and joy they experienced in raising their gifted girls. Dweck suggested interviewing a subsample of daughters to document their insights on growing up gifted and to determine if their perspectives corroborated the data provided by their mothers. In nearly all of the twenty resulting interviews, this proved to be true with the exception of one daughter. This young woman shared information about an immediate family member's ongoing dysfunction that impacted the family and that, for whatever reason, her mother chose not to disclose. In addition, this same daughter stated that she and her mother had conflicting ideas about her career choice. Each of the twenty sampled daughters participated in a one-time-only interview that lasted about one hour. Neither the mother nor daughter in the twenty mother/daughter pairs were privy to the data each provided.

All 106 interviews (the two interviews for the forty-three mothers and the twenty interviews for the selected daughters) were audio recorded with their permission and transcribed verbatim. Each case was analyzed separately, followed by a cross-case analysis to integrate the findings and reveal recurring themes and informative outliers.

The overriding concern in sharing the data was to ensure that the privacy of the mothers and the daughters was protected and that the bond between the mothers and the twenty sampled daughters was not negatively impacted. To this end, all identifying information (names, places, school names, specific awards, accomplishments, etc.) were altered or deleted from the interview transcripts. In addition, the cases were assigned number codes, and draft transcripts were submitted to each interviewee to ensure accuracy and their comfort with the confidentiality measures taken. Any additional edits respondents recommended to further ensure confidentiality were incorporated into the final transcripts.

I am profoundly grateful to the women and daughters who so willingly, openly, and courageously shared not only their invaluable feelings, insights, struggles, hopes, and dreams but also their precious time. These women all lead lives packed full of meaning. As one mother in her seventies stated, "My friends are always saying that they're bored, but for me, there are never enough hours in the day." I sincerely hope my research effort is worthy of their incredible support and generosity. Their willingness to share their stories and, indeed, their lives with me and to be fully candid and self-disclosing allowed me to present a collective and authentic portrait of what's involved in nurturing gifted females. Being invited into their lives was a privilege and a pleasure.

Because of the huge quantity of data collected from 106 interviews as well as all the sources reviewed over many years of research, the study findings are presented in a trilogy. The first book, *The Perfect Storm,* highlights the challenges gifted mothers of gifted daughters face over the course of their lives. Because knowledge is power, having an awareness of the different obstacles and roadblocks common to gifted mothers will be empowering to those embarking on a parenting journey with their atypical child. And the fact that both the mothers and daughters not only overcame tough challenges but thrived offers hope to those currently raising gifted girls. The second book, *Conquering the Storm,* presents the various strategies and approaches respondents employed to overcome challenges, some proving successful and others not so much. The third and final book, *Celebration,* shares specific words of wisdom these women wanted to offer to younger mothers of gifted daughters. These include advice about what they would have done differently in hindsight and ways they celebrate what they have achieved including individual moments of joy, special times with their adult gifted daughters, and family times that honor their collective journey.

Given the large amount of rich data collected during the interviews, not all of the valuable insights and pearls shared by these women could be included in Book One. Although all the interview data helped to give this book greater depth and complexity, I was forced to include only the data that seemed to best fit with the major themes and findings in *The Perfect Storm*. However, most of the remaining insights shared by the interviewed mothers will, most likely, be included in Books Two and Three. In addition, the subsample of twenty daughters interviewed helped to enrich the study and ensure that the data provided by the mothers was reliable, but a detailed analysis of this data set will not be included in this trilogy.

FRUIT BASKET UPSET

After completing the interviews and compiling the results, I found myself in a quandary. My reason for conducting this study was to identify the most effective strategies the sampled mothers used to raise their gifted daughters. But what I found was that these women used a whole range of different parenting approaches and that many of the current cultural labels for parenting styles seemed to be covered in the sample. Those included hummingbird, helicopter, attachment, free range, gentle, permissive, and authoritative, to name just a few! In addition, some mothers found that the strategy or style used to nurture their eldest gifted daughter was inappropriate with subsequent daughters or no longer worked as the daughter advanced through different developmental stages. As a result, many of the mothers were continually tweaking their parenting strategies. Parenting is indeed a work in process.

The other contributing factors related to siblings, fathers, extended family, schools, and peer interactions added to the complexity of trying to figure out what worked. So, not surprisingly, given the organic and dynamic nature of children and families, it was very difficult to isolate and identify causal factors related to the best way to nurture female giftedness. Solomon notes in *Far from the Tree*, after his incredible study of families with atypical offspring, that the functional families he observed showed incredible diversity while dysfunctional families did not. He states, "I take the anti-Tolstoyan view that the unhappy families, who reject their variant children have much in common, while the happy ones, who strive to accept them, are happy in a multitude of ways." So, not too surprisingly, the parenting approaches these women used to raise their successful gifted daughters, in fact, represented fifty-eight unique ways to nurture female giftedness.

But by stepping back and using a wider, more holistic lens to look at the data, two key commonalities emerged. First, the sampled mothers deeply and proactively loved their daughters while raising them. Second, nearly every one of the sampled women wasn't afraid to speak her mind and challenge the system to support her gifted girl.

This is the key finding of the study—each of the sampled mothers overcame the cultural limitations placed on both them and their daughters, and each, in her own way, became a positive disruptor to meet her child's neurodiverse needs. These forty-three women basically threw out traditional parenting manuals and commonly accepted parenting wisdom (which, for the most part, proved irrelevant for raising gifted girls) and went off script. They poked at cultural limitations and boundaries and designed outside-the-box ways to get their daughters' special needs met in our not-too-supportive society. The parenting journeys of these brave women provide invaluable examples of the creativity, resilience, and courage necessary for nurturing female genius. The motivating factor for these women was love—both self-love and a deep love for their daughters. They exhibited the kind of love psychologist Scott Peck (which belle hooks refers to in *All About Love*) described as a verb, which demonstrates the will to extend one's self for the purpose of nurturing one's own or another's spiritual growth (spiritual referring to that dimension of their core reality where mind, body, and spirit are one).

These mothers' stories highlight the success and joy these gifted mothers have experienced, but they also point out their mistakes. But despite some failures along the way, these women never gave up. They continually challenged social norms that proved unhelpful in pursuit of both their life goals and those of their gifted girls. As one mother put it, "If you suspend all the biases of everything that everyone's trying to teach you and you think for yourself, you can be part of the salvation of our species." My takeaway after interviewing each of these women was that I had been blessed with the opportunity to connect with forty-three unsung heroes. I feel honored to share their voices and their parenting wisdom.

Therefore, this study offers no script (or dogma) that prescribes the "right" way to parent a gifted daughter. Instead, it is my hope that these mothers' stories will serve as a narrative bridge across generations. This book invites younger mothers to explore their own distinctive ways to parent gifted girls, to claim their parenting voices, to imaginatively define their own paths, to challenge limiting societal norms, and to trust their own inner wisdom. I invite mothers of gifted girls to free themselves from the notion that perfection is the goal or even a possibility. I encourage them to speak their minds and become positive disruptors, or put another way, as Steve Jobs in a 1994 interview suggested to young entrepreneurs, to "poke":

> Life can be much broader once you discover this: everything around you that you call life was made up by people that were no smarter than you. And you can change it, you can influence it, you can build your own things that other people can use… The minute that you understand that you can poke life and actually something will…pop out the other side, that you can change it, you can mold it: that's maybe the most important thing…Shake off the erroneous notion that life is there and you're just gonna live in it versus embrace it, change it, improve it, make your mark upon it. Poking life—that's what we can do…I can get locked into thinking life is static, that it's locked in, the rules are set in stone, that I have to move around in it like I'm in my grandmother's good room with all the nice china. But this stifles and it makes me want to bust out and do a bull routine in a shop full of nice china.

INTRODUCTION

As gifted mothers, in order to thrive, it's important to understand the forces that currently limit us as well as how we got here in the first place. Praising gifted mothers as resilient without calling out the societal challenges that force them to be resilient tells only half the story and does little to improve the parenting realities mothers in this situation have faced for generations. To create a new culture that's more empowering both for us and our bright daughters, it helps to get clarity about the one we need to transform. Simply telling ourselves that we should just accept our current restrictive situation or fight to change it without understanding the root causes of our socialized impulses will only create anxiety and self-blame and force us to go through life with little awareness of what's really happening around us. The intersectionality of the key layers of our identity as gifted females who are parents is a critical lens that we need in order to get a realistic perspective of how to maximize our potential in today's world.

The confluence of these three facets of our identity—gender, giftedness, and motherhood status—creates a perfect storm that can lead a gifted mother to a near breaking point or provide the catalyst for transformation. An awareness of how these three facets impact us and examples of how other gifted mothers overcame them, as opposed to letting them become a cultural straitjacket, can be extremely empowering in improving the quality of both our lives and the lives of our daughters. This book describes the details of this Perfect Storm to give gifted mothers a clearer idea of the obstacles they face in realizing their full potential as bright women and gifted mothers.

Knowledge is power. By looking at the whole of our reality, we can more effectively question the cultural assumptions we've internalized and make more educated life choices going forward.

This book highlights these cultural and societal forces. The sampled mothers were able to conquer these forces by developing a growing awareness of them, ceaselessly working to overcome them, and proactively embracing their own power. By understanding the challenges ahead, gifted mothers can develop more effective strategies for overcoming them.

Part 1

GENDER

CHAPTER 1

Historical Perspective on Gender

A historical perspective on the cultural influences that play a role in determining women's life choices across generations can provide insight into how we got here and why society is so resistant to getting rid of these gendered barriers. By gaining some understanding about the world that our female ancestors grew up in as well as the environment in which we were raised, our gifted daughters can be better informed and prepared for the gendered reality they will face when venturing into the fray.

The idea that women should inhabit a separate domestic sphere and that only men should occupy the public sphere has been a constant in Western thought for centuries, extending back to the ancient Greeks. However, this "separate spheres" notion did not emerge as a distinct ideology in the United States until the Industrial Revolution during the 1800s. Before this, family members of both genders typically worked together, mostly in and around the home.

According to author and historian Professor Stephanie Coontz, in her book *The Way We Never Were*, scripted gender roles arose to resolve tensions when men moved away from the household or family farm into the newly competitive, gender-segregated world of market work.

Wives took over many activities that their husbands formerly dominated, becoming the emotional and moral center of the family. Increasingly, emerging cultural norms assigned ambition to men and altruism to women. A woman's proper sphere was now the home, placing her in charge of the family's domestic life, child-rearing, housekeeping, and religious education. Along with these responsibilities came full responsibility for her children's well-being. Assuming mothers needed help as primary caregivers, professionals began offering their expertise. This included stern warnings to mothers in the latter part of the 1800s and early 1900s, cautioning them against overfeeding and spoiling. Mothers increasingly became blamable not only for what they did and didn't do as parents but also, thanks to Freud, for their children's unconscious feelings and motivations. So if the child had a problem, it had to be the mother's fault.

Feminist psychologist Sandra Bem points out in *The Lenses of Gender* that this sexual division of labor also created an increasingly extensive network of cultural beliefs and social practices that took on a life and history of their own. These further polarized the two genders and dictated different modes of dress, social roles, and ways of expressing emotion as well as experiencing sexual desire. These gender-based scripts assigned the label of masculine or feminine to just about all aspects of human behavior and resulted in predetermining very different life experiences depending upon the sex one was assigned at birth.

French political thinker Alexis de Tocqueville visited America around this time and wrote this in his article "How Americans Understand the Equality of the Sexes": "In no country has such constant care been taken as in America to trace two clearly distinct lines of action for the two sexes." He also observed that married women in particular were subjected to many restrictions, noting that "the independence of woman is irrecoverably lost in the bonds of matrimony." He added that "in the United States the inexorable opinion of the public carefully circumscribes woman within the narrow circle of domestic interests and duties and forbids her to step beyond it."

Surprisingly, Tocqueville considered this a positive development for females despite women's confinement to the private sphere and their obligation to perform free domestic labor. Women's separation from public society was reinforced by cultural and legal arrangements such as the lack of women's suffrage, legal prohibitions against women undertaking professions like medicine and law, and discouragement from obtaining higher education. Tocqueville contended that although women's narrow sphere of domestic life resulted in a situation of extreme dependence, he believed that, as such, they occupied a "lofty position" and that America's prosperity and growing strength could be attributed to the "superiority" of its women. This ideology portrayed females as uniquely suited to home life, while males were depicted as strivers in the public arena. Stemming from this belief was the general tendency passed down through the ages that women, like children, were dependents and needed to be both provided for and protected from harm.

But in *Lenses of Gender*, Bem points out that these cultural underpinnings of chivalry and romantic paternalism have served as powerful social mechanisms to limit females' liberty and autonomy. While some viewed putting women on a pedestal was for their own good, in reality, it was more like imprisoning them in a cage. Women were kept economically dependent, ensuring that they stayed in their assigned roles as wives and mothers and politically disempowered. Reverend John Milton Williams expressed the notion of romantic paternalism in his 1893 book, *Woman's Work and Woman's Sphere: A Study in Social Ethics*, stating,

> Woman has no call to the ballot-box, but she has a sphere of her own, of amazing responsibility and importance. She is the divinely appointed guardian of the home…She should more fully realize that her position, as wife and mother, and angel of the home, is the holiest, most responsible, and queenlike assigned to mortals; and dismiss all ambition for anything higher, as there is nothing else here so high for mortals.

These compelling cultural messages, along with disparities in pay and promotion for those few brave women who ventured into the public arena, gave females limited options other than marriage. Consequently, according to Coontz, from 1900 to 1940, most married women were unable to develop a strong commitment to the labor force.

However, this all changed when World War II ushered in a major transformation and society realized the dire need for women to work outside the home. According to Coontz, the female labor force increased by more than 50 percent between 1940 and 1945, encouraged by the government's push to spearhead a rapid shift in attitudes toward the employment of married women and mothers. Three-fourths of these new female workers were married, and a majority had school-age children. The state financed childcare for women working in defense industries, and many barriers to the employment of wives, mothers, and older women were eliminated. Sadly, it took a war to give females their first experience of occupational mobility and the rewards of challenging, well-paid work.

But when World War II ended, the situation for women was drastically reversed. Managers of large American companies went to great lengths to purge women workers from high-paying and nontraditional jobs. In most cases, women were not excluded from the labor force but merely downgraded to lower-paying "female" jobs that lacked the challenges that had made their responsibilities during the war more rewarding. Coontz states that women were intentionally concentrated into a small number of predominantly female occupations where the wages were depressed, and corporate America reverted once again to the longstanding devaluation of women workers.

Conversely, immediately following the war, Coontz notes in *The Myth of Male Decline* that males were entitled to what sociologist R. W. Connell called a "patriarchal dividend"—a lifelong affirmative-action program where they could count on women being excluded from the most desirable jobs and opportunities. One example of this patriarchal dividend, according to Coontz, was the GI Bill that provided college or vocational training for the returning veterans. In the five years after the war, only about 65,000 women (of the 265,000 females who had served) were able to attend college on the GI Bill while nearly one hundred times that many men (totaling about six million) took advantage of this opportunity. In addition, because colleges favored the guaranteed tuition payments they got from the Veterans Administration and didn't want to incur bad public relations by rejecting war veterans, most of these institutions were filled to capacity with male vets, leaving little room for students who were nonveterans, the majority of whom were female. This, in part, resulted in the decline of the educational level of American women during this period.

Another example of the patriarchal dividend was the country's policy of allowing newspapers to list "Help Wanted" ads by gender, which limited women's career opportunities and directed females to lower-paying positions. It wasn't until 1968 that this policy was deemed unlawful.

During the period following World War II, women were strongly encouraged to retreat to defining themselves solely in terms of the private sphere, i.e., home and family, even if they were working outside the home. Vehement attacks were launched against those who refused to succumb to this pressure. In addition, the patriarchal dividend for males extended into the home. As Coontz elucidates in *The Way We Never Were*, marital rape was not considered a crime, and husbands had the right to decide where the family would live as well as make unilateral financial decisions for the household. Further legal limitations on women included not being allowed to serve on juries, convey property, make contracts, take out credit cards in their own name, or establish residence.

Although the 1950s reasserted the notion of female domesticity from past eras, the traditional family of the 1950s was a qualitatively novel phenomenon. This new family model was characterized by a high standard of living, a focus on consumerism, and a strong sense of community. The age of marriage and motherhood fell, fertility increased (producing the baby boom generation), divorce declined, and the degree of women's educational parity with men dropped sharply. Nonetheless, Coontz states that despite this cultural push to return women to the private sphere and prioritize American home life, other social forces were at work. There was an explosion of employment among both single and married women during the postwar period with an expansion of women's jobs in clerical work, teaching, nursing, and retail sales. The baby boom created a backlog of supply and demand pressures that provided the impetus for enticing females into the workforce, coupled with the government's push to maximize America's "womanpower" in order to foster industrial expansion and win the Cold War with Russia. Ironically, the GI Bill also encouraged employment of wives by offering men incentives to stay in school but paying family allowances so low that wives had to work in order to supplement the family income. As a result, between 1940 and 1960, Coontz notes, the United States experienced a 400 percent increase in the number of working mothers, and by 1960, nearly a third of all women workers had children under the age of eighteen with as many women working as there had been at the peak of World War II.

This schizophrenic cultural reality for females presented a huge challenge to those trying to come to grips with the incongruity of their identity. While the labor market was encouraging women to take jobs outside the home, the cultural message pushed the image of the perfect mother staying home to serve her family full time. Esther Peterson (President Kennedy's assistant secretary of labor) and Winifred Conkling highlight the mixed messages given to females by society during this period in the memoir *Restless*. Peterson asked high school females how many expected to have a home and family, and their hands shot up. Then she asked how many of them expected to work, and only a few raised their hands. Finally, she asked how many had mothers who worked, and again their hands shot up. Peterson noted that in reality, 90 percent of these girls would work outside the home when they grew up. However, as high schoolers, each girl thought she would be in that remaining 10 percent of adult women who stayed home because of the strong cultural belief that in a traditional family, a woman did not pursue success outside the home. The impact of this socialization regarding the "right" role for mothers most likely negatively impacted their perception of the reality of their current home lives if their mothers worked as well as how their mothers viewed themselves.

During the 1960s, women finally began to question the notion of social engineering for females, including the concept of separate spheres, and its impact on their lives. This sparked an ideological revolution called the "second wave of feminism." The first wave in the late 1800s and early 1900s focused primarily on women's suffrage. This second wave included demands for equality and recognition that working in the public arena was an important option for women as well as men. Although the pioneers of married women's employment in the 1950s and 1960s had been lower-middle-class or working-class women with high school educations, this new movement was initiated largely by college-educated females from the upper middle class who wished to play a part in the public arena. One of the leaders of this movement was author, activist, and mother Betty Friedan, whose 1963 book *The Feminine Mystique* asserted that women were being forced by an oppressive, socially constructed "separate spheres" ideology to define themselves solely in terms of their role as wives and mothers rather than by any biological predisposition to prefer staying at home.

However, raising the consciousness of women across the country was a slow go. As Coontz noted, as late as 1970, 78 percent of married women under age forty-five still agreed that it was better for wives to be homemakers and husbands to be breadwinners. Coontz states: "it was largely economics, rather than feminism, that led these women to violate their own expectations and eventually reorder their values. For many, work begun as an opportunity soon became an economic necessity" due to high inflation in the 1970s. As a result, Coontz asserts, feminism developed hand in hand with women's employment. Despite the increased presence of women in the workforce, strong opposition to women's participation in the public sphere continued to hold firm, coming in part from a few of the women themselves.

Two key pieces of proposed federal legislation that surfaced during this period illustrate America's conflicting ideas about women's proper role. The Comprehensive Child Development Act hoped to establish a network of nationally funded childcare centers open to everyone on a sliding scale basis. This legislation was viewed as a first step toward providing universal childcare in the United States (following the model of many European countries). A central unresolved issue underlying equal rights for women was this: "If the father works and the mother works, who is left to watch the kids?" In the early 1970s, the United States nearly passed this necessary legislation to make affordable childcare available to all, but at the last minute, President Nixon vetoed the bill. He declared in his veto message to Congress on December 9, 1971, that the bill would "implement a communal approach to child-rearing against a family-centered approach," tying it to broad-based fears of communism and labeling it a long leap into the dark (according to Nancy L. Cohen in her article "Why America Never Had Universal Child Care"). Critics, in large part fueled by fundamentalists, claimed it had family-weakening implications. In vetoing the legislation, Nixon sided with proponents of the traditional family who believed women should forsake every ambition apart from motherhood. As a result, more than fifty years later, our country still offers no solution to the lack of affordable, safe, quality childcare. The Comprehensive Child Development Act has become just a far-off dream for working parents.

Society's failure to provide childcare support to families negatively impacted some of the gifted mothers in my sample. For a number of the forty-three women, juggling childcare was a constant challenge, many resorting to hiring other women as caregivers, enlisting relatives or neighbors, searching for affordable daycare centers, switching to part-time employment based on their children's school hours, or dropping out of the workplace altogether for periods of time depending on their family's needs. In rare cases, fathers might offer support, but the mothers were still considered the primary care providers.

The second example of society's opposition to supporting women in the public arena was evidenced by the failure to pass the Equal Rights Amendment (ERA). The ERA, which would amend the US Constitution to guarantee equal rights for women, was introduced in 1923. The legislation came closest to passing in 1972 when public consensus still leaned in the direction of women's rights. Both houses of Congress passed the legislation and then sent it to the state legislatures for ratification. Unfortunately, the ERA received ratification by thirty-five of the necessary thirty-eight states. Five states later rescinded their earlier ratifications, and no further states signed on to support the amendment before the extended deadline for passage in 1982.

The reason for the failure to pass the ERA was the change in political momentum during the late 1970s and 1980s. Opponents of the amendment stressed that it would eliminate the male-only draft requirement as well as traditional gender roles. They also generated fear that ERA supporters wanted to transform society by destroying the traditional family, radically altering child-rearing, housework, the corporate world, politics, and even sex. "Stop ERA" advocates baked pies for the Illinois state legislature while they debated the amendment and hung "don't draft me" signs on female babies. They also declared that the amendment would repeal protective laws for women related to sexual assault and alimony and eliminate the tendency for mothers to win custody in divorce cases. The most prominent opponent of the ERA was Phyllis Schlafly, a conservative lawyer. Schlafly defended conventional gender roles and heckled feminists by saying, "I'd like to thank my husband for letting me be here tonight," using this for the first time in a speech she gave to the Illinois Federation of Women's Clubs on October 13, 1972. The ERA opponents' strategy proved successful. Nonetheless, several organizations continue to push for adoption of the ERA. The amendment has been reintroduced in Congress every year since 1982 but has never passed.

Since the late 1970s and 1980s, conventional wisdom about the role of women has changed significantly, according to Coontz. In 1994, two-thirds of Americans rejected the notion that it was better for everyone involved if, in a traditional nuclear family, the man was the achiever outside the home and the woman took care of the home and family. Despite this radical change in attitudes, the fight for equality stalled around the beginning of the millennium. Women increasingly seemed to be backsliding on earlier, hard-fought gains. Unfortunately, this was exacerbated with the pandemic beginning in early 2020. Women's level of participation in the labor force declined drastically when COVID-19 resulted in school closures and large numbers of women being forced to leave the workforce to care for their offspring.

In addition, in recent years, Paula England and Su Li note in "Desegregation Stalled: The Changing Gender Composition of College Majors, 1971–2002" that although the proportion of women majoring in STEM fields and other male-dominated occupations has increased steadily over time, the pace of increase has slowed. For example, the proportion of women in engineering occupations increased from 10 percent in 1992 to 15 percent in 2020. However, the proportion of women in engineering occupations has plateaued since the mid-2000s.

Finally, progress in adopting family-friendly work practices in the country has proceeded at a glacial pace while the demands and hours of work have been intensifying. In a 2021 interview on *Freakonomics Radio*, Dr. Claudia Goldin, a Nobel Prize winner for economics, states in her book *Career and Family* that the number of so-called "greedy jobs" has increased in recent decades. Goldin defines greedy jobs as jobs that demand long or unpredictable hours, often at odd times, and that reward workers more for the number of hours they work than for their productivity. Goldin argues that these jobs present a barrier to women's advancement in the workplace, because they are difficult to balance with family and other caregiving responsibilities assigned to mothers.

Many Americans are puzzled by the absence of concrete political proposals to change women's status, given that nearly sixty years have passed since publication of *The Feminine Mystique* and a vast majority of children now grow up in households where every adult is employed. As Cohen states in "Why America Never Had Universal Child Care," "the United States ranks near third to last among the Organization for Economic Co-operation and Development (OECD) countries on public spending on family benefits. That we lack anything resembling a 21st century family policy is not an oversight. It is not because American society refuses to come to grips with the reality of working mothers. Rather, it is the result of a political hijacking so fabulously successful it wiped away virtually any trace of its own handiwork." Coontz echoes this, adding that the United States has not passed any major federal initiative to help workers accommodate their family and work demands. Compared with other countries at similar levels of economic and political development, according to Coontz, the United States ranks dead last.

Perhaps hope is on the horizon as the untenable reality of American mothers trying to do it all was exposed during the COVID-19 pandemic. This increased public awareness of the need for social and legislative change to support America's mothers. However, in the absence of bipartisan agreement about what major systemic improvements for women, especially mothers, should be, this opportunity for advances in the lives of American females may be missed. In the end, despite revealing the shortcomings of public policy in relation to children and mothers, the pandemic may yet result in another setback in the fight for gender equity.

CHAPTER 2

The Role of Gender in the Perfect Storm

One of the most prevalent myths in our culture is that two separate and opposing genders exist, each with its own distinct, biologically based behaviors and characteristics. As women, we all have an awareness of how males and females are viewed by our culture, because we've been immersed in our gendered position since birth. Even if our families of origin didn't proactively marginalize us as bright girls, all other aspects of our environment (including schools, peers, and media) seeped into our consciousness, creating barriers established to minimize our life choices. And this seepage begins from day one. As Bem states in *The Lenses of Gender*, "it seems naïve to ignore the gendered selves and cognitive schemas that children develop as they become cultural natives in a patriarchal world."

In fact, Kerr believes that of all the different characteristics a baby is born with, gender is one of the most important in predicting achievement among gifted individuals, more than affluence, background, or other key factors. Studies have documented how comments about female newborns in maternity wards differ from those of male newborns, focusing on how sweet and cute the baby girl is versus the boy's strength, intelligence, and vitality.

This gendered perspective continues throughout childhood with mothers often unknowingly serving as the primary enforcer of society's misogynistic norms. A study of aggregate data for Google searches underscores the degree to which parents have internalized these cultural values. As reported by Seth Stephens-Davidowitz in "Google, Tell Me. Is My Son a Genius?" based on this data, parents appear much more concerned with the intelligence of their sons, more commonly asking Google "Is my son gifted?" versus the significantly higher incidence of queries related to the appearance and waistlines of their daughters. Parental concern may, in some cases, be a throwback to the romantic notion of centuries ago. This apprehension may stem from Tocqueville's belief about women needing to attract a mate to enjoy the "soft glories of home life."

For gifted daughters, both mothers and fathers may subconsciously wonder why their daughter is so driven to achieve when she could simply accept the "easier life" society has carved out for her: caring for her family full time while supported by a male breadwinner. Such gendered stereotypes (commonly held but rigidly fixed beliefs about how particular types of people should look, behave, and feel) can result in less parental investment in the educational achievements and career dreams of their daughters while parents place pressure on their sons to achieve financial success by competing in the public arena. As a result, both males and females are forced to grow up with the limitations dictated by society's regime of gendered expectations.

Specifically for females, this means being instilled with the belief that our self-worth is tied to pleasing others (especially males) and learning behaviors that might make this possible: being nice, polite, subservient, and attractive.

We spend our lives observing the gendered world around us, absorbing the subtle and not-so-subtle cues that inform us about our place in it. These messages let us know what's considered "normal" for females, lumping gifted and other neurodiverse girls and women into this broad category. These norms dictate the behavior that's expected of us in a variety of roles and situations while conveying the powerful message that what's valued is convergence to these expectations. Any divergence is strongly frowned upon. For example, one mother in the study commented that "if her daughter knows something to be a fact, she is going to make sure you know it" and often faces harsh backlash as a result. This mother noted, "Boys are taught from the time they are little to be aggressive and competitive, but girls are just labeled a 'bitch' if they act this way."

As a result, women's lives are spent being pruned, molded, and shaped to keep us looking uniform and behaving in lockstep. And children of both sexes are aware that society enforces different expectations and scripts based on gender and that these are more limiting for females. In *Work Left Undone: Choices & Compromises of Talented Females*, Dr. Sally Morgan Reis describes a 1995 study that found both boys and girls thought boys could do more, had more opportunities, and had fewer restrictions. Conversely, the girls struggled to identify good things about being female but came up with a number of negative aspects. Along these lines, Reis quoted Jeanne Block, a pioneer in gender research: "Socialization narrows women's options while broadening men's." Or as one of the daughters in the study described it, she felt stuck in a box because she was born female.

The reward females get for playing along with this discriminatory system is social approval and acceptance and, if we're "lucky," being financially supported to some degree as adults. Because as females we have been socialized to prioritize being loved and learned not to have needs, we manage our reputation by doing whatever it takes to fit in. With this as our goal, our life choices often don't account for what's best for us and our own inner well-being. In effect, we're continually conducting a cost-benefit analysis. We are always on the lookout for cues about what's considered appropriate to gain acceptance while minimizing what it costs us in terms of discovering who we really are and being all we can be. Typically, without realizing it, the long-term collateral damage of trying to maintain our reputation creates internal shame, because we know in our heart of hearts that we are not being true to ourselves. And as this process plays out, our awareness of what we truly value and need diminishes. The ultimate cost is losing our souls.

A famous study conducted by Yale psychologist Stanley Milgram in the early 1960s described on Harvard University's Department of Psychology website underscores the incredible power of societal expectations. Milgram's study demonstrated that humans cause themselves pain and great inner turmoil in order to conform to society's demands. The subjects in Milgram's study "shocked" participants at increasingly higher levels because they felt compelled to obey what they perceived to be a higher authority: a male wearing a white lab coat. Although the participants who supposedly were "shocked" in fact experienced no discomfort, the study subjects caused themselves real agony and distress, because they felt there was no option but to unquestionably follow orders.

Not surprisingly, the arbiters of cultural norms (the ones perceived as wearing white lab coats) regarding appropriate female behavior are those in power, typically males, whose interest is best served by maintaining the current gendered state of affairs. Ironically, it is the mothers who are put in the position of being society's key agents in this socialization process. In her book *Rage Becomes Her: The Power of Women's Anger*, Soraya Chemaly states, "If there's a word that should be retired from use in the service of women's expression, health, well-being, and equality, it's 'appropriate.'" Chemaly adds that this is a control word—a policing term used to regulate our language, appearance, and demands. With mothers as the main enforcers of cultural appropriateness, the potential and power of females, especially gifted females, is often severely limited. This process gives males the edge in the competition for status and economic rewards in the public arena. In *Waking Up White*, Debby Irving remarks, "Powerlessness creates a state of fear which puts people in survival mode. Who can be anything close to their best in this state?"

Protecting their authenticity requires females to learn to set boundaries against harmful socialization attempts and to assert themselves. Chemaly believes that the declarative word no is one they should use much more frequently when females feel cultural pressure to yield. She asserts, "It takes practice and, in some cases, years to undo socialization that might be leading you to bite your tongue or not believe that you are deserving of whatever it is that you are asking for."

Refusing to follow the script that demands subservience from females involves setting boundaries around what we will and will not do. Glennon Doyle echoes this sentiment in her book *Untamed*:

> My mother watched the spark in my eyes fade during my 10th year on Earth...Where did my

spark go at 10? How had I lost myself?…Ten is when we learn how to be good girls and real boys. Ten is when children begin to hide who they are in order to become what the world expects them to be…we begin to internalize our formal taming… "These are the feelings you are allowed to express. This is how a woman should act. This is the kind of life you are supposed to want." I wanted to be a good girl, so I tried to control myself. I chose a personality, a body, a faith, and a sexuality so tiny I had to hold my breath to fit myself inside. Then I promptly became very sick…Over time I walked away from my cages…Our children are too vast to fit themselves inside these rigid, mass-produced bottles. But they will lose themselves trying.

This idea is central to "Sad Girl Theory," highlighted by artist Audrey Wollen in a 2015 interview with Ava Tunnicliffe. Wollen proposes that the sadness of girls should be witnessed and rehistoricized as an act of resistance rather than passivity. She says,

> I'm trying to open up the idea that protest doesn't have to be external to the body; it doesn't have to be a huge march in the streets, noise, violence, or rupture. There's a long history of girls who have used their own anguish, their own suffering, as tools for resistance and political agency…It's a way of fighting back…I think feminism should acknowledge that being a girl in this world is really hard, one of the hardest things there is, and that our sadness is actually a very appropriate and informed reaction.

However, breaking free of our cages and trying to undo years of socialization can be a huge challenge, and being angst ridden, sad, and suffering seems to negatively impact girls themselves to a greater degree than society. Enforcement of societal standards is often effective, because there is a high price to pay for not accepting the established power dynamic. As the mother mentioned above, by speaking up or questioning the status quo, we call attention to ourselves, which makes us vulnerable to various forms of attack. Often when a gifted female expresses herself, it can result in painful consequences such as negative labeling, shaming, teasing, bullying, exclusion, ridicule, and, more concretely, a withholding of resources, opportunities, and other societal rewards.

In addition to speaking up, several interviewed mothers shared that their gifted daughters tended to be like bulls in a china shop and did not suffer fools gladly. As part of rejecting gendered socialization (including the "good girl" persona), these daughters were quite assertive in stating their opinions, spoke up against perceived injustice, and stood up to those they believed to have less informed positions. Although these mothers seemed generally proud of their daughters for having the strength of their convictions, some shared concern about the cultural backlash this behavior invited and admitted that they wished their daughters would "tone it down" a bit.

Perhaps these mothers' worries revealed the not-so-subconscious desire to protect their offspring from the harsh blowback they anticipated from their daughters' peers and colleagues. As one mother put it,

I think my daughter's challenges have always been on the interpersonal level…She's always had one or two close friends…But I think this assertive strand in her is just too much at times, and she doesn't always control it so that it can be a positive attribute…I wholeheartedly believe in helping our girls not be wishy-washy, but my daughter kind of goes over the edge sometimes. So she'll get herself into trouble because she just doesn't have that fine art of politically moving people to where she wants them to be. Then, she'll end up in a confrontational situation.

Another mother expressed a similar concern. She described her daughter as being "more boy-like growing up. A little coarse and a little out there…Not conforming and not trying to please people, wanting to do things her own way and not worried about the consequences." When her daughter was a young adult and working, this mother advised her that "we all are a combination of the yin and yang, the feminine and masculine, and my advice would be finding a better balance," proposing that she concentrate on her feminine side a little bit more and a little bit less on the masculine with both her dress and demeanor. The mother said, "She can be kind of salty. It's just a matter of degree." She suggested to her daughter that "if you just toned it back a tad, you would be more effective." This gifted mother felt that part of it may be age (her daughter was in her midtwenties at the time of the interview) and said, "Maybe that's part of the reason why she's still a little rough around the edges." When this mother attended a seminar with journalist Christiane Amanpour, she flashed on her daughter. "Amanpour said she was an iron fist in a velvet glove—she has strong opinions, but she can express them in such a way." This mother believed that her daughter really needed to work on developing a velvet glove.

Indeed, as mothers of gifted daughters realize, smart women face the challenge of trying to maximize their high potential in a man's world that caters to rewarding males (and their "masculine" traits like assertiveness and competitiveness) while punishing females who demonstrate these same qualities. Being "feminine" (compliant, subservient, empathetic) can indeed be a disadvantage in "getting ahead," but a female who rejects feminine qualities is equally hindered in the public sphere. This is a Catch-22 for sure.

Despite the sad reality that gender bias continues to overshadow female lives, many believe that gender inequality is no longer a serious social problem. Notwithstanding the efforts of many brave women and some men over the past few centuries resulting in progress in some areas, women still face major obstacles. Gender inequality endures and negatively impacts females in nearly all aspects of their public, professional, and personal lives. The sad fact is that males continue to rule the world, running a vast majority of independent countries (at the time of this writing, the United States has not yet had a female president), and few females occupy the C-suites of major corporations.

Stereotypes for females have been part of our society for so long that we simply fail to see them. They have become engrained in our culture and provide the basis of many social, political, and legislative restrictions today. Once we become aware of how the past is present in both obvious and very subtle ways, examples of how our gender can negatively impact our lives become difficult to ignore. Only by making inequality more visible can we devise adequate strategies to confront it. This is true on both a macro scale and in our personal lives and the lives of our daughters. Sheryl Sandberg declared in her controversial book *Lean In*, "The promise of equality is not the same as true equality. A truly equal world would be one where women ran half our countries and companies and men ran half our homes." Based on these criteria, we've got a long way to go before achieving this vision.

Part 2

FEMALE GIFTEDNESS

CHAPTER 3

Historical Overview

Statements by male authorities over the past few centuries in America reflect the cultural pressure on gifted females to remain in their "proper" sphere despite having talents that may be beneficial to the public domain. The underlying themes of these pervasive messages included the separate spheres ideology, the pathologizing of gender nonconformity, and, as this chapter will discuss, the variability hypothesis, which emerged at the close of the nineteenth century. As a result, the dilemma for a female with high potential, as Roeper notes, was "she was not supposed to be that which she could not help but be."

In the 1800s, the label of "mental hermaphrodites" was given to bright women, with the negative implication that their intellectual capabilities made them both male and female. This view held that a gifted female failed to conform to the established gender binary. Coontz quoted one marriage adviser who declared them to be "less capable of loving a man or bearing a child than a true woman." Apparently, a "true" woman during this period was characterized by average intelligence or less.

In the late nineteenth century, according to Coontz, in addition to trying to shame women with what were considered insults at the time (like mental hermaphrodite), fear-based comments about women's activities outside the home were common. Coontz states that philosopher Herbert Spencer made a veiled threat to those women who ventured out into the public arena. Spencer's fearmongering was creative but also quite foreboding. He warned that leaving the private sphere would result in females losing the "evolutionary advantage conferred by their ability to conceal the antagonism created by men's ill-treatment of them, which had previously ensured women's survival." This seems a rather gloomy take on traditional family life and a twisted way of complimenting females by praising their capacity to withstand abuse.

Coontz provides yet another example of the cultural lens regarding gifted women in the early 1900s, citing a doctor who claimed that "when women saw themselves as competent in school or work, they acquired a self-assertive, independent character, rendering it impossible to love, honor, and obey." Thus, as Dr. Jennifer Jolly notes in her article, "The Woman Question," included in *Teaching and Counseling Gifted Girls*, although women were pushing for the right to vote during this period, they were far from being considered as equals in both the classroom and workforce and were treated accordingly.

Another thesis that emerged around the end of the nineteenth century targeted women with higher intelligence and compounded the cultural pressure on women to "know their place" and conform to the stereotypical female role. According to Doreen Kimura in her book *Sex and Cognition*, this was the variability hypothesis, which viewed females as a more homogenous group in terms of intellectual ability (compared with males who were considered more heterogeneous and thus capable of producing outliers who could attain eminence). The flip side of this supposed innate male heterogeneity was that while having more individuals capable of great intellectual achievement on one end, on the other end, more males wound up as patients with extremely limited intelligence in institutions. This hypothesis flourished in the early 1900s even though it was not supported by empirical evidence but rather from "armchair dogma" about innate female inferiority. Unfortunately, this unsubstantiated theory led to the adoption of educational curricula for females that prepared them to become wives and mothers rather than for success in the public domain. The attitude was that it was unreasonable to expect women to achieve, so it was best for them not to even try. One study carried out in the 1890s by G. Stanley Hall tested children's familiarity with a variety of objects and ideas at the start of school, according to Dr. Stephanie Shields in "The Variability Hypothesis: The History of a Biological Model of Sex Differences in Intelligence." Shields states that Hall concluded, "Girls' minds excel at the common and pedestrian, whereas boys' ideas are wider ranging. Because girls are more like one another than are boys, they are, as a group, closer to the 'ordinary.'"

Fortunately, according to Shields, the first wave of females admitted to graduate school in the 1880s represented an "upstart element in the scientific community," and their work was largely responsible for the eventual decline of the variability hypothesis, because, surprisingly, they found no evidence to substantiate it. One of the most active critics of this theory was the American psychologist, feminist, and educational researcher Leta Hollingworth.

Shields points out that Hollingworth challenged the view that gifted females were a homogeneous group in terms of their intellectual ability and primarily suited for domestic duties. Throughout her life, Hollingworth conducted research to disprove the variability hypothesis. In one study, Hollingworth examined one thousand newborn boys and one thousand newborn girls, finding more similarities than differences between the genders, indicating the potential for females to accomplish great things given similar educational and career opportunities as boys. In 1914, Hollingworth proposed that channels for eminence were simply not open to women, according to Jolly in her article cited above: "Housekeeping and the rearing of children, though much commended to women as proper fields for the exploitation of their talents, are, unfortunately for their fame, not fields in which eminence can be attained… Eminent housekeepers and eminent mothers as such do not exist." Hollingworth held that there was basically no way to compare women's abilities with those of men, who have followed the greatest possible range of occupations and have at the same time procreated unhindered, as noted by Shields. Hollingworth fought for reforms that advantaged women and advocated for gifted females. In her personal life, she encountered discrimination by not being allowed to work as a schoolteacher because she was married. Ironically, this incident precipitated her going to graduate school, which began a lifelong journey as an eminent researcher and pioneer in gifted education. In 1922, Hollingworth studied gifted students and discovered special challenges for girls attempting to overcome attitudes about their inferior mental abilities. She went on to start a public school for gifted children that offered invaluable data proving environmental and educational opportunities played a critical role in developing talent. Professor Connie Phelps, who has a

PhD in gifted education, stressed that Hollingworth's findings represented a milestone in encouraging a level playing field between the sexes in the education of the gifted.

Lewis Terman was, like Hollingworth, one of the most important pioneers in the field of giftedness research. His findings helped explain the reasons for the scarcity of eminent women in society. In 1921, Terman, a Stanford University psychologist and a pioneer of the IQ test, scoured California's schools to identify 1,521 children who scored 135 or more on his new intelligence test, the Stanford-Binet (according to Daniel Goleman in his article "75 Years Later, Study Still Tracking Geniuses"). Terman's sample included 672 females. Even though the study participant with the highest score on the newly developed Stanford-Binet IQ test was a girl, because the ratio greatly favored the boys, Terman wondered if there might be some merit in the variability hypothesis after all, sparking another round of scientific dialogue and inquiry, according to Shields. However, Terman eventually reversed his position and concluded that the scarcity of eminent women was more likely attributed to motivational causes and limited opportunity rather than inherent limited mental capabilities.

One factor that also played a part in questioning the validity of the variability hypothesis was the fact that young female adults in the first half of the twentieth century began to reject their traditional roles. They had fewer children and bore them later in life. More of these females went to college and graduate school, had careers, and married later if at all. In other words, these women chose to participate more fully in the public sphere where eminence was possible. Nonetheless, the advances of females in education and careers for more than one hundred years has not completely served to stamp out the variability hypothesis. As Shields notes, though it has undergone some modifications and lost much of its social importance, this hypothesis has survived to the present day with little factual support.

Life for bright females during the first half of the twentieth century, for the most part, still demanded strict observance of the gendered role culturally scripted for females, forcing many to suppress their gifts and talents. Sadly, those professions where it was permissible for women to shine, such as teaching, nursing, social services, and motherhood, were devalued by society and afforded low status and little pay. Given the intense societal pressure to conform, most gifted girls accepted their lot and assumed characteristics associated with the female stereotype including passivity, attempting to please, and striving to be feminine and attractive. Roeper points out in *The Young Gifted Girl: A Contemporary View* that because gifted individuals are typically more aware of the complexities and dangers of the world, gifted girls in the early twentieth century often chose to live within this well-defined gender framework because it provided both protection and praise from family members, teachers, and society in general. Within this context, Reis notes in *Work Left Undone* that gifted adult women focused on catering to the needs of others and living through their children, sensing that positive feedback and love were contingent on staying within the limits of gender boundaries. However, Roeper believes this repressed lifestyle and squelching of potential was the reason so many smart women during this period struggled with depression.

But world events positively impacted this grim reality for gifted females. A major shift related to giftedness occurred midway through the twentieth century that, to some degree, helped improve educational opportunities for gifted females. Society began to focus on the need to tap into the potential of gifted individuals in its effort to win the Cold War with the Soviet Union. In 1957, after the launch of Sputnik, a Russian satellite, the perception of the United States as a technological superpower was shattered. To counteract this, the United States implemented steps to regain its technological lead, placing an emphasis on science and technology and initiating reforms in education. Specifically, the federal government began investing in science, engineering, and mathematics at all levels of education. Gifted citizens were now considered a valuable national resource. The federal government mounted an energetic effort to maximize these citizens' potential, which included providing advanced classes in math and science for both gifted boys and girls. The government also enacted reforms to establish gifted education, all of which included girls. As a result, society's separate spheres ideology became tamped down as the realization finally set in that gifted females could in fact serve a utilitarian purpose in the public domain.

But progress for gifted females during the 1950s happened slowly. Given that society's needs were focused on the products of science and technology, which had traditionally been part of the male world, there was much resistance by the men in STEM jobs to welcoming females into this domain, according to Phelps. Thus, mostly males were identified as gifted by proud parents and teachers during this period who assumed the STEM world was the future for gifted students. In addition, identifying individuals with high potential presented a Catch-22 for bright women. If a girl was identified, she was thought to have the mind of a boy, because like the pathologizing of gender nonconformity in past eras, it was not considered possible to be both gifted and female. Sadly, Hollingworth's hope that the introduction of quantifiable measures like the Stanford-Binet test would promote the identification of more gifted girls wasn't fully realized.

So despite society's concerted effort to nurture giftedness that began in the 1950s, long-held cultural and societal expectations continued to limit academic achievement and place barriers on talent development for gifted females. An example of this is shown in a story shared by a close friend of mine. Kay was identified as gifted in elementary school as part of the Sputnik program in Southern California. She thrived in the advanced classes, but both Kay and her gifted female cohorts were eventually dropped from the accelerated math program at the start of high school, because it was deemed inappropriate at the time for females to pursue careers in math-related fields.

Despite these obstacles, a number of women who came of age in the 1950s courageously claimed their giftedness by getting the best education possible. But it took the sexual revolution of the sixties and seventies to increase opportunities for women to actualize their potential. The second wave of feminism, otherwise known as the Women's Liberation Movement, which spread across the country during the sixties and seventies, was a milestone in the history of gifted females. It now became a civil right for women to have access to opportunities to develop their potential and break away from traditional gender roles and stereotypes. As Bem describes it in *Lenses of Gender*, "This legacy of naturalizing gender conformity and pathologizing gender nonconformity held sway within the field of psychology until the early 70's when feminism finally took hold in both psychology and the culture at large." In addition, Roeper states that giftedness was no longer narrowly defined by quantitative indicators like IQ scores but rather was seen more holistically, encompassing unique personality characteristics including socioemotional and cognitive differences from the general population. But like released inmates who've been imprisoned most of their lives, these high-potential women faced a complex landscape based on male models of success that appeared to offer opportunities but for which they had no practical skills and no support system. As Reis puts it, in many ways, it was the best of times and the worst of times, but at the very least, for women with high potential, it was an exciting time in which they could breathe some less constrictive air.

Additionally, the Women's Movement helped ignite interest in learning more about gifted females. Research focusing on issues related to gifted girls began in the 1980s. The pioneers of this endeavor include Dr. Barbara Kerr, Dr. Sally Reis, Dr. Linda Silverman, and Dr. Joan Smutny, to name just a few, whose recommendations underscored the need for accelerated and enriched educational curricula for gifted girls as well as boys. In response, the different levels of government attempted to push for programs aimed at promoting excellence in gifted girls, according to Phelps. The National Science Foundation's Gender Equity programs began in the early 1990s and led the way in funding research and creating policy on the education and guidance of gifted girls in STEM fields. Despite these efforts, the National Research Council report in 1993 forecasted concerns about America's talented students, deeming it a quiet crisis.

Society's deeply engrained beliefs and attitudes about gender roles most likely contributed to this crisis. Although Roeper believes that the gifted female in recent history is a psychologically different person from her gifted female ancestors, as stated in *The Young Gifted Girl: A Contemporary View*, and reality has changed in some respects for women over the past two centuries, in many ways some things have stayed the same. For example, a gifted female's self-perceptions as well as the cultural script that's constantly forced on her by today's ever-present media and social network find her with one foot strongly rooted in stereotypical gender roles of the past while the reality and pressures of today's socioeconomic needs, as well as her own drive and motivation, are yanking her other foot into a very different future.

The cultural messages aimed at our gifted daughters today (and coming from multiple sources) are shockingly similar to those from two hundred years ago. According to Coontz, New York City economist Sylvia Ann Hewlett wrote in her 2002 book *Creating a Life: Professional Women and the Quest for Children* that "the rule of thumb seems to be that the more successful a woman is, the less likely it is she will find a husband or bear a child." Maureen Dowd agrees, lamenting in her 2005 article "What's a Modern Girl to Do?" that she would have done better at landing a man if she had become a maid rather than a high-powered columnist at *The New York Times*. In this same article, she shares a 2005 report by researchers at four British universities that found that a high IQ hampered a woman's chance to marry while it was a plus for men. The prospect for marriage increased by 35 percent for guys for each sixteen-point increase in IQ; for women, there was a 40 percent drop for each sixteen-point rise. Finally, Michael Noer warned men in a 2006 *Forbes* column entitled "Don't Marry Career Women," defining a "career girl" as one having a university-level (or higher) education, working more than thirty-five hours a week outside the home, and making more than $30,000 a year. Noer states that recent studies found professional women are more likely to get divorced, more likely to cheat ("When your spouse works outside the home, chances increase they'll meet someone they like more than you"), and less likely to have children, and if they do have kids, they are more likely to be unhappy about it. Coontz summarizes this pervasive message: "The main reason that educated and high-achieving women have trouble finding or keeping mates, according to observers past and present, is that they won't play dumb enough to assuage a man's ego or act submissive enough to put up with unfair treatment." Sounds like something straight out of the 1800s.

CHAPTER 4

The Role of Female Giftedness in the Perfect Storm

Cultural scripts about female giftedness are equally as oppressive as society's dictates about appropriate gender roles. Being exceptionally bright can at times feel more like a liability than a gift because of the conflict gifted females often must deal with. This conflict involves the choice to maximize their potential and address their inherent desire to self-actualize or succumb to societal pressures to dumb down, follow gender norms, and fit in with their more neurotypical peers. In addition, the constant tape playing in the mind of most gifted girls is how, and if, they will be able to deliver on the high intelligence and talent they are being praised for while at the same time fulfill their culturally assigned roles as wives and mothers. One profoundly gifted daughter shared that the ongoing assumption from the time her off-the-charts IQ was discovered in elementary school was that she was going to cure cancer. She deemed this her giftedness burden.

Being gifted impacts females differently, and there is in fact no single gifted female type. A given female's lived reality of giftedness depends upon many factors including where she falls on the giftedness range. IQ levels of giftedness are broken down differently depending upon the source, however. Some experts and organizations define mildly gifted individuals as having an IQ of 115–129, moderately gifted as 130–144, highly gifted as 145–159, exceptionally gifted as 160–180, and profoundly gifted as more than 180 (occurring in 0.01 percent of the population). As noted earlier, NAGC defines an IQ of 160 or higher as profoundly gifted while other organizations consider profoundly gifted as those with an IQ of 180 or higher. Other factors that distinguish gifted females from one another are their predominant type of gifted abilities (such as intellectual, creative, artistic, leadership, athletic, musical, linguistic, psychomotor, and/or social-emotional giftedness), additional neurodivergent characteristics, learning disabilities for twice-exceptional females, physical and mental challenges, and how the gifted individual chooses to apply her gifted talents if at all. The giftedness umbrella can encompass underachievers (sometimes referred to as selective consumers) and overachievers. Giftedness is not synonymous with achievement despite what some in the gifted field assert. It may or may not lead a gifted girl to do well academically or result in fame, fortune, or culturally recognized success as an adult. Many factors affect its expression, but no matter what, a gifted female remains gifted throughout her lifetime.

That said, gifted individuals typically see and feel the world differently than the neurotypical population and exhibit unique thought processes, interpersonal skills, emotional responses, and physical reactivity. This uniqueness can make them feel out of sync, sometimes even with gifted peers, and negatively impacts them in a variety of other ways due to the possible mismatch between their abilities and skill levels and their emotional, physical, and spiritual development. The gifted individual can appear to be incredibly mature at times and, at other times, extremely immature. This asynchronicity can often be overwhelming for gifted females, because it places them outside normal developmental patterns. And it's exceptionally challenging for gifted girls trying to adapt to a school environment structured for more neurotypical age cohorts. In *Off The Charts*, Stephanie Tolan describes the Columbus Group, made up of five experts in giftedness—Dr. Christine Neville, Dr. Linda Silverman, Kathi Kearney, Martha Morelock, and Tolan—who gathered in 1991 and defined giftedness in this way: "Giftedness is asynchronous development in which advanced cognitive abilities and heightened intensity combine to create inner experiences and awareness that are qualitatively different from the norm."

GEARING UP FOR BATTLE

As humans, we are born with an engrained need to categorize, and putting individuals into groups based on intelligence level is common practice, beginning when we're quite young.

Researchers have found that at the preschool level, very young children seem not to differentiate between girls and boys in terms of their notions about intelligence level. However, researchers Lin Bian, Sarah-Jane Leslie, and Andrei Cimpian (as discussed in "Why Young Girls Don't Think They're Smart Enough") discovered that, unfortunately, starting around age six, this perception begins to change. Girls are less likely to believe that members of their gender can be "really, really smart." At this age, they also begin to avoid activities said to be for children who are "really smart." These findings suggest that gendered notions of brilliance are acquired at a young age and impact girls' interests as well as their willingness to challenge themselves. Sadly, the stereotype that females are not naturally brilliant seems to be implanted very early on in our young minds.

As young girls, a number of daughters in the study countered this mindset regarding gender-stereotyped activities and chose to socialize mainly with boys. For example, one mother of two gifted daughters stated, "My oldest was always much friendlier with boys. She thought boys were much more interesting—actually both my girls did—because they did much more fun things. They never had much patience for girl drama." Perhaps, like the daughters of many other mothers interviewed, these gifted girls found that the games and activities for the "really, really smart" kids that the boys were involved in were more interesting and challenging. Additionally, these bright boys may have been more like true peers for their bright daughters, because research has found that gifted girls are in fact more like gifted boys in many ways than they are like girls of average intelligence.

Another developmental curve ball for gifted girls occurs around middle school or even a year or two before. During this time, females who are exceptionally bright begin to be negatively judged, which impacts their standing in the social pecking order. This social rejection can be related not only to the girl's intelligence but also to her interests, appearance, and unique personality characteristics. This may be particularly devastating for many smart girls who served as leaders in the elementary grades and whose peers previously looked up to them. As one mother mentioned, her daughter led a charmed life up until fifth grade when social conflicts took over her life. Gifted girls at this age frequently find they are forced to choose from less-than-desirable options in an attempt to survive in the world outside their home.

And even if a gifted girl develops the necessary coping skills for herself, watching the cruel way other girls are mistreated may be as painful for her as if she were experiencing this abuse personally—similar to subjects in Milgram's study who felt the pain of those they mistakenly believed they had shocked. This proved to be the case for one daughter in the study who became very upset in the seventh grade after witnessing how mean kids were behaving toward each other. According to her mother, "She'd observe kids who'd been in elementary school together being really close to one person until another person came along and then turned on them. My daughter never had any tolerance for that kind of cruelty…As a result, she gravitated to hanging out with older, more mature people and had a lot of male friends. She didn't suffer fools wisely."

Kerr points out in *Smart Girls* that as gifted girls enter adolescence, their social skills and attractiveness to boys become more important to both peers and parents. In many cases, the impact of giftedness upon a daughter's likeability begins to worry her parents, who want her to be happy, which typically means "fitting in." Parents may start to praise their daughters' appearance more and unconsciously prioritize popularity over intellectual accomplishments.

As a result, upon entering their middle school years, gifted girls become more aware of the culture's strict gendered guidelines about manners and appropriate behaviors (which includes downplaying their "smarts"), and many grasp that these directives negatively impact their ability to self-actualize. So if gifted females adapt to these norms, it can be like shooting themselves in the foot. These gender stereotypes for females with high intelligence form a type of psychological straitjacket, limiting behaviors that enhance success.

Good news, bad news—Kerr believes that some gifted girls are quite adept at adjusting to gender scripts, because by virtue of their sex and atypical intelligence level, they had lots of experience early on adjusting to the dominant group in an effort to fit in. Kerr shares that what makes this situation the most poignant for her is that the giftedness of these girls must so often be applied to fitting in rather than focusing on achieving their dreams. In some cases, however, a gifted girl may take on the formidable task of trying to do both: to be popular while still pursuing her dream through academic success. In a 1995 article "To Be Gifted or Feminine: The Forced Choice of Adolescence," Silverman aptly described this scenario:

> Essentially, the gifted young woman is faced with Sophie's Choice: if she chooses to be true to herself, to honor her drive for achievement and self-actualization, she breaks some unspoken rule and faces disconnection, taunts, and rejection from both male and female peers. If she chooses to give up her dreams, to hold herself back, to redirect her energies into the feminine spheres—preoccupation with boys, clothes, appearance, observing her tone of voice, choice of words and body language, remaking herself to become attractive to the opposite sex—she is accepted and rewarded for her efforts.

Since there is little immediate value in choosing achievement over social acceptance, a girl would have to have incredible self-assurance to make that choice.

This was true for one of the daughters I interviewed who found this struggle to be mentally and emotionally exhausting. As this daughter put it, "In high school, I didn't want to subsume my academic focus in favor of partying and popularity, but I also never wanted to be an outcast. So I understood that I had to achieve this by sheer force of personality, and it took a huge amount of work to hold that together! As a result, I think I had a sort of breakdown when I went to college."

However, the majority of the sampled daughters refused to put on the gender straitjackets for gifted females. Many donned other gear to protect themselves during the battle waged against them primarily in middle school, high school, and, for some, even college. This "gear" came in several forms—thorns and shells (described by Kerr) as well as masks. Many of the fifty-eight daughters chose to wear thorns during adolescence to defend against societal pressures to be normal. They rebelled against authority, became intolerant of the status quo, and tended to be more self-righteous and aggressive. This prickliness made social interactions a bit of a challenge for these gifted girls and often caused some friction in the mother/daughter relationships as well. In one case, however, both the mother and daughter (now a pediatric anesthesiologist) believe in hindsight that these thorns served the daughter well. They enabled her to separate from a bad peer group in high school and blaze her own trail in an environment that wasn't at all supportive of bright females. However, it did result in her music teacher throwing an eraser at her during band practice, which led to a fiery parent-teacher conference in the principal's office.

Conversely, a handful of the daughters chose to develop a shell to protect themselves from the pain of being different. The mothers described these gifted girls as becoming more private, shy, introverted, and modest, starting in middle school, and emerging from their shells as adults while quietly pursuing their passions. These daughters may have been more introverted by nature than the others in the sample, and when faced with the social challenges experienced by gifted preteens, they preferred their own company (and intellectual stimulation) over contending with a hostile crowd. The following is an excerpt of the interview with one daughter (a brilliant young woman getting her PhD in biology from a top university at the time of the interview) who effectively used a shell to survive this difficult phase.

INTERVIEWER (ME): CAN YOU REMEMBER SOME DIFFIcult times in your life when you were growing up?

Daughter: I think the main one for me was high school, because I didn't have a ton of friends, and I was stressed out and sleep deprived. But I think that the good thing was, especially about my mother, that she never pressured me to do things other than I wanted to do. I mean by not asking "Oh, aren't you going out with friends?" or asking kind of leading questions like that and kind of letting me make my own choices rather than trying to push me one way or the other…I was really pretty shy in high school. I think that the thing that made making friends in the eighth grade year easy was that the school was so small, and you had a group of people that you took anywhere from like six to seven to eight classes with them, so you would be with them all day. But then, starting freshman year, those groups kind of got broken up a little bit, because people were branching off to be able to take different things. So you didn't have a core group that you were with.

Interviewer: Can you remember how you dealt with this?

Daughter: I just kind of studied and did gymnastics fifteen to eighteen hours a week and read books on the weekends, and that was life.

Interviewer: Did you feel comfortable telling your mom about issues or concerns that you had when you were growing up?

Daughter: I think when I was little, yes. But I've also been the kind of kid who likes to show to the authority figures that, you know, I like to please them and show them that I'm a good kid and all that. So I think that if I had issues, it might make me look like a bad kid…like, if I was fighting with a friend, I might not have told her about that. So yeah, I would try to hide. I got through it. I wasn't particularly happy in high school, but I mean I did what I needed to do. I got studying done, and I did gymnastics, and I liked gymnastics and all that. I definitely played the "if I get through this, college will be better" mantra game.

FINALLY, MASKS WERE CHOSEN BY SEVERAL OF THE daughters who attempted to cover up their giftedness and, like chameleons, blend in with the appearance and behaviors of their age cohorts. One mother noted that her younger daughter, who always felt like she was in her big sister's shadow academically although she was equally as capable, adopted this strategy. According to her mother, by middle school, this daughter chose a different approach than her big sister and took on the persona of "the quintessential dumb blond to avoid the social retribution that comes with being exceptionally smart. She'd toss her little blond ponytail, and people would ask, 'Don't you wish you were as smart as your sister?' And she'd reply, 'Oh, yeah!' knowing she was every bit as bright but hid it well. She didn't let her grades slip, but she did it quietly, whereas my older daughter was much more in your face with it—totally, totally competitive." Another mother described the mask her daughter put on, pretending to be very extroverted and social: "My daughter is not outgoing socially, and yet she can pretend to be that way. What she does is…she's actually quite shy and withdrawn, but she puts on this outside persona, which takes on a leadership role, and people see that, and then they can't get through this to see the real person my daughter is."

Another mother shared an interesting example of her daughter who chose not only to don a mask but entirely different personas. This daughter (who was raised in a rural area and attended three different elementary schools) came up with a completely different and very creative form of protecting her inner core and dealing with stressful experiences: she developed false personas. This highly gifted girl first took on a different persona in elementary school during an after-school class. The mother said, "She did something kind of weird. She can put on an accent really, really well, so she decided that she was Scottish. So she had this identity that she was the little Scottish girl." She finally confessed to her mother about three-quarters of the way through the class and said she didn't want to go anymore—she didn't want to keep acting out this false identity. Then during her sophomore year in college, her mother assumed her daughter was doing okay, because, as she stated, "She was going to class, getting good grades, and all that, but she called and said, 'I want to drop out.' About the same time, her professor called me and asked to speak to her guardian, and I said, 'Well, I'm her mother.' And he said, 'Your daughter told us you were dead!' (This mother paused at this point and shared, "This is a terrible story…I'm not really fond of this, but I can kind of laugh at it now.") So her daughter had established a completely different identity and knew she had to drop out, because she just didn't want to maintain it anymore. According to her mother, "I think as my daughter got more depressed, she didn't want to be herself—she wanted to be somebody else…so she became a girl from the Netherlands." This mother had a talk with her daughter, who later told her mother it was a very important talk. Her mother said, "You don't have to do anything you don't want to do anymore, because you're an adult now. You don't have to go to school to please me or just because you think you have to. But you can't live at home." So the daughter rented an apartment, found work doing "crappy things" ("which was part of what convinced her to go back to school"), saw a therapist, and took medication. By the end of spring, she transferred to another university. She then went on to get a PhD and is a university professor, a happily married mother, and very close to her mom.

But what happens to some bright girls who either don't or simply can't conform or don protective gear? One mother of two autistic daughters shared a heartbreaking example of this. The older daughter has a master of science degree and works in radiology. The younger is currently working on her bachelor of science degree (because she hadn't yet completed undergrad, she wasn't included in the sample of fifty-eight daughters). The mother said, "Both of my daughters were comfortable doing different activities and with different social groups until the age of ten or eleven. The girls—then preteens—started dressing a certain way and speaking a certain way and having their hair a certain way. Neither of my daughters wear makeup or get their hair done—they're not 'girly' girls. So they became more and more different from their peer group as they got older." Their mother said it was very painful to watch this, especially when her older daughter lost all her friends and became extremely unhappy and distressed.

It is important not to gloss over the deep pain many of the gifted girls experienced at this stage when they began to perceive themselves as weird and felt a deep sense of loneliness. And it is also critical to appreciate the pain their mothers felt witnessing their daughters go through this and their desperate desire to fix it. Most of the daughters in the study suffered significant social or emotional challenges going through this preteen and adolescent stage. Only about 15 percent of the daughters, according to their mothers, apparently did not spend much psychic energy or experience much angst trying to survive during this passage to adulthood.

For many gifted girls, resorting to thorns, shells, or masks can lead to inner conflict, as they are typically keenly aware that they are out of alignment with their true selves. However, the desire for fellowship is often universal. In his book, *Escape from Freedom*, Erich Fromm quotes Honore de Balzac (I apologize for the androcentrism used), "Man has a horror for aloneness." Fromm described the terror many feel of being alienated from one's community and the tremendous desire to belong. It seems that nothing, according to Fromm, is more difficult for an individual to bear than the feeling of not being identified with a larger group.

One mother stressed how traumatic it was for her daughter going through this stage and noted that it impacted her on a long-term basis:

> "I think that we have a tremendous challenge with young women to build their sense of self-esteem and confidence, because females can be hideously mean to each other, at certain ages, particularly during the middle-school years, which are the most devastating. A girl can be your best friend today and then call you that night and say, 'You know, I'm not even going to talk to you tomorrow, because I hate you.' And it's that roller-coaster that gets in the way of everything—it's an emotional roller coaster and, as a mom, you spend a lot of time and angst figuring out how you can keep [your daughter's] confidence level up—that self-worth level up."

This mother continued:

> "My daughter [now a successful attorney, married with gifted children] got through that ugly middle-school period, but I think it's hard…and it's not the same at all for boys…It marks girls in ways that are very recognizable where they are not really sure where or how they fit into the social structure or clique structure of high school. I think it marks them…When they're going into puberty with all

this physical upheaval and emotional upheaval. It just breaks your heart...My daughter just kind of muddled through this."

In her wonderful story "I Stand Here Ironing," Tillie Olsen perfectly captures the angst of this situation for young, gifted girls by describing her adolescent daughter:

> She was too vulnerable for that terrible world of youthful competition, of preening and parading, of constant measuring of yourself against every other, of envy, 'If I had that copper hair,' 'If I had that skin...' She tormented herself enough about not looking like the others, there was enough of the unsureness, the having to be conscious of words before you speak, the constant caring—what are they thinking of me?

However, while the good news is that gifted females are typically very socially aware, the bad news is that, according to Silverman in "The Social Development of the Gifted," they can quickly pick up social cues and are better than boys at imitation. As a result, gifted girls often figure out what's necessary to fit in and may try desperately to adapt. They are typically overly sensitive to what others think and have an exceptional ability to read the room (and, sadly, the message they get back typically does not favor female intelligence). This ability can be an asset, especially later in life, but it often results in these girls hiding parts of who they are and may lead to overcompensating for differences in a variety of dysfunctional ways including wasting valuable psychic energy on the various machinations required to fit in.

SCHOOL DAYS (OR DAZE)

Roeper described the vulnerability gifted individuals face in our educational system in *The Eye of the Beholder*: "Many of us feel we are not legitimate in the eyes of those in charge. We've accepted that there is a hierarchy of values and rights....And in our schools, we find that gifted children don't feel that their needs are legitimate in the eyes of their teachers." Not surprisingly, because of their gender, gifted female students often are especially disempowered.

Many gifted girls and their parents struggle to find an educational environment where the girls will be challenged and where their inherent love of learning will be nurtured. Unfortunately, gifted females find that the educational options available to them, in many cases, could be termed, at best, lacking (and, at worst, harmful) and are often not suited to their special needs. The school histories of the sampled daughters from kindergarten through high school revealed the never-ending challenge of finding a positive learning environment for these gifted, "box-resistant" girls.

A number of the sampled mothers shared their daughters' long history of being in constant flux during their school years. This involved changing schools, or grades and programs within schools, or dropping out of school for varying periods of time in search of a more nurturing educational environment up to and even through college. Nearly half of the studied daughters switched elementary schools, some two to three times. About 15 percent changed middle schools, and an equal number transferred to a different high school.

While transferring a child to a different school sounds like a simple solution, I think it should be noted that this often is a lot more complicated for the mothers involved than it may seem. The time, stress, and energy to find, research, and visit other schools in the quest for a better learning environment can be draining. In addition, completing all the documentation necessary to make such a change, applying one's best social-emotional skills to overcome possible barriers to admittance by the school's gatekeepers, and the huge task of psychologically preparing your gifted daughter for this upheaval in her daily life can be exhausting, especially when combined with feeling uncertain all along if this change will in fact solve the problem.

In terms of public versus private schools, more than 60 percent of the fifty-eight daughters attended public schools from kindergarten through twelfth grade. Three of the daughters attended only private schools, and two attended only parochial schools, while nearly 25 percent went back and forth between private/parochial and public. One daughter was homeschooled the entire time, and two others were homeschooled for only a little more than a year (one in early elementary and one in eighth grade). This small number of homeschooled cases is most likely the result of social conditions at the time. Most daughters were of school age in the 1980s, 1990s, and early 2000s when homeschooling was very much the exception, in part because of a lack of resources and public support, a nascent internet, and few local support systems available. So these three families were frontrunners in choosing to opt out of the traditional school system during this time.

The academic needs of the fifty-eight gifted daughters were addressed to varying degrees and in a variety of ways. The key factors involved were the quality of their local public school system, the availability of good private schools, and/or the family's access to and ability to pay for private resources outside the public school system. In the large number of cases where services for gifted students were unavailable or ineffective, the mothers went to great lengths to help establish gifted programs, start gifted schools, set up special activities outside of school, and/or pursue legal action to fund or gain access to the necessary services. Unfortunately, despite these efforts, a few of the gifted daughters had minimal access to any challenging educational opportunities outside the home from kindergarten through high school, but with the love, support, and encouragement of their mothers, they went on to thrive nonetheless.

In terms of the specific educational alternatives provided to a number of daughters in the sample during elementary and middle school, eleven of the fifty-eight were placed in gifted pull-out programs (although many mothers commented on the fact that these programs often fell short, offering only one to two hours a week of more advanced instruction), twenty were enrolled in full-time gifted programs, five were assigned to independent study programs, and four took enrichment classes. Several girls enrolled in alternative programs or schools in their district that were not specifically targeted to gifted students but were more appropriate for their needs. Fifteen of the fifty-eight were moved ahead in school, and several of these radically accelerated, skipping two or more grades. Two of the daughters attended a private school for gifted, and one went to a university laboratory school.

Twelve of the daughters took college classes while in high school, twenty-four took advanced placement or honors classes, two were in an International Baccalaureate (IB) program, and two went to a college prep magnet school.

Four of the girls studied in Europe while in high school, and three managed to complete the requirements for a cosmetology license as high school students. One daughter went off to a private boarding school ninth through twelfth grade, and three girls attended a state residential program for gifted high school students.

Because teachers have been found to believe and reinforce one of the most prevalent sex stereotypes—that males have more innate ability while females must work harder—according to Reis in "Social and Emotional Issues Faced by Gifted Girls in Elementary and Secondary School," it was not uncommon for some of these daughters to find themselves the only female in their advanced classes or programs. For example, one daughter who was in the IB program was the only girl in it. Seven other sampled daughters found themselves the only female in accelerated science and math classes. In one instance, a daughter who had outrun the math program at her private high school along with six other male students was taught an advanced class by one of the student's fathers who volunteered his services. He was a well-known pioneer in tech who recognized the gifted girl's high math ability but commented that her responses were "too prolix"—a less-than-helpful critique, it seems, based perhaps on gender differences in style. Another daughter found herself the only female in vocational education classes that she took in addition to her college prep curriculum.

Conversely, five of the fifty-eight girls attended all-girls high schools, thereby opting for a single-sex learning environment that they believed to be more empowering for female students. This opinion is supported by Judith Harris Rich in *Nurture Assumption*: individuals feel uncomfortable about violating the norms of their group because of the conflict between the desire to do well and the feeling that doing well would conflict with the status quo. And because it's less acceptable for females to be academic superstars, especially in fields like STEM that are dominated by men, they may downplay their ability. But in contexts where gender is less salient such as all-girl schools, females perform better in science and math, with women's colleges producing a disproportionate number of outstanding scientists.

Four of the fifty-eight daughters in the sample attended public schools that offered no gifted services, with three of these girls eventually switching to private schools. Sadly, this alternative is typically unavailable to families without the necessary resources to make this possible. Another four of the gifted daughters were not accepted into their school's gifted program in elementary school, but three of these girls were identified eventually as twice exceptional in middle school, high school, or community college. The remaining fourth student was identified as gifted as a young adult, but due to serious health issues and the fact that her family's financial crises resulted in frequent moves, she missed more than one-third of elementary school, resulting in a less-than-optimal learning experience for her during these early years.

Finally, two daughters were accepted into their school's gifted program but rejected the offer to participate. One wanted to stay with her friends in the mainstream class, and the mother of the remaining girl made this decision because she felt that her older daughter had struggled so much by being labeled gifted, as in "different," that she just wanted her younger daughter to have a "normal" school experience. Some common concerns among gifted students (and, in some cases, their parents) about participating in special services for gifted include anxiety about being labeled "nerdy," the assumption that they would not benefit from the program, that they would not measure up, and/or fears about being too academically pressured.

For a few of the sampled families, the problem of trying to find a good educational fit for their gifted girl reared its head even before elementary school. One mother shared about her daughter's preschool experience.

> "By age three, my daughter had a vocabulary bigger than her preschool teacher's. One day, the teacher called and said, 'Your daughter used a bad word today. We went to the farm, and she called one of the animals an odiferous ovine, and we can't have them using bathroom language.' And I asked, 'What do you think ovine means?' She thought it referred to ovaries. And I said, 'No. Ovine is to sheep as bovine is to cow as canine is to dog as feline is to cat.'"

This mother said her daughter had learned this word from reading adult-level books about animals since she was a toddler.

For other families in the sample, the realization that finding an appropriate learning environment was going to be a challenge hit when their girl started elementary school and they became aware their daughter had already mastered the work required for kindergarten if not several grades beyond. This was described by a mother who, with her husband, purposely (and at great expense and effort) moved to a home in a neighborhood with a "highly ranked" school system, attended by the offspring of professors from one of the top universities in the country, right before their bright daughter started kindergarten. The mother was taken by surprise when she went to the first parent-teacher conference, and the kindergarten teacher suggested she find a better placement for her gifted girl, noting that she would not get the support and challenge she needed for her advanced academic skills in her current "outstanding" public school. Unfortunately, because the public school system in their community had such a great reputation, there were limited private school options and no schools targeted to meet the needs of gifted. After finding one private school that the parents thought might work, this daughter refused to leave her elementary school, wanting to stay with her group of friends. Sadly, she went on to suffer being underchallenged throughout elementary school.

One mother shared an extremely difficult school experience. When her daughter started elementary school, the program for gifted students was a pull-out program that students attended one day per week. However, the coordinator of gifted services for the district was interested in new approaches to gifted learning and saw a need for something more. So a group of parents collaborated with her (brainstorming, researching, and visiting other gifted programs around the country) and created a full-time program for the most highly gifted kids with IQs over 150. The students would attend the gifted center full time, five days a week. The mother described her daughter's school history up to this point:

> "My daughter was an odd duck…She started school young because she had the very last cut-off for birthdays, but she was so far beyond the kindergarten

class that she was spending part of the day in first grade and part in second grade. The teacher wanted to advance her to second grade, but the district was opposed to double promotion. When she was in the second grade class, they were all turning nine, and she was over two years younger than most and still smarter than everybody by far. After a couple of months, she eventually was double promoted, but the story becomes kind of sad in that by fifth grade, the teacher didn't know what to do with her as far as giving her advanced materials, and my daughter was reading long novels and could do all the other work. So the teacher had a closet in the classroom about two feet by three feet, and she told my daughter that she would make this her own spot. She gave her a rug and flashlight and said this would be her personal 'reading spot.' So my daughter spent her days in fifth grade in the teacher's closet…And the teacher would kind of just forget about her…I was outraged. I was just livid. It was just beyond me that this teacher couldn't provide anything better for my daughter than her closet and a flashlight… It was horrid, and I thought, *Okay, I want to take a picture of the closet and go to the school board and shout and scream, "Look at this spot on the floor where you're putting my child in the dark in the closet! This is the best you can do? Are you kidding?"* But my daughter was happy there. She was like, 'Oh, good! I get to be in the closet away from all those kids.' She couldn't stand their behavior problems in class. She hated them making fun of her and her books. So school was not a real fun experience, and she was definitely not learning in the classroom. She already knew what they were doing in math and science and everything else, so why be in the class with the kids giving her trouble? She was just as happy to be in the closet. I was horrified, but I didn't make a huge fuss about it, because I just wanted to get her through this year, because that's the year we worked on implementing the full-time program, and I thought, *If we can just get through this year, she'll be somewhere else next year.* The next year, for sixth grade, my daughter was in the new full-time gifted center program."

Another gifted daughter in the sample was a student in a large, urban public school system that offered no special instruction for high-ability students. (In fact, this daughter was never officially identified, because her district offered no services for gifted at all.) Her mother got divorced when the daughter was ten and worked full-time to support her two children while taking college classes at night. They had very limited financial resources during this period, and according to the daughter, "Emotionally, my mom was broken—we were really struggling." During this difficult period for her mother, this daughter was facing her own issues, especially at school, and in the eleventh grade, she made the choice to drop out. This devastated her mother: "Nobody in our family ever dropped out of high school. I thought I had lost her. I really did." But unbeknownst to her mother, the daughter had a plan to get her graduate equivalency diploma (GED) through the district's alternative education program. To be accepted into this program, a student either had to be truant or pregnant. The mother told her daughter when she got into this program for truancy rather than pregnancy, "Well, you made the right choice there!" She lived at home, worked odd jobs, and eventually enrolled at the local state commuter college that, fortunately, offered a special program to promote students of color (which she was) in STEM careers. With the support of a scientist who she interned with during the summer after her junior year in college, she returned for her senior year, switched her major from psychology to premed, and completed nearly all of her premed requirements in one year. This young woman eventually went on to earn her MD/PhD from a leading medical center.

One of the subsample of fifty-eight daughters who were interviewed shared one final example of the challenge gifted females face from kindergarten through high school. This gifted girl was "saved" by her involvement in a work-study program offered in high school. Her mother commented, "She surprised us all. While she was in high school, she took a work-study program and did office work for [a large global high-tech corporation] and was asked if she wanted to put a radio together. And she did. She was never very good at math, but before we knew it, she became an engineer." The daughter expanded on this: "When I started working [at a high-tech firm] and I saw all this neat equipment all over the place, I got interested in it and decided that I wanted to pursue it. So I just kind of made the decision to do that." She stated that up to this point, she hadn't been challenged "at all" in school. "I would write my essays on the bus on the way to school and get As, and it was a detriment. I dropped out of math in the tenth grade. My guidance counselors let me. My parents didn't say much, and that was a mistake." She stated the reason why she dropped out of math in tenth grade: "I just didn't like school anymore. In fact, in my senior year, I was only in school like a couple of hours a day. I was working two jobs—I had an afternoon apprenticeship in accounting and was the manager at [a fast-food restaurant] at night." She added, "The apprenticeship came up through my high school—it was a work-study program." Despite dropping out of math in tenth grade, at the start of twelfth grade, this gifted student got one of two jobs offered to high school students (by the global high-tech firm). "How I managed to get this job is a good question, because it was an accounting job. And for the life of me, I don't know. I must have done well in the interview. I don't know! It was a big mistake [dropping out of math in tenth grade], because I later went to work for [the global high-tech firm] and decided I wanted to be an engineer, and all of a sudden, I didn't have any of the prerequisites. I had to go to junior college to get tutoring to be able to take those courses so I could be an engineer." But she admitted, in hindsight, that this may have been a positive development: "Graduating at seventeen and not being sure of exactly what to focus on, junior college was a good experience. It was only one year, but it was a year well spent for me just in terms of getting my feet back on the ground and getting ready to go to college!" She continued,

> "And when the work-study program ended, they offered me a permanent position, and I stayed at (this corporation) while I was at the junior college. They then moved me into a position for engineers, because I was going to go to engineering school. So I moved to swing shift and was working on the assembly lines, working with microscopes, solder-

ing lines, fixing resistors and stuff, and worked with an engineer to get me ready for college—he was kind of a mentor to me."

This gifted female went on to get bachelor's and master's degrees in engineering and worked for a top university in its lab. Her mother stated that she was published, traveled, and gave talks, and after a few years, she was enrolled in a PhD program in engineering. The daughter eventually dropped out, having completed all but her dissertation, to have children. She is now a mother of five neurodiverse children and toys with the idea of eventually teaching at a community college. She noted, "Teaching is something that I really would enjoy doing. I don't think I'll go back to the corporate world just because of having to work summers, and by the time [my youngest] is out of school, I'm going to be sixty [laughter], and I probably can't go back to work then."

FEELING LIKE "OTHER"

As these examples and the majority of the fifty-eight daughters' academic histories underscore, the process of making it through kindergarten to college can seem like running a gauntlet, adversely affecting gifted females who are outside the norm—like swans in a system built for ducks. This "ugly duckling" situation is further compounded for individuals who are both gifted and learning or neurologically disabled (labeled twice exceptional). According to the NAGC, the term twice exceptional, also known as 2E, describes gifted children who have the potential for high achievement but also have one or more disabilities including learning disabilities, speech and language disorders, emotional/

behavioral disorders, physical disabilities, autism spectrum disorder, or other impairments such as attention-deficit/hyperactivity disorder (ADHD). Because of their cognitive disabilities and, possibly, other atypical behavioral characteristics, these individuals' giftedness may be harder to identify and may go undiscovered throughout their lifetime. Additionally, the twice-exceptional girl may become increasingly frustrated as she progresses through school, being told of her high intellectual potential but stymied by disabilities that cause her to fail and feel like a misfit. A mother of a highly gifted daughter described this situation: "It was a relief for our younger daughter to finally get special ed status—she realized there was something going on and couldn't understand why, if she was so smart, she was having so much trouble. Because even though she was labeled gifted, she didn't feel smart—there was so much she wasn't able to do." This daughter had taken an IQ test, so she knew she qualified for the gifted program, but she shared a dream she had with her mother. In this dream, she had an image that she was in a room with lots of doors and with a bunch of people who were disabled in some way. The blind could exit through one door, the deaf could leave through another, and so on. She said, "I was left in the room all alone, because my needs were not visible." This was really tough for her to deal with, her mother noted sadly.

It's likely that many gifted females experience this ugly duckling syndrome. But unlike the fairy tale, their essential "beauty" (giftedness) is rarely discovered or valued. As a result, they go through life feeling like misfits who somehow ended up in a brood instead of a bevy. As Ginny Kochis, writer and a mother of gifted, put it in her article "Want to Have Your Heart Broken? Take a Look at an Angry

Gifted Kid," giftedness sometimes is not a "gift" so much as simply a difference, a biological variation from the norm. Regrettably, in many cases, this lifelong sense of otherness can cause bright girls and women to feel an ongoing sense of shame rather than realizing they are stuck in a world, surrounded by individuals of normal intelligence. (Shame has been defined by social scientist Brené Brown, in *Daring Greatly*, as "the intensely painful feeling or experience of believing that we are flawed and therefore unworthy of love and belonging.") This sense of being different, however, can sometimes be two sided, with gifted females experiencing a combination of enjoying, and feeling pride in, their unique mental richness and abilities while at the same time feeling abnormal and deserving of rejection. Tillie Olsen describes this perfectly when the mother in her story refers to her gifted adolescent daughter:

> Sometimes, to make me laugh, or out of her despair, she would imitate happenings…at school. I think I said once: "Why don't you do something like this in the school amateur show?" One morning she phoned me at work, hardly understandable through the weeping: "Mother, I did it. I won, I won; they gave me first prize; they clapped and clapped and wouldn't let me go." Now suddenly she was "Somebody" and as imprisoned in her difference as she had been in anonymity.

But even for gifted girls fortunate enough to be in more supportive and academically challenging educational environments with their bevy of intellectual peers, this sense of being an "ugly duckling" may persist. Because gifted individuals are a very diverse population with a wide range of intellectual, emotional, and behavioral characteristics, they may be quite dissimilar from one another. Tolan explains the dynamics of this situation in her article "Self-Knowledge, Self-Esteem, and the Gifted Adult." She states that individuals at the other lower end of the IQ scale, who have more limited mental capacity, seem to be considerably more alike. However, moving upward on the intelligence scale, as mental abilities become less restricted, no individual can possibly have "all the many capacities available to the extraordinary, beyond-the-norms, human mind." As a result, each gifted individual will exhibit a constellation of these capacities that differs from the constellation of any other gifted individual. This heterogeneity among the gifted population, Tolan poses, may be why so many gifted people fail to recognize their own high intelligence level—they observe what other gifted people are like and don't see a reflection of themselves. And sadly, they often fail to find a true peer who shares a similar intellectual constellation.

Along these lines, a gifted individual raised among other gifted folks with highly gifted parents and siblings and in an area of educational privilege would likely have trouble recognizing herself and her offspring as anything other than average. Since their brightness is normal for them and for their family and community, they almost uniformly assume this must be normal, which causes confusion as they venture outside their bubble.

CAGED CHEETAHS

Most mothers in my study learned that our society (and most notably our school systems) is not focused on nurturing giftedness, especially female giftedness. Many communities' inability to even acknowledge giftedness and therefore provide services to address these special needs creates a hostile and isolating experience for gifted girls. Not only is the tenderness and care society often shows to those on the lower end of the intelligence quotient rarely shown to gifted individuals falling two to three standard deviations on the upper end, but often the opposite occurs. In our competitive, market-driven culture, gifted individuals are perceived as being born already having a leg up. Others envy them because they assume gifted individuals have unearned advantages in the dog-eat-dog race to success. In other words, many believe that gifted girls don't need any help—they'll be just fine.

But many gifted mothers know that without services for their girls at the upper end of the intelligence spectrum, they will not be just fine. And even when the evidence of this is right in front of them, school administrators often continue to ignore, deny, and dismiss the scale of suffering that these students experience. These administrators frequently resort to a Catch-22 excuse that if a gifted girl can't cope (showing behavior including acting out, underperforming, or becoming the class clown) in a system that is failing her, she most likely was never gifted in the first place. And although the cultural myth that equates giftedness with high achievement may seem to hold true for some gifted girls who conform and do glowingly on measurable indicators of "success" such as grades, awards, and/or achievement tests, this level of academic performance may be masking the harm they may experience due to their hostile, anti-intellectual learning environment. For these girls, it is frequently only their mothers who know the sad reality about what's really going on. Their daughters are not flourishing despite all the academic accolades and appearances to the contrary.

In her brilliant article "Is It a Cheetah?" Tolan provides an excellent metaphor for gifted children "caught" in our educational system. She states,

> The child who does well in school, gets good grades, wins awards, and "performs" beyond the norms for his or her age, is considered talented. The child who does not, no matter what his innate intellectual capacities or developmental level, is less and less likely to be identified, less and less likely to be served…A cheetah metaphor can help us see the problem with achievement-oriented thinking. The cheetah is the fastest animal on earth…But cheetahs are not always running. In fact, they are able to maintain top speed only for a limited time, after which they need a considerable period of rest…This is an animal biologically designed to run…While body design in nature is utilitarian, it also creates a powerful internal drive. The cheetah needs to run! Despite design and need however, certain conditions are necessary if it is to attain its famous 70 mph top speed…It must have plenty of room to run…If a cheetah is confined to a 10 X 12 foot cage…it may pace or fling itself against the bars in restless frustration…A school system that defines giftedness (or talent) as behavior, achievement and performance is as compromised in its ability to recognize its highly gifted students and to give them what they need as a zoo would be to recognize and provide for its cheetahs if it looked only for speed… Schools are to extraordinarily intelligent children what zoos are to cheetahs. Many schools provide a

10 x 12 foot cage, giving the unusual mind no room to get up to speed. Many highly gifted children sit in the classroom the way big cats sit in their cages, dull-eyed and silent. Some, unable to resist the urge....pace the bars, snarl and lash out at their keepers, or throw themselves against the bars until they do themselves damage.

And for our daughters who are twice exceptional, this educational environment may be even more harmful. Again, the myth that giftedness means high academic performance comes into play for these children. This high-performance level may be nearly impossible for a gifted, twice-exceptional girl to achieve unless she receives specialized help. In some school districts, students must be both in the top 99 percent of the class academically and score high enough on an IQ test for specialized gifted services. Using these criteria, chances are that any student who is 2E won't be considered gifted and therefore won't qualify for gifted instruction. For some, the reverse may happen—the twice-exceptional female may be deprived of services typically provided by the school to special education students because she has been labeled "gifted," and therefore, the school administrators may feel she's not in need of extra help.

Finally, some other girls labeled gifted might be good at masking their learning struggles, appearing to be model high-achieving gifted students while struggling on their own with twice-exceptional issues and, therefore, not officially identified as 2E. Some interviewed mothers lamented that because their daughters were not officially diagnosed as twice exceptional, their girls often received little or no support for dealing with these disabilities. While other mothers shared that sometimes even if their gifted girls were identified as 2E (and therefore had an Individualized Education Plan, or IEP, and/or a 504 plan to ensure equitable access to an appropriate learning environment), services still remained unavailable to them. As a result, the school system often fails many twice-exceptional gifted girls twice, leaving them feeling like they are supposed to be smart but with little understanding of, and support for, what's "wrong" with them.

SLICING UP THE PIE

In addition to most schools' underlying ethos of teaching to the norm, the cultural notion of rugged individualism is imbedded into our educational systems. We are all socialized to believe that everyone should make it on her own, independent of government or community resources or support. Competition is valued over collaboration, and this "every man for himself" attitude breeds scarcity fears that permeate all aspects of our lives as well as our daughters'. From our parenting beliefs ("I'm not enough—other mothers are doing more") to our schools ("Resources are limited, so not every student can get a fair share of the pie"), our culture exalts those on top and blames victims for their failures. For many parents fighting for help for their children, the fear of them failing to succeed in a society based on rugged individualism that provides little to no support is a constant terror. We're all afraid of our children winding up as adults in a zero-sum society as "them"—those on the bottom.

The idea that there is not enough to go around is, in fact, a very sad reality for most school districts (and communities in general), given grossly inadequate state and federal funding. Consequently, in many districts, parent groups representing children with different learning needs often find themselves fighting each other over scraps to ensure a decent future for their offspring. So rather than parents working together in a win-win, collaborative approach to improve education in their district and demand the necessary resources for all children to thrive, many mothers feel compelled to do something they would prefer not to: fight to meet their own child's needs in a zero-sum game. As economist and author of *The Sum of Us* Heather McGhee claims, we all suffer because our society was raised deficient in social solidarity.

The incredible lack of funding earmarked for gifted students on the federal level is stunning. According to the Department of Education website, roughly a mere $6 million is allocated annually to support innovative educational research projects for gifted and talented students. And the NAGC states that although federal law acknowledges that gifted children have unique needs, it offers no specific provisions, mandates, or requirements for serving these children. As a result, gifted education varies widely across the country, leaving gifted education up to the whims of local legislatures and the availability of local resources. This proved true for the sampled mothers from various states; great variability in both the quality and quantity of services existed for their gifted daughters, depending upon where they lived. One mother recounted her ongoing struggles to help her gifted children who were floundering in the school system where they lived on a mountain top in a rural area of the South. She finally decided to homeschool them for a few years, but the public outcry from their small community in which they had a family business was such that she was forced to reenroll them and attempt to find enrichment activities outside of the school environment.

Another mother in a different part of the country noted that quality gifted programs were available to both her daughters starting in third grade. They were then able to attend an excellent, state-funded boarding school for gifted students in high school. But this was, for sure, the exception for most of the study families. In fact, identifying gifted students is mandated in only thirty-two states and funded in fewer, while most teachers across the country receive only minimal instruction on the identification and enrichment of gifted children. There is no legal obligation to serve exceptional students. "It's never been federally required," says Pat O'Connell Johnson of the US Department of Education, according to journalist Jill Tucker. As Dr. Gail Post points out on her website, gifted students have traditionally received less than 1 percent of most school districts' special education budgets, resulting in many gifted students not receiving any services or receiving profoundly inadequate services that fail to address their needs. And, sadly, this bleak financial reality transforms many committed educators from service providers into service rationers, forced to parcel out limited services while facing tough budgetary constraints and strict laws and mandates.

DEVALUING GIFTEDNESS IN OUR SCHOOLS

In addition to the lack of financial resources allocated for gifted students, many school districts have few, if any, staff with the knowledge and expertise to assess gifted students' needs or the skills necessary to educate them adequately. Complicating this situation is the fact that gifted students are a highly diverse group, so no one curriculum that a district might develop has a high degree of success in meeting the unique needs of all the gifted students it serves. For example, given the different levels and types of giftedness, the asynchronicity levels, and the wide variety of needs for twice-exceptional students, gifted programs, like a one-hour-per-week pull-out program, often serve as Band-Aids and may even further a gifted girl's alienation and resentment of the educational system. She finds herself once again in an educational setting where she doesn't fit or is bored.

Dr. Deborah Ruf has studied different levels of giftedness and researched the fit between educational systems and the needs of gifted students. In the article "Why It's Sometimes Hard to Find the 'Right' School for Your Gifted Child," Ruf identifies a key obstacle for gifted children. Basically, this is the way most school systems are structured. In almost all cases, schools group and educate children by age rather than by ability or level of performance. This practice results in instruction being too slow and repetitive for gifted children (or "cheetahs"). These students don't get to learn nearly as much as they could from an environment that's a better fit for them. This can affect them on many levels including their happiness, excitement for learning and life, and behavior and cooperation. Ruf shares the findings of researcher Dr. David Lohman, who found that within a typical first grade classroom, the achievement range of the students is already twelve grade equivalents. This means that some first graders are already performing at the high school level in some areas, while others are performing at the kindergarten level—a grade behind. Ruf stresses that age alone is a convenient but inefficient way to group learners and that grouping kids this way makes about as much pedagogical sense as grouping them by height.

Another major problem with many educational systems relates to the performance criteria used to assess both school districts and teachers. This "bottom line" is based on how well their students do on achievement tests for each grade level. According to Ruf, the unfortunate result of this approach is that educators end up teaching mainly to the top of the bottom third of the students to bring up the grade average results. Ruf points out that since most students pass proficiency tests or are close to doing so even before they enter the grade, teachers focus solely on the bottom third of students. When Ruf asked a second grade teacher about whether the students who, at the start of the year, already demonstrated reading nearly two years above grade level also needed to be challenged, she responded, "No, they'll just be fine." The teacher added that these advanced students allowed more time for her to work with those children most "at risk." The teacher's rationalization for this (and, most likely, the story she needs to tell herself to comply with the common narrative within the district) is that it's far more important for the advanced children to gain appropriate life experiences with their age mates than for them to move forward academically. Ruf disagrees and argues that while social-emotional learning is important, this should not necessarily be the main focus of reading or math classes. And she cautions parents of gifted students to "just be aware that schools are not set up for every learner, no matter what they try to tell you."

In their article "Bore-Out: A Challenge for Unchallenged Gifted (Young) Adults," Dr. Ellen D. Fiedler and Dr. Noks Nauta explore a recently recognized condition related to understimulation termed bore-out. They describe the symptoms of this condition as exhaustion and a depressive mood coming from ongoing boredom. According to Fiedler and Nauta, bore-out occurs when gifted "find themselves in tedious, unstimulating situations, feeling as if time is barely dragging by, and as if their day-to-day lives have no purpose." The authors cite a Boredom Scale developed in 2013 by psychologist Gaby Reijseger et al. that includes self-report statements to assess bore-out such as these: "Time goes by very slowly, I feel bored, I spend my time aimlessly, I feel restless, I daydream, the day never ends, there is not so much to do." One of the interviewed daughters in my study used the term "waiting" to describe similar feelings, sharing that her entire four years in a highly ranked public high school were spent just waiting to be presented with information that triggered her love of learning and her need to be intellectually challenged. Fortunately, this gifted female experienced more intellectual challenge in college and went on to become a professor at an esteemed university. But four years "waiting" in high school is a long time to languish or for a gifted mind to be encaged.

One of the interviewed mothers, a veteran elementary school teacher and professor with a PhD in curriculum and instruction, described gifted students' daily reality in mainstream classrooms, saying,

> "When they're in a classroom and feeling so frustrated because they got it four days ago and this teacher is still going over it, they find it hard to understand why they're feeling that way. Teachers will feel like these kids are antisocial or they're too emotional or they're all those other dysfunctional labels, but gifted brains really don't want just to sit in idle. If any of us are in a workshop where it just seems really boring and we've already seen the material, we may take out our phones, or we may make notes to ourselves or just get up and leave."

Unfortunately, the option of just getting up and leaving is considered unacceptable for students in most schools today.

Paradoxically, while society fails to provide gifted students with the intellectual challenges and additional resources they might need to maximize their potential, at the same time, it holds high expectations for these students and conveys the message that they need to accomplish great things. The implication is that these individuals are inherently lucky and need to give back irrespective of all the obstacles society places in their path. Several interviewed daughters mentioned that they had suffered under the weight of feeling pressure to live up to the highest levels of their potential—all the while feeling unclear about how to pull this off.

It should be noted, however, that a number of interviewed daughters recounted less-than-ideal learning environments even in schools providing specialized services for gifted students. Many gifted pull-out programs provided enriched curricula on a very time-restricted basis. One hour per week of being intellectually challenged can hardly compensate for the nearly thirty hours spent being bored throughout the rest of the week. And because there's a tendency to assume that all exceptionally intelligent individuals strongly resemble each other, even in some of the self-contained classes or schools for gifted students set up around this false narrative, the situation may not be ideal, given the wide variation in different levels and types of giftedness as well as social-emotional needs. This was the situation for a profoundly gifted daughter interviewed for the study who attended a gifted school within a school. She said, "I went to [the self-contained, gifted school] full-time for three years with thirty-seven highly gifted kids. And

I know, for a while, they were either thinking of hiring a school psychiatrist, or they really should have, because everybody there either was seeing somebody or should have been." This daughter continued, "My wonderful sixth grade teacher lasted two years in teaching at the full-time gifted program—I don't think anybody realized exactly how hard on people that was going to be...Imagine, if you will, being a teacher at like the X-Men's school where you've got kids randomly electroshocking people and turning into hurricanes and mutating into things." When asked by the interviewer, "So it was like a free-for-all?" the daughter responded,

> "Yeah...which was good in a certain way and really bad in a certain way...I was definitely the one who got picked on, which was really good actually because it needed to happen...To a certain extent, I think that the kids who are bullying you are sort of doing you a favor, because it's kind of like the butterfly who has to fight its own way out of the cocoon. And when you're somebody like me who was like the little kid sitting under the desk, somebody sort of has to beat social-normal into you. So by providing, you know, not positive feedback, they at least were playing the role of the rest of the world, which was really useful, because it was during that time that I developed a sense of humor and figured out that you can't always sit under the desk and was taught how to attain a certain level of social respectability...I think [this situation] scared my mom to death...When they finally got me and all of us into a place where everybody was like us, they

assumed that suddenly we would all be…We would form our own society of 'gentle geeks,' and everyone would be happy, rainbows, puppy dogs, etc., which, shockingly, was not the case. But we were so bad, and this is really funny…we were so bad that in the sixth grade, as an attempt at behavior modification, they made us read *Lord of the Flies*…It was a good program, but you know, good things and easy things are not the same thing. If my mother was looking to create a great utopia for me, that's not what happened. But it was a place where we could all start to turn into the people that we would be later on, and that was good."

Unlike this daughter whose giftedness was identified early and who had a group of caring individuals attempting to meet her unique learning needs (albeit not perfectly), many gifted girls' needs are frequently not identified or, if so, they are not actively addressed within their school systems. Sometimes this is because many gifted girls, like females in general, have been socialized to be polite, not express their needs, and not "make trouble." As a result, they may hesitate to complain or even question the reality of their lives. As Ruf notes, some gifted children's temperaments are simply more flexible than others, and they conform to school expectations whether those expectations fit them well or not.

Consequently, mothers of gifted daughters may be unaware of the mismatch between their daughters' educational needs and what's being offered in the mainstream classroom. This situation may be exacerbated by the fact that in addition to the daughter not speaking up, the schools may withhold information from the parents about the high level of their daughter's intelligence and her special learning needs. Several interviewed mothers mentioned that their daughters' schools never informed them of their girls' results on the achievement, performance, and even IQ tests administered by the district, and it was only years later that they learned their scores from secondhand sources. One mother who in fact worked for the school district had a colleague inform her, years after her daughter graduated from high school, that her daughter had received the district's highest score ever for admittance to the gifted program. While many administrators and teachers in the district were aware of this, the mother was intentionally kept in the dark. A handful of other gifted mothers in the study shared similar stories. Given that knowledge is power, a mother who is unaware of her daughter's less-than-ideal learning environment can obviously do little to improve this situation, in many cases, unless her daughter goes against gendered constraints and speaks up or acts out.

Another sad outcome of the educational system's failure to acknowledge, nurture, and value gifted individuals is that it often creates a dysfunctional and isolating reality for many gifted students and their mothers. The suffering that results for gifted students, especially females, from the negative way people act around them and react to them can often profoundly change who they are. It can cause emotional pain, leading to psychological and even physical distress. This can devastate their mothers as well. Gifted educator and advocate Dr. Christine Winterbrook notes in her book *Gifted Women: On Becoming Ourselves* (coauthored by her daughter, Abby Noel Winterbrook) that gifted girls frequently struggle at school because the work moves too slowly or they feel different, cannot relate to classmates or their teacher, or are uncomfortable in a learning environment with little gifted culture. She goes on to stress that these feelings may then be internalized, resulting in physical and mental conditions including nausea, anxiety, or headaches.

CREATING DYSFUNCTIONAL MINDSETS

In addition, less-than-nurturing school environments can negatively impact gifted girls' personal notions about what it means to be really smart, leading to what Dweck terms in *Mindset: The New Psychology of Success* as a "fixed mindset." The stage for this limiting belief system is typically set in elementary school where the curriculum rarely challenges gifted students to do any real critical thinking. As a result, they often sail through grade school with little effort, rarely do poorly on tests or make mistakes, and start to equate being smart with having all the answers and, as one daughter put it, placing great value on being the "smartest jerk in the room."

But as they continue in school, the work gets harder, and these gifted students are eventually faced for the first time with a challenging academic environment. In the upper grades and beyond, gifted students confront the reality of more difficult subject matter, a tougher workload, smarter peers, more stringent and competitive grading, and less personalized instruction. For a number of both mothers and daughters in my study, this didn't occur until they went off to highly competitive colleges. This made the situation even more daunting, as they were cut off from their traditional support systems, resulting in lots of calls home for guidance from parents and, in a few cases, taking a break from school until they could adjust their mindset. One mother who had gone through the public school system got accepted into one of the most selective colleges in the country as a premed student. She was floored by the level of competition, especially in her science classes, and eventually dropped out of the premed track. It seemed like, decades later, she still regretted this decision, on some level, despite having a rich professional and personal life.

For students who have developed a fixed mindset based on their earlier school experiences, this new tough reality means they have to put in effort to do well, and without having developed the skills and discipline, they need to figure out how to apply themselves to learning properly. Often, they find themselves floundering. Because of their mindset, gifted girls falsely deduce that they in fact are not smart, resulting in self-doubt, anxiety, and a drop in achievement. Sadly, this is another way our culture and educational institutions fail gifted students: gifted children receive the message early on that easy success means they're intelligent and that making mistakes and having to work hard in school means that they're not. How ironic that in the real world, as Dweck notes, the hallmark of successful individuals is that they love learning, seek out challenges, value effort, and persist in the face of obstacles.

Conversely, for gifted students who do manage to survive and even thrive in academia and in their careers, another threat exists: they may become addicted to success, as described by Harvard Professor Arthur C. Brooks. Brooks highlights that success itself has addictive properties, given that praise stimulates the brain's neurotransmitter dopamine, which underlies all addictions. Research demonstrates that many workaholics willingly sacrifice their own well-being to keep getting hits of success, choosing specialness over personal happiness. According to Brooks in his article "'Success Addicts' Choose Being Special Over Being Happy," some scholars believe that the desire for success may be inherent to human nature. Brooks quotes psychologist William James: "We have an innate propensity to get ourselves noticed, and noticed favorably, by our kind." But as discussed above, "success," specialness, or eminence takes incredible effort, sometimes bordering on the pathological. In the 1980s, physician Robert Goldman, according to Brooks, found that more than half of competitive athletes would be willing to take a drug that would kill them in five years if it meant winning every competition. Brooks adds that, sadly, no matter what the outcome, most success addicts never feel successful enough, and many suffer from depression and anxiety. And because our culture values overwork, success, and fame, it provides fertile ground for gifted individuals to develop a mindset that breeds success addiction, which frequently comes at a steep cost—negatively impacting the relationships and love that enable a gifted individual to lead a well-balanced, happy life.

THERE'S MORE TO IT THAN IQ SCORES

A helpful way of identifying and understanding giftedness, despite the diversity shown in advanced mental abilities and unique constellations of abilities, is to focus on the common personality traits of gifted females. These similarities in personality for bright females show that high intelligence is only one indicator of giftedness. The sampled mothers identified a number of characteristics related to giftedness in both themselves and their daughters that have also been cited by researchers in the field. During the interviews, the mothers frequently mentioned key gifted traits like a powerful drive, heightened emotional sensitivity and intensity, perfectionism, heightened concern for justice, relentless curiosity, divergent thinking, creativity, high energy levels, and a powerful life force. In addition, many of the mothers commented on how their daughters often talked a blue streak, asked never-ending questions, could become lost in thought or an activity, and searched for patterns. One daughter shared that her incessant mantra as she powers through her day is "Focus forward."

These qualities, which come together to create a unique profile for each gifted individual, can be wonderful but also challenging for the daughter and her mother. In one case, a sampled mother wondered why she didn't try to homeschool her profoundly gifted daughter when she was struggling from a lack of challenge in elementary school:

> "Why didn't I homeschool her when things weren't going well? But I guess it's because I had a baby at home…It really kind of intimidated me. I mean, I knew what she needed as far as math and science, and I thought, I'm not really very good at that, and I'm not ready for that. And you know, she was intense and demanded a lot of attention. She talked all the time. I mean, honestly, she talked all the time! I'm telling you I think I'm the only parent that sent their kid to summer camp and turned around and said, 'Yes!' Everybody else is like 'Oh, how did you leave your child?' but I'm thinking, *Oh, you don't know!*"

Another mother described a scenario with her daughter that underscored her daughter's deep concern for justice as well as her strong will to stand up for herself. "My daughter always stood her ground—I mean always! Sometimes she should have bitten her tongue, but she never did." She said when her daughter was in the early grades,

> "She would stand up for her rights. She would say, 'I don't know why Mrs. So and So said I shouldn't have been talking. I wasn't just talking. We were talking about a problem in school. So I told her that, and I got in trouble, and I don't care, because that was what I was doing.' So at times, I'd say to her, 'That's being disrespectful.' And she'd say, 'Mom, I wasn't being disrespectful. I think she was being disrespectful to us, because she didn't ask us what we were discussing, and instead we got into trouble, and she didn't ask us about what was really going on.' I think she was born like that, because even when she was little, she would stand up for her own rights. She would stare me down—stare me down! My eyes would want to blink, and I'd think, *I'm not going to give into this little two-year-old here.* And so I knew early on…she was just born that way."

Another quality several mothers stressed as a major attribute of their daughters was their keen sense of humor—a common characteristic of giftedness that, for some reason, seems to have gotten short shrift in gifted research. For gifted individuals, the ability to combine learning and laughter brings more liveliness and joy to their learning experience, enables them to express anger or frustration in a more socially acceptable form, and serves as a more acceptable way to question the status quo. In addition, resorting to humor can ease intensity and discharge nervous excitement.

Basically, it can serve as a way to slow down the incessantly spinning hamster wheel of the gifted mind. Finally, gifted females can use their developed sense of humor to promote bonding with their like-minded peers. However, because their unique brand of humor is often so highly developed, it can be challenging to find others who get it.

One interviewed mother with seven children said all her gifted daughters had a good sense of humor but noted that this was not always a blessing.

> "In fact, I think that's been very difficult…When they're getting spouses and boyfriends, [these non-family members] would come into the family and kind of sit there dumbfounded, because there's this kind of underground kind of humor based on our heritage—a lot of punning and backwards and forwards and people making jokes and nobody laughs, but everybody knows it's there, and there's just kind of a gentle grumble. I have one son-in-law who to this day still will ask me, 'That was a joke, right?'"

Another mother noted,

> "The thing I like best about my three gifted daughters is they've got a very odd sense of humor and really think outside the box. I don't think any one of my kids would be described as a 'conventional thinker.' My oldest daughter said the best thing about college is that people finally understood her humor. They were more on an intellectual level with her. A funny example is, you know, the mathematical symbol for infinity is an eight lying on its side. For a while, her

group of friends would make the infinity sign by holding up five fingers on one hand and three on the other and then turn them sideways so all their fingers were pointing sideways. Nobody else would get that this was the infinity sign except smart people into math."

A frontrunner in identifying personality characteristics unique to the gifted was the Polish psychiatrist, psychologist, and physician Kazimierz Dabrowski. His work first garnered attention in the gifted world in the later part of the twentieth century because it offered insights into who gifted individuals *are*, focusing on their unique traits, rather than society's more common approach of focusing on what they can *do*. In her article "Overexcitability and the Gifted," gifted education leader Sharon Lind states that Dabrowski identified five key traits (translated from Polish into the terms "overexcitabilities" or "super-sensitivities") that he believed caused the gifted individual to experience reality more intensely. These are:

1. Psychomotor (lots of movement, fast talking, nervous habits, sleep trouble, inability to sit still)

2. Imaginational (visual thinking, love of fantasy, daydreaming, innovating, worrying, embellishing)

3. Sensual (strong positive or negative reactions to the way things feel, smell, taste, or sound, and/or an acute awareness of earth's beauty or artistic masterpieces)

4. Intellectual (a love of reading, learning, puzzles, intellectual challenges, an advanced ability to concentrate, and/or an insatiable curiosity)

5. Emotional (need for meaningful connection, the ability for deep empathy, compassion and sensitivity, intense emotional reactions, and/or a striving to be the best you can be)

Dabrowski's colleague Michael Piechowski noted that living with overexcitabilities can create rather turbulent inner lives for gifted individuals. He described this in a paper presented in 1991 as "a different quality of experiencing: vivid, absorbing, penetrating, encompassing, complex, commanding—a way of being quiveringly alive." And when one or more gifted family members has oversensitivities, it can create lots of high energy, intensity, and excitement on the home front!

In her many writings including *Out of Sync: Essays on Giftedness* and coauthoring *Guiding the Gifted Child*, as well as coediting and coauthoring *Off The Charts*, Tolan has significantly contributed to providing a more holistic perspective on giftedness. The foundational ideas in her works offer a lens focusing on gifted individuals beyond the limited focus on IQ. And she holds that the personality characteristics found in gifted children—heightened emotional sensitivity, intensity, a lively sense of humor, heightened concern for justice and morality, and the desire to make certain that actions are consistent with their values—continue into adulthood, creating a different life experience for the gifted adult. This, according to Tolan, can be positive but also, at times, painful or even destructive. Because our culture views emotionality as unacceptable, gifted women may be compelled to suppress their heightened emotions in order to advance in their careers. In addition, for gifted individuals with a strong sense of justice and morality, dealing with some of the ugly realities of the workplace may prove intolerable. Finally, getting one's social needs met may prove challenging if the gifted individual's career puts her in a situation with few or no intellectual peers. Tolan believes these difficult situations are exacerbated if the woman doesn't understand or accept her giftedness, creating the context for her to blame herself for being "weird" and socially inept rather than appreciating the fact that she may be a swan among ducks in her given work environment.

In her article "Can You Hear the Flowers Singing? Issues for Gifted Adults," psychologist Deirdre Lovecky used observational data from a study of gifted adults to identify five traits that represented the central features of their giftedness and elucidated how these could be both positive and negative factors in a gifted person's life.

The first of these traits is *divergency*. Divergent thinkers are often innovative, independent, intrinsically motivated, and able to see all sides of a situation. They frequently challenge the status quo and, per Lovecky, "bring color to the lives of others." Conversely, they may be frustrated when others in the group disagree with them. They struggle to support fatuous ideas, and because they often fail to adhere to common social conventions or mandates, they may find themselves misfits in social situations, facing pressure to conform at the cost of maintaining their unique identity. Lovecky describes the highly divergent thinker as "often a minority of one," which may lead to a sense of alienation and even existential depression.

Lovecky believes a second trait, *excitability*, is manifested by a high level of emotional reactivity, energy, and nervous system arousal. Lovecky notes that unlike individuals with hyperactivity, gifted adults can focus and concentrate for long periods; they function well and productively, enjoying challenges and taking risks. This characteristic allows them to thrive in whatever field captures their interest, although because of their high energy level, they may be competent in a variety of areas. However, it may be hard for them to self-regulate, needing constant activity and stimulation to ward off boredom. For some, their passion for novelty may find them abandoning projects that become stale. They may leave others to reap the rewards for their innovative ideas. Lovecky believes this lack of gratification may lead to chronic depression.

A third trait is *sensitivity*, described as a deep sense of identification with others, causing the gifted to form intense attachments and sense the emotional tone of interactions—"they think with their feelings." Gifted adults are often dedicated to various causes, responding to the needs and rights of others no matter the personal costs. Unaware of their own shortcomings, these folks are highly moralistic, focused on doing the "right" thing. As a result, they may fail to understand why others don't share their passion, leading them to feel intolerant of those whose concerns they judge to be superficial.

A fourth common trait for gifted adults, according to Lovecky, is *perceptivity*—the ability to appreciate the different aspects of a person or situation and quickly get to the heart of the problem. Thus, they can help others understand themselves, although, paradoxically, they are typically unaware of their own gifts. Because they can often see behind the curtain, they are able to recognize truth, resulting in an aversion to ambiguity, deceptiveness, and hypocrisy. Lovecky holds that these folks have a touch of magic about them because of their intuition and insight. They also tend to be highly self-aware, able to evaluate their own behavior, needs, and motivations and, as a result, determine what's in their own self interest, irrespective of what others may think. However, others may feel intimidated by these gifted individuals' ability to so quickly get to the core of the matter, while the gifted individual may not understand why others act in ways that are counterproductive to solving the real issue at hand. Lovecky points out that the greater the discrepancy between the inner self and outer face, the less comfortable gifted people feel.

Finally, using the Greek term for "having a goal," Lovecky identifies a fifth trait common to gifted individuals that she calls *entelechy*. This term describes the unique type of motivation, inner strength, and vital force directing them to be all they can be. This drive often serves as a model for others to self-actualize and creates the context for deep connection or "golden moments" of friendship where both parties are working together to maximize their potential. However, this may result in the gifted individual feeling overwhelmed in trying to meet others' needs at the expense of meeting her own, eventually shunning relationships in order to achieve her dreams. In *Off the Charts*, edited by Neville, Piechowski, and Tolan, Annemarie Roeper expands on this idea, in "Asynchrony and Sensitivity," stressing that while the ability for cognitive learning is in the brain, it's the heart that provides the motivation for learning, for inner growth, for self-actualization. She believes that we miss the essence of giftedness by excluding the emotions.

This powerful drive, or entelechy, was demonstrated by nearly all the mothers and daughters in the study. After completing an interview, I often found myself a bit exhausted after learning about all the achievements of the sampled mother and daughter. One example that comes to mind is of a single mother who, at the time of the interview, was in her sixties, completing her PhD, and actively involved in educating her gifted grandchildren. As a single mother, when her four children were young, she taught elementary school and had to supplement her income to support her family. She sewed wedding dresses after school ("For many years, I actually made more making wedding dresses than I did teaching. But teaching is my love") and delivered newspapers at night while her children slept in the back of her station wagon. She said, "One year I remember getting up at two o'clock in the morning to deliver newspapers. I would pile all the kids in the back of the station wagon with pillows and blankets, and I would deliver my newspapers, and they could sleep while I was doing that." This gifted female raised four highly functioning adults and continued this legacy by being actively involved in nurturing her many grandchildren.

Another creative way of describing giftedness is presented by therapist Paula Prober in *Journey into Your Rainforest Mind*, where she portrays gifted individuals as intense, multilayered, colorful, creative, highly sensitive, overwhelming, complex, idealistic, and influential. And like the rainforest, gifted are often misunderstood, misdiagnosed, mysterious, and confronted with too many chain saws. Prober believes that the rainforest metaphor cuts through much of the controversy around identifying and serving gifted children: "If people are compared to ecosystems, then people as meadows, desserts, and oceans are all valuable and beautiful. It is just that the rainforest ecosystem is the most complex."

Gifted specialist Shulamit Widawsky presents a unique approach to understanding the differences in intensity and quantity of experiences for gifted individuals. Her theoretical way of visualizing this process is the Funnel and Cylinder Analogy. She states in her article "Experience and Processing: The Funnel and Cylinder Analogy of Giftedness" that "the average individual takes in, analyzes, and synthesizes experiences in proportion to their general age and emotional abilities. The 'gifted' person may take in levels of experience that they are not able to process evenly. They are taking in, analyzing, and synthesizing experiences out of proportion to their general age and emotional abilities. This disproportionate system creates what is generally called asynchronous development."

One of the interviewed mothers, who was a professor in gifted education, found Widawsky's theory of giftedness helpful in her work. She described Widawsky's use of a funnel and cylinder as being very applicable to the gifted mind, with the cylinder representing the child's chronological age and the funnel representing the child's giftedness level. The greater the child's giftedness, the wider her funnel, which means she experientially/intellectually takes in more than her age peers of average intelligence. As a result, in certain situations, the child with the greater funnel can feel overwhelmed and not sure what to do with the onslaught of stimulation. This mother stressed, "The funnel to me represents one of the ways gifted are amplified. I feel like we owe it to children when we're identifying them as gifted to also help them understand their social-emotional lives, because if all we do is focus on the academic piece, then we are going to have children who are really struggling with feeling differently, experiencing reality differently, and thinking of themselves as a 'dork.'" As John Lennon put it (according to Philip Norman's book *John Lennon: The Life*), "There was something wrong with me, I thought, because I seemed to see things other people didn't see."

Author and gifted mother of neurodivergent children Kochis shares in a blog post "Want to Have Your Heart Broken? Take a Close Look at an Angry Gifted Kid" how the metaphor of the funnel and cylinder has shown up on brain scans of gifted individuals where the neural pathways (or "hubs" as scientists refer to them) tend to be denser in individuals with higher IQ levels. According to Kochis, "the denser the neural hub, the more efficient the processing of information." The scans provide physical evidence of a gifted person's increased processing speed. Kochis explains that this demonstrates that gifted children think, feel, and react more deeply to every sense and situation: sounds are louder, smells are stronger, and emotional reactions can be off the charts. "It is difficult for a child to navigate big feelings under the best of circumstances. Imagine trying to do so while under direct sensory and emotional assault… They're actually caught in the throes of an emotional trigger and unable to manage the feelings they're experiencing."

Obviously, these traits of gifted individuals can be both a blessing and a curse in the daily life of the gifted as well as in the lives of their loved ones, especially their primary caregivers (who most likely are dealing with their own gifted characteristics)! These traits can present a huge challenge for the gifted individual herself in trying to find her place in the world but also for those around her when her overexcitabilities may be triggered, resulting in extreme anxiety, rumination, bouts of depression, and/or intense emotional reactions. As these dynamics play out and the gifted female becomes more aware that she is being misunderstood and that her special needs are not met, she may resort to more desperate measures, creating a downward spiral and increasing frustration and negativity in those around her.

Two experts in the field of giftedness, George Betts and Maureen Neihart, recognized the need to capture the lived reality of gifted students whose behavior, feelings, and needs may make it difficult for both parents and teachers to appreciate and acknowledge their brilliance. In "Profiles of the Gifted and Talented," Betts and Neihart's model delineates six different profiles of gifted individuals impacted by their special abilities in different ways. Based on the researchers' experience working with gifted in a variety of settings, they concluded that the gifted cannot be seen as one group but rather as individuals whose giftedness is demonstrated (or not) by the influence of their families, education, relationships, life experiences, personalities, and genetic makeup. Because the behavior, feelings, and needs of a gifted child may change frequently when they're young, it may be more difficult to determine which gifted profile applies best in their case. But as they pass into adulthood, they most likely will settle into one or two of the profile areas listed below.

- Type I THE SUCCESSFUL: Discover what "sells" at home and school…Convergent thinker…Learn and tests well…Eager for approval…Liked by peers…Positive self-concept…Unaware of deficiencies

- Type II THE CREATIVE: Divergently gifted…Challenging when needs not met…Often go unidentified…Question authority…Don't conform…Haven't learned to use the system…Receive little recognition for accomplishments...Struggle with self-esteem...At risk as eventual drop outs

- Type III THE UNDERGROUND: Middle school females hiding giftedness...Want to be included in non-gifted peer group...May be radical transformation from earlier grades...Their needs are often in conflict with expectations of parents and teachers

- Type IV THE AT-RISK: Angry with adults and with themselves...Defensive...System has not met needs for many years...Burnt-out or spaced-out...Depressed and withdrawn or act out...Interests are outside realm of regular school curriculum...Poor self-concept

- Type V TWICE EXCEPTIONAL: Physically or emotionally challenged...Learning disabilities...Limited English proficiency...Typically not identified gifted...Programs don't integrate their varying needs...Discouraged, frustrated, rejected, helpless, powerless or isolated...School system tends to focus on their weaknesses

- Type VI THE AUTONOMOUS LEARNER: The end goal for all students...Few demonstrate this at an early age...Work effectively in school system...Use the system to create new opportunities...Strong, positive self-concept...Positive attention and support for accomplishments...Respected by adults and peers...Leadership roles...Independent, self-directed...Feelings and Attitudes: Self-confident, Self-accepting, Enthusiastic, Accepted by others...Behaviors: Appropriate social skills, independent workers, develop own goals, follow through with plans, work without approval, follow strong areas of passion, creative, stand up for convictions.

Having an awareness of the various personality traits and different gifted profiles can prove invaluable for gifted females in two key ways. First, it helps reframe what the gifted individual (and those who love her) previously believed were abnormal or pathological qualities. Many have shared that knowing that their uncommon characteristics are in fact common attributes related to their intelligence provides a positive interpretation for behaviors that up to this point were frequently deemed odd, problematic, and even weird.

Secondly, based on this self-awareness, gifted individuals can learn to adapt and restrain or control their reactions resulting from these traits rather than cause major disturbances or conflicts in social interactions, if they so choose. But doing so sometimes demands trade-offs, resulting in the gifted individual feeling the need to deny what she's feeling. In *Untamed*, Doyle shares an example of this about her daughter:

> Tish was born concerned…By the time she was six, I'd given up on happy.…Act happy. Just pretend. This is our social contract with the world, kid: ACT HAPPY. Suffer silently like the rest of us, for the love of God…When I realized that Tish was me, I remembered that acting happy was what had almost killed me…She shows us what we need to notice, think, and feel in order to stay human. She is the

kindest, wisest, most honest person I know. There is no one walking the earth I respect more. Tish is our family's conscience and prophet.

This reinforces, again, the question of what we as a society lose by forcing gifted females to fit the mold and follow the cultural script.

The value of developing a broader view of giftedness was echoed by a handful of the mothers in the study. For example, one mother who specializes in gifted education stated,

> "When I've shared with parents of gifted about Dabrowski's intensities and sensitivities, it's like a big light bulb would turn on, because it gives a name to situations they've encountered. It's like 'Oh, I'm not weird, and my kid's not weird, and we're not crazy after all.' It just normalizes what they've experienced. 'Oh, yeah, there's actually a theory—someone's researched this, and there's more than one person in the world who is like this, and it's okay.'"

Along these lines, another mother shared that she finally realized she herself was gifted (rather than just weird) after becoming aware of these gifted personality traits.

> "I always thought there was something really the matter with me. It wasn't until [at age forty-five] I became friends with a counselor who turned me on to the sensitivities of gifted people, and I started understanding there wasn't anything really the matter with me…I had started working with

gifted kids before this…but I never saw it as being me. I got my PhD but, again, never saw it as being me. And then, when I turned my attention to the sensitivities and intensities and looked at characteristics of giftedness beyond the academics, I started realizing the reason I create so many programs and feel so passionately about things…I started putting it together. So my focus [as first a teacher and then as a professor] has shifted—it's not on who gets the one hundred percent and achieves all these things but more the characteristics of giftedness."

This confirms that when gifted females learn about and come to an awareness of their differences, it can be incredibly empowering. When they are able to describe both to themselves and to those close to them that they are not broken, crazy, or in need of being fixed, this can be freeing, and it goes a long way in helping them thrive.

SELF-DOUBT IN A PATRIARCHAL SOCIETY

Failure to recognize one's own high intelligence is especially true for gifted females. This was underscored by the number of interviewed mothers who believed initially that their bright daughters inherited their intelligence from their fathers. Psychologists Pauline Rose Clance and Suzanne Imes conducted a study in 1978 described in their article, "The Imposter Phenomenon in High-Achieving Women: Dynamics and Therapeutic Intervention." They found that "despite outstanding academic and professional accomplishments, women who experience the imposter phenomenon persist in believing that they are really not bright and have fooled anyone who thinks otherwise."

Based on these findings, they developed the concept termed "imposter syndrome"—a state of mind in which the bright female feels like she is incompetent or not intelligent enough to meet the demands of her current situation and fears that others are going to eventually find this out.

Research has attempted to discover how females develop these internal barriers in the first place. Dweck's extensive research, described in *Self-Theories: Their Role in Motivation, Personality and Development* and *Mindset*, found that bright girls were often quick to give up when faced with a difficult problem, while conversely, bright boys embraced the struggle. Boys in fact had what Dweck termed a "hardy response to failure" where they remained focused on mastering the problem in spite of difficulty. She observes that the boys and girls *interpreted* a challenging situation differently. Bright girls, when confronting hard problems, were much quicker to *doubt* their ability and lose confidence, and as a result, they become less effective learners. Dweck attributes this behavior to the difference in the mental attitude or mindset—beliefs they develop about themselves to organize their world and give meaning to their experiences. These different psychological worlds can lead the sexes to think, feel, and act differently. Smart girls typically hold the belief that their ability was something they were born with (a fixed mindset) whereas the boys thought their ability could be developed and grow through effort (a growth mindset). Dweck and her team traced the origin of the more limiting mindset of bright girls to the differences in praise from parents and teachers. They found that girls were more often praised for how smart they were versus the praise boys got for what they did—tackling hard problems, making mistakes, and developing different strategies that, even though they failed, showed they were trying. The more empowering feedback that the boys received is termed "process praise," which Dweck believes is given more often to boys, starting in infancy, leading to their embrace of challenge. Conversely, girls who have been praised for who they are—being smart and compliant—develop a fear of doing anything that might disprove this assessment, resulting in a more vulnerable and helpless response when facing a tough problem.

Others have backed the lens up even farther in attempting to explain why more females fall prey to imposter syndrome, focusing on larger historical and cultural forces and examining social contexts. Most research in the 1970s and 1980s focused on internal barriers, finding females to be their own worst enemies with their lack of self-confidence resulting from internalized misconceptions regarding their ability. These findings tended to, in effect. blame the victim, given that historically, the pervasive cultural belief has been that women's abilities, work, and accomplishments are of little value. In those instances where women have been successful in the public domain, they often believe this is attributable to luck or other external factors rather than their own ability. This misconception is frequently reinforced by our culture.

In their article "Stop Telling Women They Have Imposter Syndrome," Ruchika Tulshyan and Jodi-Ann Burey echo this and question why successful females doubt their abilities and tend to blame individuals (like the females themselves or parents and teachers) for this response rather than the systems that they believe foster and exacerbate it. These writers hold that the treatment many bright women get in educational settings and later in work environments often chips away at their self-confidence. This can lead to anxiety, depression, and feelings of being, once again, an ugly duckling. By placing blame on individuals rather than cultural forces like sexism and patriarchy, women's emotional reactions get pathologized. The negative label of "imposter syndrome" ascribed to females, according to Tulshyan and Burey, directs our attention toward fixing them instead of fixing the environment where they learn and/or work so they can succeed.

In challenging situations, gifted males, unlike bright females, often find other males to serve as successful role models and mentors, discover that their progress is validated, and rarely have their competence questioned. Typically, gifted females experience the exact opposite; they frequently face battles with micro-aggressions, unrealistic expectations, and negative assumptions formed by cultural stereotypes. As a result, many bright females feel that they don't belong in male-dominated realms like STEM. Tina Opie, associate professor at Babson College (quoted by Tulshyan and Burey), stresses that when individuals from marginalized backgrounds try to hold themselves up to a standard that no one like them has met (and that they're often not expected to be able to meet), the pressure to excel can become too much to bear. According to Tulshyan and Burey, academic institutions and corporations still promote imposter syndrome by, in part, being mired in the cultural inertia of the good ol' boys club or "bro" culture.

One of the mothers in my study offered an example of this sad reality. She stated that her gifted daughter doubted her exceptional abilities: "All the time—she thinks way too much about everything; she doesn't understand the power of who she is…My daughter doesn't listen to me when I tell her how brilliant she is. She always says, 'Mom, you're prejudiced,' because I love her." This highly gifted daughter decided on a master's program instead of a PhD (where she would have received grants and not racked up $70,000 in loans that's she's paying off), but she was afraid to go into the PhD program. Her mother said, "She didn't think that she was good enough…Just like her sister-in-law who chose a master's program. You've got Joe Blow bubbas in the middle of nowhere with PhDs behind their names that can't think fast enough to walk across the street, and you've got two girls who've graduated Phi Beta Kappa from outstanding universities afraid to go into a PhD program. What the hell is wrong with that?"

Part 3

MOTHERHOOD AND GIFTED WOMEN

CHAPTER 5

Historical Overview

The context in which gifted mothers care for their daughters in today's culture has been dictated by powerful forces that have shaped motherhood since our country's inception with the objective of "what's best for our patriarchal society" as the primary goal. Knowing how we arrived at this socially constructed motherhood role will, hopefully, enable gifted mothers to understand the cultural pressures and constraints in their path as they attempt to deconstruct and reconstruct an approach to nurturing gifted females that more appropriately addresses the unique needs of both the mothers and their offspring.

In her amazing book *Caste*, Isabel Wilkerson states, "Each of us is in a container of some kind. The label signals to the world what is presumed to be inside and what is to be done with it…the label is frequently out of sync with the contents…and this hurts people and institutions in ways we may not always know." This insight regarding the different labels given to how we look or what we do encourages an understanding of the label "mother" and the whole concept of motherhood in our culture. The commonly accepted notion of motherhood is an artificial construct—something that doesn't exist in objective reality but is just made up and generally accepted as fact. Viewing our parenting approach through a lens that acknowledges how motherhood was constructed and tweaked over past generations, as well as the current social, economic, and political influences prescribing how we "should" parent, allows gifted females to see our role as mothers with greater awareness. This understanding is helpful to each of us in creating our own singular motherhood identity and approach to nurturing our neurodiverse daughters. Being aware of the power of culture in our lives can help free us, as gifted mothers, from becoming captives of our conditioning and thereby able to create our own counterrealities. We can become the outside-the-box women and parents we need to be to best address both our needs and those of our gifted offspring.

Adrienne Rich, one of America's foremost intellectuals, stresses in *Of Woman Born: Motherhood as Experience and Institution* that since our country's inception, motherhood has been seen as an institution, with prescribed behaviors for women, that is fundamental to American culture. As such, says Rich, motherhood has provided a reference point for social, political, and religious agendas of all sorts and an arena in which Americans have wrestled with their ambivalence about female power, the needs of families, and even the social order. In her book *Modern Motherhood: An American History*, Professor Jodi Vandenberg-Daves notes that as an institution, the concept of motherhood has been extensive in its power, encompassing laws that define legitimate forms of maternity, control reproductive rights, and restrict access to resources while more generally defining what constitutes a good and bad mother based on current cultural mores.

In *The Way We Never Were*, Coontz underscores the pressure women have faced to conform through the years.

For mothers, the more successfully they adhere to the script of a "good" mother, the more they must suppress aspects of their personality that do not fit this ideal. Since women have historically been expected to do the work of managing emotions (be even-tempered, moderate, reasonable, soft-spoken, and never angry), many have learned to enact the cultural expectations regarding motherhood, anticipating what society, partners, and offspring want, need, or demand. Mothers are expected to perform in ways that are considered acceptable. The more mothers are defined in terms of this ideal motherhood myth, the more it's possible for society, as well as our loved ones and community, to ignore, punish, or even reject women who fail to live up to this ideal.

Because of this powerful public rhetoric, Ann Hulbert, author of *Raising America: Experts, Parents, and a Century of Advice About Children,* believes that motherhood in America is often the source of both our deepest happiness and most intense anxieties. Generally, societal dictates require mothers to form deep and everlasting attachments to their children, no matter what, and to be long-suffering models of loyal and loving attentiveness. And they must accomplish all this very often with little support from partners or a social safety net. At the same time, mothers are expected to resist the ever-present corrupting enticements to selfishness and irresponsibility constantly being promoted by our consumer culture. Consequently, Hulbert cites a claim by a historian in the 1950s: "In no other country has there been so pervasive a cultural anxiety about the rearing of children."

Society's institution of motherhood disallows mothers the freedom to be who they uniquely are—real, vulnerable, and wholly human. Instead, according to Dr. Brené Brown in *Braving the Wilderness: The Quest for True Belonging and the Courage to Stand Alone,* mothers are saddled with the resilient, self-sacrificing-woman trope that undermines their humanity and allows little time for self-actualization, not to mention self-care. They are tasked with the burden of playing Superwoman, which involves the 24-7 responsibility of being the primary caregiver. And for gifted mothers, this situation is exacerbated by their own special needs as well as those of their gifted children.

Throughout history, women have struggled in silence to rise to society's motherhood demands, and in doing so, they have made a huge, unacknowledged contribution to humankind. But at what cost? The social construct of motherhood undermines the humanity of mothers by disallowing them the freedom to cry, feel, grieve, hurt, rage, be vulnerable, fail, and, for sure, quit. It also denies mothers the support necessary to maximize their potential in other areas if they so choose—representing a personal loss for these females, and notably gifted females, as well as society in general.

Sadly, most women must face the challenge of being primary caregivers on their own, because Americans individualize social problems, as Caitlyn Collins points out in *Making Motherhood Work*. Many mothers scramble to figure out unique ways to survive within society's rigid motherhood structure that decrees child-rearing to be a private responsibility and views work-family conflicts as personal problems. Because of these beliefs, says Collins, the United States has no national work-family policy to support caregiving, no universal healthcare, no universal social insurance entitlement, no guaranteed income, no paid parental leave, no universal childcare, and no minimum standard for vacation and sick days.

According to Vandenberg-Daves in *Modern Motherhood: An American History*, mothers throughout history have been nothing if not resilient and resourceful in attempting to meet their own needs as well as the needs of their children, both individually and collectively. Many have had to tiptoe around society's prevailing and often irrelevant motherhood dictates that have proven detrimental to their family's welfare. Not surprisingly, gifted mothers, who by definition fall outside "average" in intellectual capabilities and potential as well as in their social-emotional makeup, have an especially tough time adjusting to society's motherhood standard. As a result, generations of gifted women have had to adapt, resist, and parent in their own innovative ways in a culturally hostile environment. In doing so, many of these women have often unknowingly served as change agents, rebelling against the limits imposed by society and bringing about transformations in the prevailing motherhood construct. Nearly all of the gifted women in my study fall into this category. They proactively rejected the cultural boundaries limiting both themselves and their daughters.

Unfortunately, however, gifted mothers' wisdom has never been valued, documented, or included in public policy discussions regarding child-rearing in America. As Vandenberg-Daves comments, nothing has been more constant in our country's history than the fact that women have always been significantly underrepresented in the centers of political and economic power. Consequently, generations of women have been burdened with an inadequate and ill-informed social policy structure related to caregiving and have little power to shape the conditions in which they raise their children. The limitations imposed by these policies not only hinder their work as mothers but limit their access to achievements outside the family realm that has been historically defined as a male preserve. Is it any wonder then that few gifted women, especially those who are mothers, have achieved eminence in the public arena?

A key reason that mothers' input is not actively solicited in family policy decisions relates to the value and visibility of caregiving in our society. Dr. Anne-Marie Slaughter (who holds many esteemed titles, one currently being CEO of a think/action tank) views this as the central issue for the twenty-first century and one that has been ignored or downplayed for far too long. Slaughter points out that even when issues related to equality for females are addressed, care feminism has long taken a back seat to career feminism. As she passionately asserts in her article "Rosie Could Be a Riveter Only Because of a Care Economy. Where Is Ours?" there is a severe lack of investment in a care economy in our society that, sadly, was not recognized in large part by the feminist movement despite being one of the great struggles for human freedom of the twentieth century. Slaughter states,

> Advocating for child or elder care may be less glamorous and newsworthy than breaking glass ceilings to become the first woman in a role traditionally reserved for a man, but both are necessary if we are ever to achieve true gender equality…We have to see care work as the essential work that it is, the work that makes other work possible, the work that develops young brains and determines the extent to which our children will be able to learn and live up to their potential.…the work that determines who we really are as a society.

Gifted mothers' efforts to nurture the potential of their offspring, and to achieve the goals of both career feminism and care feminism (if they so choose), can provide an invaluable approach to all women trapped by rigid motherhood ideals constructed mainly by males with little first-hand knowledge about life as a primary caregiver. Looking back at how we arrived at our current motherhood model—highlighting the obstacles faced as well as the strategies used in attempting to transform it to meet the needs of real women raising real children—is useful to gifted mothers wrestling with the limitations imposed by the social construction of motherhood today.

I want to stress, however, that this analysis is not meant to minimize the importance and meaning that some gifted females find in focusing solely on nurturing their offspring and family within the private sphere. In her powerful book *Maternal Desire*, Daphne de Marneffe stresses that for those who champion motherhood, it's often narrowly defined in the context of service rather than the mother's deep desire to experience herself as an agent choosing to focus on her personal exploration of parenting—finding motherhood not as a step backward but rather a step forward toward greater awareness and a truer model of the self. De Marneffe believes that too often our culture frames the reality of motherhood as a matter of how little time one can spend with her children and not do them damage. "When the activities of mothering are interpreted as self-limiting, they tend to be treated dismissively," according to de Marneffe.

A number of gifted women in my study found full-time mothering deeply satisfying and filled with meaning. The role brought them extraordinary pleasure. And the benefit to society from carrying out this role is invaluable both in maximizing the potential of their gifted offspring and in contributing to a more caring culture. Acknowledging and honoring the voices and lived realities of these gifted mothers is critical in shaping society's future policies regarding motherhood in America.

THE BIRTH OF "MOTHERHOOD" IN AMERICA

During colonial days, society placed little value on women's usefulness to society beyond their ability to have children. Their role was to bear children and struggle to keep them alive, which meant working from dawn to dusk, providing food, shelter, and other necessities, caring for sick family members, and maintaining family life. This task fully occupied the adult lives of most of the female population. If these mothers did harbor any thoughts about other life choices, they were denied access to apprenticeships that would have made it possible to become a skilled tradesperson. Fathers, who were considered morally stronger, were responsible for the spiritual education of their offspring, because women were not thought to be up to the task. Vandenberg-Daves quotes a Puritan minister who captured the zeitgeist of the time: "Persons are often more apt to despise a Mother (the weaker vessel and frequently, most indulgent)."

Legally, children belonged to their father, whose duty was to raise them to be decent, God-fearing, and self-supporting, according to Ellen Ross in *Love and Toil: Motherhood in Outcast London, 1870–1918*. For female offspring, this meant getting married, which was the only legitimate avenue to social acceptance. What followed for young women, in most cases, given the absence of effective birth control and the legal denial of a woman's right to refuse sex, was motherhood. This was her sole role as determined by society's "motherhood mandate": the decree that motherhood was women's biological and social destiny. Sadly, because of the high rates of maternal mortality of this era, many died in childbirth. As a result, only a few mothers lived long enough to see their children grow up, and the average length of marriage, according to Coontz, was less than twelve years.

After the American Revolution, the maternal "weaker vessel" of colonial times morphed into the morally superior parent. The newly formed nation offered women a kind of compromised maternal citizenship—"republican motherhood," according to Vandenberg-Daves. Because of their (newly ascribed) virtue, mothers would be able to support the new republic not by having a vote or the ability to hold office but rather by raising honorable sons (not daughters) who were able to carry on the country's experiment of self-government. Our nation's Founding Fathers envisioned a private patriarchal family and passed laws to ensure women's confinement in what would come to be seen as a "separate sphere"—the family home. Despite these harsh limitations, Vandenberg-Daves claims, republican motherhood elevated the cultural role of women as mothers were now assigned the teaching of reason to their children. As a result, more educational opportunities for females were promoted so that, as mothers, they would be able to better nurture the young minds of their offspring. In *Women of the Republic: Intellect and Ideology in Revolutionary America*, historian Linda K. Kerber notes,

> ...in postwar America the ideology of female education came to be tied to ideas about the sort of woman who would be of greatest service to the

Republic. Discussions of female education were apt to be highly ambivalent. On one hand, republican political theory called for a sensibly educated female citizenry to educate future generations of sensible republicans; on the other, domestic tradition condemned highly educated women as perverse threats to family stability. Consequently, when American educators discussed the uses of the female intellect, much of their discussion was explicitly anti-intellectual.

But as the nineteenth century approached, as Kerber states in her article "The Republican Mother: Women and the Enlightenment—An American Perspective," the concept of republican motherhood faded into the notion of moral motherhood. Now, in addition to their other responsibilities, mothers needed to attend to their children's immortal souls. To effectively carry out this role, the character and behavior of mothers had to be beyond reproach—they were expected to show affection, be soft-spoken, and restrain themselves from expressing emotions considered inappropriate. In other words, they were expected to not be human. Self-sacrifice was the key to carrying this off. Children were now thought of as innocents, serving as vehicles of redemption who could transport mothers from materialism and egotism to a world of new and higher feeling. In this new world, the ideal mother lived through her children. And as Vandenberg-Daves notes, "Mothers should do so even when fathers were intemperate or uncooperative."

These developments turned the home into a place set apart from the outside world. The home front became a place of moral training of children, leisure for men (a precursor, perhaps, to today's "man cave"?), and refuge from the competitive world of economic striving, according to Howard Zinn in *A People's History of the United States: 1492 to Present*. This family structure became more feasible with the growth of a middle class, the production of goods shifting from home to factories, and the work of fathers moving along with them into the public sphere. At the same time, the press helped popularize feminine domesticity by promoting ideas about cooking, housekeeping, and consumption of goods for the family. This kept women too busy for much of anything beyond the boundaries of home. Their lives were centered almost exclusively on activities in the private domain, which included preparing their daughters for similar lives in the future.

Thus the female world was closely knit, isolated within the confines of family. And for most female offspring, coming of age simply meant moving away from their family into their husband's home. As part of their socialization, mothers were expected to pass along to their daughters the values of culturally sanctioned selflessness, which eventually found expression in their roles of wife and mother. As sociologist Dr. Sharon Hays states in *The Cultural Contradictions of Motherhood*, this period's ideology of moral mothering, with all its trappings, provided the early underpinnings for the child-centered mothering model prevalent today.

Hays affirms that this ideology created the context for women's heightened sense of self-consciousness and introspection related to how they parent that remains widespread among mothers nearly two hundred years later. As Vandenberg-Daves comments, Abigail Alcott, an artist and sister of Louisa, documented her parenting angst in 1833, asking, "Am I doing what is right? Am I doing enough? Am

I not doing too much?" Historian Sylvia Hoffert, according to Vandenberg-Daves, found that considerable parenting anxiety like this was common and connected to the era's changing motherhood ideals. While the benefits of the moral motherhood ideal had increased women's authority in the family, sadly, it exacerbated mothers' susceptibility to guilt, anxiety, and regret. As stated by Vandenberg-Daves, children's health, development, and spiritual destiny were now measured solely by the mother's individual actions as opposed to the broader impact of the father, extended family, and community members.

As this shows, and as Coontz notes, during this period, caring for others became a woman's main duty. This resulted in her personal autonomy being denied while, conversely, the self-reliance and independence for men was promoted. Consequently, Western tradition came to view caregiving and independence as mutually exclusive traits. The use of the term "individualistic" to describe men's nature became acceptable only in the same time period that established the cult of domesticity for women, according to Coontz. Gender divisions were thus fortified—males were assigned all the character traits associated with competition (ambition, authority, power, logic, and single-mindedness), while females were assigned traits associated with cooperation (gentleness, sensitivity, altruism, empathy, and submissiveness). As a result, gifted females of this era were pressured to sublimate their superior intellectual abilities and drive to focus all their intensity and abundant energy solely on domestic tasks.

Because women were excluded from the public arena, mothers were severely limited in their ability to meet the economic needs of themselves or their children. As men embraced individualism and economic self-reliance, women were increasingly powerless dependents, left out of the notions of human rights to life, liberty, and the pursuit of happiness as evidenced by the Constitution. Coontz notes that between 1872 and 1900, the courts ruled that women were not entitled to the rights of "citizens" and even questioned whether they qualified as "persons" when it came to the applicability of constitutional rights. They were legally excluded from voting, professional training, and most colleges.

The experience of mothering changed very little after the birth of our nation. Being a mother meant, as it had in the past, struggling to meet the needs of a family, frequently on limited resources. During this period and until the 1900s, families were large, averaging more than six children, not including stillbirths and child deaths, which were common. As in colonial times, motherhood represented a physical feat, with only a few women living long enough to see their children grow up. Obviously, self-actualization for mothers was not even in the vernacular during this era when mere survival was a priority.

MOTHERHOOD IN THE LATE 1800S TO MID-1940S (PROGRESSIVE ERA)

The earlier ideals about republican and moral motherhood diminished as the nineteenth century drew to a close. During this period, known as the Gilded Age (1870s–1900s), the seeds for privatization of family values were sown. The roles of wife and mother lost their transcendent moral and political significance. Gradually, families became more insular and increasingly required to shoulder their own financial weight, with society providing few buffers from outside forces. Coontz comments that as motherhood became divested of any larger social and political meaning, women labored primarily for the personal comfort of their husbands and children.

This change in the institution of motherhood during the late 1800s occurred amidst other dramatic social and economic upheavals—and the world for mothers was turning upside down. Much of the population was shifting to industrial employment, an urban environment, and a cash economy, leaving mothers with onerous chores in the absence of time-saving technology. They dealt with the health hazards of urban living before modern infrastructure and medical advancements came along.

In addition, the growing factory system caused by industrialization established an even more rigid division of labor. Middle-class families adapted by putting fathers more firmly on the market side of the line and women and children on the household one. However, working-class families assigned only married women to the private sphere, sending men, unmarried women, and youngsters out of the household into paid work. By 1870, women comprised 16 percent of the labor force, but as late as 1900, a mere 5–9 percent of married women worked for wages. Women's economic second-class citizenship became apparent over these years. Unions fought to keep female workers out of their shops, and if women managed to find work, they earned measly wages, averaging less than half of male earners.

The twentieth century ushered in further changes for mothers and their families. Hays states that the average size of families decreased from six children to two or three, and the infrastructure in many communities improved. This helped provide clean water, indoor plumbing, electricity, and antibiotics and lessened the physical work demands for many mothers. But new negative societal factors began to impact families across the country. During this period, more and more industries began to mass produce and seek buyers for their products. By 1900, the volume of advertising multiplied dramatically, and by the 1920s, America's consumer culture was widespread. Coontz points out that this resulted in a new commonly held belief that the American citizen's first importance to their country was no longer that of citizen but of consumer. This is not unlike the prevalent beliefs of our current zeitgeist. Since women were thought to buy most of the personal commodities and products for use in the home, much of the consumer campaign was aimed at them. Sadly, advertising campaigns often appealed to, and exacerbated, mothers' insecurities.

For example, consumer capitalism in the dawning age of mass advertising played on mothers' fears about the proper feeding, growth, and "normalcy" of their children, according to Hays. Throughout history, mothers had received expertise on caregiving from the wisdom gleaned from other women who had been there and done that. However, science and medicine entered the nursery, offering freedom from fear of death and disease for children. Women's tradition of maternal advice sharing was abandoned. Vandenberg-Daves states that between the 1880s and 1940s, physicians solidified a near monopoly on "legitimate" knowledge of children's health, which, of course, came with a fee and promoted the message that mothers who didn't follow their advice were responsible for child mortality and morbidity. In professional journals and popular pamphlets, physician authors—who based their knowledge of children on scientific and medical authority but had little to no experience as primary caregivers—urged mothers to turn a deaf ear to Grandmother, whose influence was increasingly seen as particularly pernicious. Hays notes that during this same era, child psychologists introduced new theories of child development that emphasized the critical importance of early childhood experiences in shaping personality and development.

As a result, with the birth of America's mass consumer culture as well as major developments in psychology and science, mothers began to feel singularly responsible for ensuring that their children had the perfect childhood and often blamed themselves for falling short of this goal. For gifted women, who tend to be more perfectionistic and tasked with nurturing the special needs of their offspring, these new pressures to provide care at even more exacting levels must have been particularly onerous.

An example of one product aggressively promoted by professional health experts was infant formula. Formula companies' pursuit of profit was advanced with the help of physicians, in part, by their push for hospital over home births. In *For Her Own Good: Two Centuries of the Experts' Advice to Women*, Barbara Ehrenreich and Deirdre English state that while only about 5 percent of births took place in hospitals in 1900, the number was nearly 50 percent by the end of the 1930s, and by 1955, it was 95 percent. According to these authors, physicians strongly recommended hospital deliveries and minimized mothers' fears by claiming that they provided pain relief through powerful drugs (which typically handed over control of the birthing process to male physicians), gave hope for safer deliveries, and improved infant health through formula samples provided immediately after delivery.

In addition, new meanings were attributed to motherhood by the burgeoning fields of science and medicine that extended well beyond birth and infant care. According to Hays, for the first time, motherhood was not only a special kind of female nurturing but a highly complex technical calling. Child development was increasingly measured with norms for heights and weights, and in the 1920s, developmental schedules regarding physical, mental, and emotional milestones appeared. This new ideal of scientific motherhood increasingly cast mothers as compliant consumers of expertise in arenas once controlled by women. Hays states that physicians' growing authority in areas of healthcare, once left to women, greatly complicated women's trust in their intuitive knowing and judgment about the care and feeding of their offspring. Compounding this sense of maternal insecurity was the reality that the advice and wisdom of these experts was often conflicting and confusing. However, the cultural expectation was that any good mother would inherently know, or at least learn, how to deal with this ever-expanding and frequently contradictory field of medical advice. How this was supposed to happen remained unclear.

In the 1920s and 1930s, with reduced infant mortality and improved treatment of infectious diseases, medical experts increasingly turned their focus to managing the care of "normal" children, including their emotional and intellectual development, according to author Ellen Ross. Hays argues that the twentieth century saw a shift in the focus of motherhood from moral motherhood to psychological motherhood, as the culture increasingly demanded mothers to be perfect because they were responsible for their children's mental health. Determining the most functional psychological makeup for mothers began to dominate the attention of helping professions and mass media, as developments in psychology proved increasingly critical to motherhood in the twentieth century. Hays says that like the nineteenth century's ideal of moral motherhood, the new focus on motherhood based on science and psychology both burdened and privileged mothers. This perspective promoted the notion that what mothers did mattered more than any impact fathers might have on their children's development. Mothers were now viewed as responsible for their children's psychological as well as physical development. As Hays affirms, 24-7 vigilance was the price mothers had to pay for their hard-won place on the pedestal of scientifically and psychologically nurturing a teetering civilization.

But the psychological advice of the early 1900s reflected experts' underlying concerns about the fallibility of maternal instinct and even maternal love. More and more, according to Hays, psychologists and child development experts expressed ambivalence about the once-admired emotional sensibilities and impeccable motives of mothers. Because mothers were now deemed responsible for the psychologically complex management of their children, experts in the field concluded that mothers were woefully in need of their help. By the 1920s, mothers were exhorted to worry about the cognitive and emotional maladjustment that could plague even normal childhoods. New behaviorist ideas about the importance of properly training children to fit more easily into a world requiring discipline and regularity came from widely read experts like Emmett Holt and John Watson. In their book, Ehrenreich and English quote Dr. Watson describing the ideal child as one who never cries unless actually stuck by a pin...who soon builds up a wealth of habits that tide him over dark and rainy days—puts on such habits of politeness and neatness and cleanliness that adults are willing to be around him at least part of the day...who eats what is set before him—who sleeps and rests when put in bed for sleep and rest—who puts away two-year-old habits when the third year has to be faced...who finally enters manhood so bulwarked with stable work and emotional habits that no adversity can quite overwhelm him.

Needless to say, very few neurodiverse, asynchronous, gifted daughters (or even gifted sons!) fit into this androcentric, "ideal child" category. Although most experts of this period pushed efficient child-rearing methods such as right habit training, this parenting approach was fortunately countered by a few like Maria Montessori and John Dewey, who advocated for individual personality development rather than standardized parental conditioning for children. Ann Hubert states that the overriding cultural concern of the time was that children faced a future of greater complexity and possibilities than their grandparents ever imagined. This sparked a fresh generation of experts motivated to correct the incompetence and inconsistency of mothers and the social woes they would cause in failing to prepare their offspring for such a future.

To maximize opportunities for child development and growth, mothers were now tasked with closely observing their children and knuckling under to expert opinion. Ads reinforced messages about ensuring children's proper emotional and intellectual development through consumer products and educational services. As a result, this pressure to be constantly watching to ensure their children's adherence to norms and assessing the minutiae of their aptitudes created tremendous anxiety in mothers, who felt they were on their own in carrying out this high-stress task. Under the influence of a cultural fixation on quantifying normality, from Apgar scores and height and weight charts to measures of developmental milestones, mothers' insecurities soared.

The new concept of adolescence further complicated the parenting challenges of this era. According to Hays, rapidly changing childhood norms promoted individual youthful initiative and more independence for older children outside the family such as movie going and unchaperoned dating. Parenting advice literature reflected cultural worries about mothers' relationship with teen daughters, promoting the notion that generation gaps were emerging between them. Again, society's conclusion was that mothers needed fixing in order to address this "problem."

The cultural belief at this time was that fixing mothers' psychological problems was best carried out by experts. The commonly recommended treatment approach was individualized therapy with the goal of empowering mothers to solve their children's problems more effectively. Consequently, the mental health experts during the first half of the 1900s helped to create, give credence to, and then treat the key cultural diagnoses of modern motherhood. They assessed these as maternal overinvolvement and underinvolvement (assigning these traits the labels of the "smothering mother" and the "rejecting mother"), which became a big fear in the 1940s and 1950s (along with other stereotypes like the nagging wife, the neurotic mother, the woman who hated housework, and wives who questioned their gender roles). Hays notes that most parenting literature suggested that these maternal psychological issues, not the common issues assigned to fathers like withdrawal and tyranny, represented a bigger threat to children. Underlying these concerns was the overriding angst of experts and society in general that many mothers were rejecting their place within the home and trying to gain power by "wearing the pants."

Occasional flare-ups of ambivalence about the whole enterprise of mothering during this period helped to substantiate these fears. In addition, certain realities occurred to lead one to question whether women during the early decades of the twentieth century were sufficiently committed to mothering. Declining birth rates, the growth of women's labor force participation, and a vocal suffrage movement raised the disturbing specter of modern women rejecting their time-honored roles. Although this first wave of feminism was mainly focused on the right to vote, according to Vandenberg-Daves, it also promoted equal contract and property rights for women and opposed ownership of married women by their husbands. In addition, feminists of the period suggested opening the public sphere so that women might combine motherhood and careers. Vandenberg-Daves notes that some, like psychologist and feminist Ethel Puffer Howes, proposed that denying the possibility of individual female achievement for married women outside the home was a proposition "which no normal woman of spirit and intelligence will accept for a moment." Like males, females needed the opportunity to choose both. However, Vandenberg-Daves points out that opportunities to put these ideas into practice were best suited to privileged married women who could afford help and could therefore build careers on a part-time basis, relying on husbands for economic support and other women for childcare assistance.

Although the suffrage movement met with massive opposition (Marina Koren states in "Why Men Thought Women Weren't Made to Vote" that the leading theory was that mental exertion could jeopardize reproductive health and voting would cause women to think) in 1920, passage of the Nineteenth Amendment granted women the right to vote. However, the mostly male experts and influential social commentators at the time continued to reject the notion that women—especially mothers—could have careers or become active in politics. Antifeminist propaganda depicted men as unhappy caregivers and women in the public arena as aggressively masculine. These critics wondered, with more females pursing education and responsibilities outside the home, who would assume the role of full-time mother. Hays points out that there was no clear alternative model to the traditional one, where mothers stayed home to care for their children, and none could adequately address the needs of working families. The lack of affordable and accessible childcare options was the result, in part, of a culture that still prized individualism and nuclear families that solved their own personal problems, leaving many mothers overwhelmed as they struggled to balance work and family obligations (and now had to think in order to vote!).

The Great Depression in the 1930s brought about some changes. Kerber states that more than a third of married women joined the workforce as their husbands were laid off or took wage cuts. Nonetheless, public acceptance of such employment plummeted, and married women continued to face increased legally sanctioned discriminatory employment practices. Vandenberg-Daves notes that federal laws and business policies at this time discouraged the hiring of married women and mandated that they be first fired if a reduction in force was necessary. In fact, twenty-six states passed laws prohibiting employment of married women. If married females did find work, they were often given lower status and lower-paid jobs. And management policies frequently excluded women in general from advancement no matter how productive they proved to be. The cultural pressure against working married women, combined with these discriminatory employment practices, was the major reason women failed to develop a strong commitment to the labor force prior to World War II. And sadly, because few women earned enough to give them any options other than marriage, self-actualization outside the home was not a dream that many young, gifted girls could aspire to during this era.

Around this time, parenting experts shifted their thinking from an emphasis on discipline and self-control in nurturing children to a focus on permissiveness and self-indulgence in the midtwentieth century, according to Hays. And in addition to raising more high-functioning children, this permissive parenting approach would supposedly be helpful for the economy, which was increasingly dependent on individual consumption. According to Ehrenreich and English, this represented a 180-degree turn away from early twentieth-century theories that promoted the rigid discipline and schedules of behaviorism. These authors describe the ideal permissive mother of the time to be one who is willing to "use endless techniques to get around rigidities and rituals and stubbornness."

Concurrently, a growing sense of anti-maternalism in the country increasingly blamed mothers for all social ills. The consensus was that many mothers' failures as parents resulted from the way they had constructed their identities wholly around their role as mothers. This is a clear case of blaming the victim. As the midcentury approached, the onset of World War II offered proof that mothers were at fault for raising offspring chock full of psychological problems when psychological screening methods used by draft boards identified more than two million men unfit for service due to psychiatric issues. Hays states that the high number of men found psychologically unfit led to a renewed focus on the role of mothers in child development. Experts and society at large began to blame mothers for their offspring's psychological problems including their inability to think for themselves and get along with others, suggesting that mothers had not done enough to nurture their children's emotional well-being.

Fortunately, mothers themselves pushed back against the cultural limitations on their role around this time. They questioned both their life choices and how best to socialize their daughters. Vandenberg-Daves notes that historian Linda Rosenzweig found excellent evidence documenting the closeness between middle-class mothers and daughters during the midtwentieth century but also found emerging struggles between them over traditional values. Mothers tended to grow more supportive of their daughters pursuing educational goals and career aspirations but were still concerned about them straying too far from conventional sexual mores and standards regarding proper appearance and behavior. Parents often felt the need to guard the sexual virtue of their daughters to ensure their marriage prospects. Mothers rarely wanted to gamble with what was still their female offspring's best hope for economic and social stability: marriage to a suitable man. Not unlike today, mothers in the first half of the twentieth century tried to help their daughters navigate a world of new, albeit limited, opportunities while facing sexual discrimination and dangers in the public arena. Undoubtedly, this challenge was intensified for gifted mothers attempting to nurture the potential of their gifted daughters while increasingly examining their own possible career options.

MOTHERHOOD DURING WWII AND THE POSTWAR IMPACT

A temporary solution to many mothers' growing ambivalence regarding their role came about with the onset of World War II, when a major shift occurred in what was perceived of as "women's work." As the United States geared up for war, the government began to encourage less traditional roles for women and mothers. Mothers were called upon to support the war effort in two critical ways: they were expected to send their sons off to fight, and they were strongly encouraged to take jobs in the labor force to boost industrial production. In addition, 350,000 women served in uniform. It's interesting to note that Hitler derided America, calling it degenerate for putting its women to work. Apparently ignoring Hitler's criticism, according to Coontz, between 1940 and 1945, the female labor force in the United States increased by more than 50 percent; 75 percent of these new workers were married, and a majority were mothers of school-aged children. As traditional barriers to wives, mothers, and older women disappeared, females experienced the rewards of challenging, well-paid work on a large scale.

But along with this came the stress of being mothers, with husbands off at war, and holding down jobs both inside and outside the home. Society soon realized that care facilities were essential to these workers' ability to do paid work, and Congress responded by allocating $52 million ($800 million today) for daycare centers for the duration of the war.

However, after the war, female workers experienced a swift turnabout. Hays states that management went to great lengths to purge them from the auto plants as well as from other high-paying and nontraditional jobs. In most cases, women were not fired but were downgraded to lower-paid "female" jobs. But many remained undeterred, with more women working than before the war even though the available jobs lacked the pay and challenges that had made wartime work more satisfying.

Vicious attacks began against women who did not define themselves in terms of home and family. According to Hays, those who sought further education opportunities or employment equality were accused of symbolic castration. A woman without a child went from being a social disadvantage or personal tragedy in years past to being considered a quasi perversion. And once again, the culture targeted women with conflicting and demoralizing messages. While on the one hand women were judged as unnatural if they did not seek fulfillment in motherhood, on the other hand, most psychologists and other experts insisted that most modern social ills could be traced to mothers who invested too much energy and emotion in their children. For this, mothers earned the diagnosis of being too much mother and too little wife.

More generally, a culture of fear and pressure for everyone to conform overtook the country immediately following the war. Senator Joseph McCarthy of Wisconsin led an obsessive pursuit of communists and subversives that began in the late 1940s and lasted through the 1950s. Only a few politicians were courageous enough to stand up to this reign of terror (such as Senator Margaret Chase Smith, who in 1950 called for an end to character assassinations and upheld every American's right to criticize, to think independently, to hold unpopular beliefs, and to protest).

Understandably, after the social upheaval of the war, the popular thinking was all about a return to "normal." Hays notes that many people felt that the war had disrupted traditional social and family structures, and they sought to restore a sense of stability and order. Life in America became centered around home and hearth. Coontz states that this was the first wholehearted effort in American history to create a home that would meet all the family members' needs, and both sexes were pressured to seek their identity in their parental and familial roles. Consequently, Americans plunged into neotraditional family life in a big way. The country experienced a dramatic rise in early marriages, high birth rates, and rigidly enforced gender roles. Mothers were coerced into enforcing even stricter gender norms for their children. According to Hays, experts admonished women to accept their role as wife and mother, which meant honoring their husbands as head of the household and limiting any interests deemed too distracting from their primary responsibility as wife and caregiver. As a result, the United States population increased by nearly 19 million between 1940 and 1950, and this baby boom continued until the midsixties.

Although one-fourth of Americans remained in poverty in the aftermath of the war, many families enjoyed an improved quality of life. With the availability of antibiotics and immunizations as well as other medical advances, healthcare improved, resulting in a decline in infant and maternal morbidity and mortality. Greater economic opportunities were available to families such as federal GI benefits, which, while helping men, caused a big decrease in women's educational parity over time, according to Hays. The GI Bill made it possible for nearly half of adult males to attend college, which, upon graduation, improved their income levels. As a result, many families were able to get by on just the father's salary while any additional income mothers brought in helped ensure the family's middle-class lifestyle. This included paying for TVs, cars, and family trips. Women's "extra income" also paid for extracurricular activities, which mothers were now supposed to actively seek out and facilitate for their kids. With the increasing presence of TV in the home, mothers were also tasked with managing and limiting their children's TV viewing while attempting to counter the incessant consumerism it promoted. America's consumer culture took off after the war, with advertising increasing by 400 percent between 1945 and 1960. Coontz quotes Ernest Dichter, a motivational researcher, who describes the objective of marketing for this era and one of the basic problems of prosperity is "to demonstrate that the hedonistic approach to life is a moral, not an immoral, one." Corporate America was increasingly perfecting its strategies to turn Americans into consummate consumers.

The end of the war ushered in an age of mass psychology, according to Vandenberg-Daves, and the role of mother was assigned even deeper psychological significance, based largely on theories derived from Freud's belief in the invisible and unconscious forces impacting children's personalities. The interactions between American mothers and their children were scrutinized even more closely than before the war, and the mother's parenting responsibilities were amplified. Conversely, fathers and grandparents were gradually viewed as secondary figures in charge of nurturing the mental health of their offspring and child-rearing in general.

Parenting experts found their largest audience to date with the help of radio, TV, and the press, which increasingly invaded the private sphere, as Arlie Hochschild states in *The Second Shift: Working Families and the Revolution at Home*. And with the sudden growth of the suburbs, young mothers, cut off from the support of extended family, turned to these parenting experts in lieu of their female relatives. Several experts like Dr. Benjamin Spock became cultural phenomena. His book *The Common Sense Book of Baby and Child Care*, published in 1946, is the most widely read childcare book ever written. It provided calming, supportive advice to mothers of this era, according to Hochschild. Spock allowed for a wider range of behaviors and feelings in children and encouraged a gentler, more thoughtful approach to discipline than was typical of previous ones. He strongly discouraged the custom of making the mother the scapegoat for anything that went wrong with her children. Many women welcomed his view that parenting was a complicated job and that being raised by a perfect mother would not prepare her children for life in our imperfect world. What micromanaged mother during these years wouldn't embrace this message? Spock's less rigid and more thoughtful parenting advice most likely appealed greatly to bright mothers of neurodiverse children. Spock basically asserted that "bringing up your child won't be a complicated job if you take it easy, trust your own instincts, and follow the directions that your doctor gives you." However, as Hochschild notes, Spock's advice, while encouraging women to trust their own instincts, still recognized professionals as the ultimate parenting authority. He wasn't without a few critics, though, who complained that he made it all look too easy. Vandenberg-Daves quotes a mother who was not a Spock fan: "Don't you realize that when you always emphasize that a child basically wants to behave well, and will behave well if he is handled wisely, you make the parent feel responsible for everything that goes wrong?"

Ambivalence about being returned to the home front full time, and the reality of closing career horizons after participating in the public arena during the war, was a common issue for mothers. In addition, any creative thinking about the institution of motherhood was frowned upon. Experts expended much more energy pressuring women back into a rigid motherhood role than promoting a scripted fatherhood role for men. Marriage and motherhood were linked to female normalcy and considered a sign of psychological, physical, and sexual health. The repressive cultural message for females from generations past emerged again based on society's fears about rising rates of higher education for women. This dictum was "books and babies don't mix." In *Modern America*, Vandenberg-Daves shares a quote from a writer in *American Home* about educated women who chose not to have children that describes them as "ignorant, lazy, or selfish" and having "no place" in American society.

The underlying message to women was that their primary responsibility was, first and foremost, to be a mother, which required providing round-the-clock service to their family. The generally held belief, says Vandenberg-Daves, was that domestic women were "normal" women; ambition was unfeminine, and unfeminine women were a menace to society, because being both wife and mother required deference, subordination, and acceptance of their role. Women were at the same time encouraged to pour their emotional energy as much into nurturing men and the maintenance of their heterosexual coupling as they put into mothering. However, they were cautioned to make sure they weren't smothering family members with too much care. Author Azar Nafisi provides a valuable insight relevant to how many women, especially gifted mothers, probably felt during this period in her book, *Reading Lolita in Tehran: A Memoir in Books*: "To have a whole life, one must have the possibility of publicly shaping and expressing private worlds, dreams, thoughts, and desires, of constantly having access to a dialogue between the public and private worlds. How else do we know that we have existed, felt, desired, hated, feared?" This repressive retro-motherhood role must have been suffocating for many women, but when combined with the intensity, sensitivity, drive, energy, and intellectual potential of gifted mothers, it most likely created a never-ending struggle to maintain their mental health. Hulbert tells of a physician during this period describing a female patient who defied postwar norms by postponing marriage and earning a PhD. The doctor eventually had her committed to a psychiatric institution essentially for defying current gender codes.

But even women who followed society's dictates and assumed the role of mothers were not free from criticism. Mother-bashing became popular as the war raged on. Philip Wylie's 1942 *Generation of Vipers* gained considerable public attention. In it, he blasted American mothers for having sinister motives that emasculated their sons and for controlling their offspring with a monstrous motherlove. Wylie claimed that thanks to modern conveniences, women had too much free time, creating the context for them to interfere excessively in the lives of their children, especially sons. Other experts blamed mom for social problems in ways previous generations would have been shocked to imagine. Vandenberg-Daves notes that a wide range of social issues including juvenile delinquency, neurosis, immaturity, lack of combat readiness, alcoholism, homosexuality, and rape were all the result of bad mothers. Psychiatric and medical experts claimed that dysfunctional mothers were responsible for creating serious mental health problems in their children. Sadly, but not too surprisingly, most women suffered in silence during this era, dealing not only with crushing parenting challenges but also with society's blame for what, in many cases, were childhood matters beyond their control.

Along these lines, sociologist Ferdinand Lundberg and psychiatrist Marynia Farnham, authors of *Modern Woman: The Lost Sex*, argue that large numbers of women in the post-World War II era were psychologically disordered and that this was negatively impacting the men in all aspects of their lives as well as the women themselves. Their solution was to encourage American women to reclaim their household domesticity and, in doing so, restore the country to its prewar social order. In their national bestseller, they claim that women who rejected femininity or embraced feminism (most apparently by working in the public sphere) were likely to ruin their children.

If the girl has the good fortune to have a mother who finds complete satisfaction, without conflict or anxiety, in living out her role as wife and mother, it is unlikely that she will experience serious difficulties. If, however, the mother is beset by distaste for her role, strives for accomplishment outside her home, and can only grudgingly give attention to her children, has regrets for whatever reason at being a woman, then, no matter how much or little of it she betrays, the child cannot escape the confused impression that the mother is without love, is not a satisfactory model.

An overriding societal concern was fear of emasculating American men by women's rejection of "femininity." According to Hays, with more women, including mothers, seeking work outside the home during WWII, society foresaw a crisis in the making. J. Edgar Hoover, director of the FBI, claimed that mothers who worked outside the home risked creating children who were "driven first to perversion and then to crime." Hays notes, however, that Hoover's own mental health was later called into question and suggests that his views on women's roles may have been influenced by his own personal struggles with gender identity and sexuality.

Ehrenreich and English shed light on what men were most likely experiencing in the aftermath of the war, given these more rigid gender roles. As seen by some of the experts discussed above, they echoed the growing sense that somehow males during this period felt they lost power and were no longer "real men." While engaged in the war effort, purportedly the most masculine of endeavors, the average

American male returned home, these authors note, to "find himself driving a blue Ford (like the hundreds of others on the highway) between a job he found no meaning in and a tract house he could identify only by looking at the street number." Thus the flip side of the 1950s busy mother, housekeeper, and household finance manager who reigned in her small domestic sphere was the one-trick-pony dad who perceived his only function was to bring home a paycheck.

In America's zeal to return to "normal" after the war, delineating strict gender roles for both men and women—who had experienced dramatic lifestyle changes during the war and, in many cases, the trauma of war—became critical. However, this pressure to be "normal" resulted in a social powder keg that exploded twenty years later. (As the song goes, "How can you keep 'em down on the farm after they've seen Paree?") For mothers—who had been employed in well-paid war-time positions outside of the home and simultaneously served as the head of the household while the men were off fighting—being told to return to the old cultural constraints of their subservient role in the private sphere (and to be criticized while they were at it) proved impossible over the long haul. And American men, experiencing their own readjustment struggles, were unhappy and disillusioned as well, in some cases suffering from post-traumatic stress disorder (PTSD). In effect, the reinstatement of the rigid pre-WWII gender system made captives of both sexes. In hindsight, it's obvious that a revolution was brewing under the country's façade of "normalcy."

MOTHERHOOD FROM THE 1950S TO LATE 1960S

In the artificially fabricated "good life" of the 1950s, the family was made the hub for fulfillment, fun, and recreation for all family members. Coontz stresses the unprecedented glorification of self-indulgence in family life during these years in which formality was rejected in favor of livability, comfort, and convenience. These family ideals were primarily targeted at middle-class mothers living in the suburbs who, for the most part, did not work for pay. These women were led to believe that they had it all: a nice house, the latest conveniences, a spouse who brought home a paycheck, and healthy children. Many middle-class mothers who fit this category and followed prescribed norms appeared very much alike. They followed the same script and had the same goal of achieving and maintaining the supposed easy life offered by their middle-class status.

Even though this era epitomized female domesticity, employment rates of single women rose dramatically, according to Hochschild. In addition, the surge in consumption created such a demand for products that it sparked a huge need for married women in the workplace. In fact, the necessity for workers outstripped the supply, resulting in both higher wages and a relaxation of employment barriers for women. Although most middle-class suburban housewives did not work for pay, many 1950s wives and mothers did work outside the home, adjusting their hours around the period their children were at school. Between 1948 and 1958, the number of employed married women with children was about 80 percent. Interestingly, many of these women stated that they were working both for personal fulfillment and economic needs. And in a big cultural shift, Vandenberg-Daves notes that married women who worked to pay for that something "extra" for their family were sometimes even publicly praised.

But Ehrenreich and English point out that during this relatively calm period for America, a storm was brewing on the other side of the world. While Americans spent the years after World War II in a great national celebration of private life, the political geography of the world was changing radically. The menacing threat of communism gripped the country and seeped into the darkest recesses of the American psyche. Fallout shelters stocked with canned food donations dotted the American landscape, and schoolchildren were taught to hide under their desks in case of a nuclear attack. As a seven-year-old, I remember donating the earnings from my lemonade stand to my school club, whose purpose was to help fight communism. The overwhelming fear of the "Red Threat" was due in part to the fact that while middle-class Americans had been enjoying all the new comforts their consumption-led economy could bring, the Soviets had been working feverishly to catch up and surpass us in GDP and military might. Waking up to the impending reality of the Cold War, as it was labeled, Americans began to see child-rearing as a key factor in our battle against the newly formed Soviet Union.

The Cold War contributed to a major shift in the country's attitude toward married women in the workforce in the late fifties. Coontz states that government policy during this period encouraged the expansion of married women's employment not only to foster industrial expansion but also because of the increasing fear that the Russians would gain educational and technological superiority if Americans did not use their "womanpower" more effectively. There was little concern about increasing female employment in the workplace to enhance American mothers' personal fulfillment, but rather mothers needed to leave the private sphere to work for the benefit, once again, of a country at war.

The media stoked Americans' fears of communism by portraying it as the antithesis of American values. Communists were soulless, according to the press—they had abolished religion, centered life solely around production and growing their economy, and devalued the sanctity of the family by having the State serve as the primary caregiver while their females did heavy labor outside the home. But according to Ehrenreich and English, experts in America were forced to acknowledge that communism did provide a benchmark that could be used to determine how American children, their parents, and American values measured up. This resulted in widespread suspicion that Americans in fact had no values. American intellectuals appeared to suffer from a massive case of "alienation" while housewives across the country exhibited ennui and frustration with their limited role. For gifted mothers with overexcitabilities, the emotional impact of this deep-seated cultural angst must have been quite disturbing.

Over the 1950s, the search by parenting experts, educators, and the government to discover key values fundamental to American society that mothers should instill in their children proved disappointing. What emerged was that the central moral and spiritual value for most Americans was, ultimately, the importance of the individual personality. Ehrenreich and English cite a 1960 Presidential Commission on Goals for Americans that declared "the paramount goal of the United States…is to guard the rights of the individual, and to enlarge his (note the wording) opportunity."

Obviously, the powers that be in America realized that this self-centered, individualistic approach needed to be countermanded to defend against the Soviet Union's increasingly consummate focus on enhancing the power of the State. Americans needed to internalize John F. Kennedy's 1961 challenge "Ask not what your country can do for you—ask what you can do for your country" to have any hope of winning the Cold War. Not surprisingly, blame for this crisis of commitment to one's country was placed squarely on the shoulders of America's mothers who, historically, were charged with providing moral training to their children and inculcating them with appropriate social values. Mothers needed to ensure that the home served as a refuge from the individualistic, "dog-eat-dog" world of the public arena. As such, mothers were required to counter the worst effects of competition and individualism in America's capitalistic society. Coontz shares that most conservative writers during these years were adamant that American culture required females to counteract male individualism by walling off the family from competitive forces. Mothers were encouraged to raise their children in a noncompetitive environment but also to prepare them for geopolitical battle against the Red Threat.

Because this was viewed as their most important responsibility during the Cold War, mothers were once again given mixed messages about their accepted place in society. There was a demand for increased womanpower in the workplace (primarily for lower-level positions, certainly not for positions that would tap into the potential of gifted females), but conversely, mothers were strongly discouraged from taking jobs in the public sphere that would negatively impact their ability to nurture future citizens. Is it any wonder women were themselves ambivalent about their role whether they worked for pay outside the home or not?

Although a few experts at this time did appreciate the ambivalence women were experiencing, David Blankenhorn with the Institute for American Values had a warning for employed women, according to Coontz. He affirmed that employed mothers do not a family make, because the family is about caring and collective goals, building life's most important bonds of affection, nurturance, mutual support, and long-term commitment. These values must counter what he obviously considered the jungle outside the door. He held that the goals of employees in the workplace are primarily individualistic: social recognition, wages, opportunities for advancement, and self-fulfillment. Apparently, recognition and self-fulfillment were considered "male" goals. This view, once again, underscores society's role in minimizing the possibility that gifted females could become eminent despite their high potential.

Sadly, as Hochschild notes, Spock joined the experts' chorus during these years, shaming mothers who worked outside the home, but he did propose that the government should give a comfortable allowance to stay-at-home mothers of young children who would otherwise be compelled to work. Spock affirmed that productive, well-adjusted citizens were our country's most valuable possession and the care provided by a "good" mother during early childhood was critical. "It doesn't make sense to let mothers go to work making dresses in factories or tapping typewriters in offices, and have them pay other people to do a poorer job of bringing up their children."

But the country's powers that be disagreed, viewing this as anathema to America's anti-communistic, "every man (mother) for himself (herself)" core belief. Society in general felt strongly that mothers should be able to carry out their responsibilities with very little systemic support, although getting a little advice from the experts now and then was viewed as critical. In a foreshadowing of today's culture, society provided a weak proxy of support to mothers in lieu of actual resources by practicing anticipatory praise—placing mothers on a pedestal and giving lip service to their amazing ability to handle these overwhelming responsibilities all on their own. Although the government did provide limited childcare during World War II, it was promptly discontinued after the war. With America's strong individualistic bent, the culture viewed solutions to establishing balance between work outside the home and primary caregiving as a private concern. As a result, mothers were supposed to magically manage these conflicting demands without concrete support from the public when resources like universal, high-quality childcare and paid family leave would have been invaluable to many overwhelmed, overworked American women.

And to add to their stress, any complaining by mothers, per Vandenberg-Daves, was seen as a symptom of a psychiatric disorder. Women who had trouble adjusting to the extremely rigid prescribed purpose of their lives were labeled mentally ill. They were typically diagnosed as neurotic, perverted, or even schizophrenic. Coontz cites a study conducted in the 1950s where the sampled females were forced to accept their domestic roles and obey their husbands' dictates by means of institutionalization and shock treatments. Further, all women, even those who repressed any negative thoughts or objections about their plight, were mistrusted by the dominant culture and were not permitted to serve on juries, buy or sell property, have credit cards in their name, enter into contracts, or establish residence. In addition, they were not allowed to hold certain jobs such as bartending or serve in the military. So pervasive was this misogynistic attitude toward working mothers that widely circulated publications like *Life* and *Esquire* published articles in the fifties describing them as a menace to society and labeling the whole notion of mothers who worked for pay a disease.

Many women, especially gifted mothers, struggled to adapt, sometimes at great cost to themselves, their families, and society. Friedan writes that many gifted women felt trapped in their domestic roles and failed to reconcile their desire for intellectual stimulation and personal fulfillment with the expectations of society. Many felt isolated and sought to find meaning and intellectual peers by returning to school or through volunteer work and civic engagement. Typically, they received no remuneration for their services.

In her book, Vandenberg-Daves profiles a woman named Carolyn Teach Denlinger. She apparently was a very bright student who loved learning but was forced to drop out of college after a year due to illness. She married at nineteen and became filled with anxiety and discontent, lambasting herself in her diary for her lack of drive, her weight, and her inability to be the kind of mother she thought she should be. "I seem to put almost everything before my children," she wrote. "I growl and snap at them especially when I'm reading. I must try to cultivate a more pleasing personality and more patience." Denlinger deeply missed participating in the world of ideas and connecting with people who shared her interests. "I wish I could follow conversations like [the one her husband and a male friend had discussing philosophy and theology] better but they use terms I don't know. I served popcorn and Kool-Aid." Her frustration with her expatriation from the outside world surfaced on many occasions like when she returned to her college ten years after dropping out to attend someone else's graduation ceremony. She blamed herself for her unhappiness in the domestic role, eventually deciding to seek help from a psychiatrist. Her doctors prescribed a coping aid promoted for housewives in the 1950s, a "mother's little helper" of a drug called Dexamyl (amphetamine and barbiturate). Approved initially as a diet drug, it was marketed to housewives by suggesting they would be happy doing household chores. One ad portrayed a woman smiling blissfully while pushing a vacuum.

Denlinger was regretful that her time out of the labor force most likely disallowed her the opportunity to work in her field of historical preservation. Like many others who had much to offer intellectually and creatively, Denlinger was stifled by cultural expectations. The most potent of these was perhaps that she should become a mother despite not liking children. Like millions of other women, she believed it was her fault that she failed to find happiness in her circumscribed domestic role. This common delusion among women of being inherently wrong and believing that failure was always their fault has (according to Catherine Lacey in her introduction to Joy Sorman's novel *Life Sciences*) been smuggled into our culture in the Trojan horse of a thousand old stories. Importantly, this narrative of failure has been reinforced by medical professionals and experts who echoed this sentiment over generations, as Sorman stresses in her novel about the medical establishment's inability, or perhaps refusal, to take seriously women's physical complaints related to their struggle.

One study cited by Vandenberg-Daves reported that middle-class women in the sample had expressed dissatisfaction with their marriages at twice the rate of men. Additionally, both husbands and wives admitted that women had to make more adaptations to wife and mother roles than men did to being husband and father. Another case cited by Vandenberg-Daves was a gifted woman who said, "I was doing a lot of reading about metaphysics, and one day while I was rinsing out dirty diapers, I thought, *These things are incompatible*. So I stopped the reading—I couldn't stop the diapers." The angst and struggles of women during this era help us understand why many "happy housewives" of the fifties dreamed of different lives for their daughters. For example, Vandenberg-Daves cites a poll taken during this period in which a staggering 90 percent of women said they wanted their daughters to live different lives than they had. They wanted them to marry later and attain more education.

A major historical event that impacted society's ideal of the best parenting approach for mothers happened during this decade. Ehrenreich states that on October 4, 1957, Americans were jolted into a terrifying new reality that distracted them from worrying about "values" and forced them to confront a concrete challenge. On that date, the Russians launched the world's first orbital satellite. Sputnik 1 rocked America's world of child-raising experts, educators, and parents. Prior to this, psychologists had been willing to concede that communist children came across as cooperative and pleasant to a degree that seemed almost unnatural compared to the Dennis the Menace personality of many American children. Public opinion expressed alarm about losing the Cold War and turned with exasperation against American parents, especially mothers and their offspring, who they now viewed as malingerers. Believing that American parents has been overindulging their children for years, experts declared the party was over and no longer pushed any type of permissive parenting. Ehrenreich and English note that the Sputnik scare, combined with rising competition for entry to colleges, set off a kind of hysteria among upwardly mobile parents who put new intellectual pressure on offspring of the fifties and early sixties.

The flip side of this intense pressure on mothers to produce citizens who could win the war against the Soviets was the boost in status they received as key players in this global competition. Because experts determined that to win the Space Race, America's children needed constant intellectual stimulation, mothers themselves were now assigned the proxy role of serving as tutors and psychologists and tasked with maintaining an appropriately stimulating, challenging, and intellectually nurturing environment within the home. As such, they were seen as critical in ensuring the survival of American society, and gifted mothers were seen as more than qualified for this challenge.

Even Dr. Spock was transformed by the Cold War. As Hulbert puts it, the doctor now worried that mothers were allowing their offspring to be too demanding and were becoming fanatical in their devotion to their children's self-regulation and self-expression. He admitted that his earlier message of "don't worry" no longer seemed to work. Permissiveness had become a catch-all code for the moral breakdown in American society. Spock now cautioned that mothers' role as servants, accommodating their children's every need, risked creating not just tyrants but aimless adolescents who succumbed to conformity, apathy, and delinquency.

Hulbert states that in the early 1960s, with the dawn of a new decade, a cry went out that America's kids had been "Spocked" when they should have been spanked. Experts sounded more panicked than ever about child-rearing practices while, conversely, increasing numbers of women were challenging the harsh constrictions of their motherhood role. Hulbert states that the harried working mother and the hurried child became the standard of the times. A major factor in creating more harried working mothers was the growing demand for women workers, especially in the lower-paid clerical, retail, and service sectors that drew women into the labor force. Many mothers entered employment outside the home when their children were in school or no longer living at home. This was a pattern that would expand throughout the rest of the twentieth century, although the age of children with working mothers increasingly lowered over the course of time.

MOTHERHOOD DURING THE SECOND WAVE OF FEMINISM AND THE SEXUAL REVOLUTION

By the 1960s, American child-rearing practices had been called too permissive for several years, and as the decade progressed, the result of these supposed wayward parenting practices became more apparent. Hulbert comments that Spock, in 1968, was dispensing stodgier counsel to parents than ever before. He began preaching against "today's child-centered viewpoint" of mothers. Instead, he stressed, mothers were supposed to be thinking about what the world, neighborhood, and family would be needing from the child to ensure he will grow up to meet such obligations. But while the experts were fretting that children had been overindulged with permissiveness, Ehrenreich and English state that no one happened to notice for quite some time that one member of the family—Mom—had never even had a taste of it. Permissiveness was allotted to the kids, and secondarily to Dad, but there was only so much to go around. Children had few demands placed on them, and dads were often free to relax after dealing with the jungle outside the door, but the tender mercies of permissiveness rarely rained down on Mom. Someone had to manage the family, provide round-the-clock care, and carry out all the domestic responsibilities, leaving little time for a mother to relax, enjoy, or indulge. Even as a consumer, mothers' primary concerns were translating the family's demands into the appropriate foods, supplies, toys, and home furnishings. Ehrenreich and English argue that by some curious asymmetry in society's ideology about the perfect family, everyone else in the family lived for themselves while mothers lived for them.

Moving well into the 1960s, parenting experts, America's mothers, and their offspring had their final falling out. A revolt against the oppressive banality of rigid gender roles and stricter demands on America's youth (exacerbated by drafting young men for war) broke out and spread to the point that even the vice president publicly weighed in on the situation. In 1968, Agnew took a side, describing the growing number of political activists as spoiled brats who never had a good spanking. Although this schism between authority figures and younger Americans calling for change was labeled a "generation gap" by the media, this analysis of the issue was too simplistic. Not only younger voices demanded reform. Along with America's youth, women of all ages, including a significant number of housewives, burst out of their repressed gender box. Mothers who for years appeared to have accepted their restrictive domestic roles collectively shared their rage with other women, sparking the second wave of feminism. As Vandenberg-Daves puts it, these women were simultaneously demanding access to the public domain and criticizing American culture for restricting them to subservient positions. Their collaborative rage was a reaction to a culture that historically showed little concern for their needs.

As a result, the restrictive script for mothers and the nuclear family began unraveling as women finally gained a voice in defining the terms of motherhood. Although in 1970, Hulbert notes, Spock was still trying to put the genie back in the bottle by praising women as specially qualified for "working at unexciting, repetitive tasks"—part of the skill set that made them "indispensable as wives, mothers, nurses, secretaries"—the media was forced to acquiesce to the radical change in the marketplace. For example, after a sit-in in 1970, *Ladies' Home Journal* was forced to include feminist articles in a special issue, to publish articles related to working women and women in the economy in future issues, and to appoint a female as editor in chief. In addition, feminists around the country began to organize powerful challenges to the silencing, privatizing, pathologizing and economic disempowering of women. Female activists published critiques of women's historical confinement and questioned society's mandate that all women had to reproduce. They also focused society's attention on the way in which motherhood, as it was constructed in a patriarchal society, was part of the oppression of women and pushed, often successfully, for policy changes to empower women.

Despite the economic and legislative seeds of this feminist movement planted by past generations, even well-educated wives continued to have little control over personal or household assets. In the second half of the twentieth century, wives were still unable to open a credit account without their husband's permission. Many housewives were more like dependents of rather than equal partners to their husbands. Prior to the changes demanded by activists in the late sixties and seventies, according to Hochschild, marital rape was not recognized as a crime, abortion was illegal (and, as of 2022, is again in nearly half the states), domestic abusers were basically given a free pass, and a housewife's role was little more than that of a servant.

However, the second wave of feminism helped American women openly define their own needs. It was now socially acceptable for females to opt out of motherhood altogether. Women were free to combine mothering with other needs and pursuits. Specifically, feminism meant freedom for mothers to freely consider opportunities for self-actualization outside the home. Vandenberg-Daves cites an older mother who described a different way of parenting that was increasingly acceptable in seventies: "My job was not to entertain them; it was to love and discipline them." As we shall see, this more mother-centered parenting approach differed radically from the intensive parenting model of today as well as the parenting model, with all its pressures on mothers, practiced during the Cold War era.

Feminists pushed to raise female awareness and empower mothers, insisting that women needed social supports like childcare, educational opportunities, and professional opportunities—not to supplant marriage and motherhood but to complement it. Mass protests for women's rights, along with feminist authors and activists like Betty Friedan and Gloria Steinem and publications like *Ms.*, helped to transform cultural attitudes regarding the institution of motherhood. The traditional division of mothers as private, emotional, and unpaid caretakers and fathers as breadwinners, disciplinarians, and representatives of the family in the public arena began to crumble as more Americans became open to new ways of thinking.

But even within the feminist movement, the cultural ambivalence about motherhood was increasingly apparent, with some feminists celebrating motherhood while others strongly denounced it. It seemed that a common critique across the divide was around the way women had been forced to construct their identities wholly around their role as mothers. Although some activists focused on liberating women from their most onerous childcare tasks and their imprisonment in the private sphere, in general, the second wave of feminism fought to promote and enhance the value of the motherhood role. In her book *Motherhood Reconceived: Feminism and the Legacies of the Sixties*, historian Lauri Umansky argues that the feminist movement that began in the late 1960s vigorously and positively addressed the notion of motherhood. She challenges the critics of feminism who maintain that the women's movement denigrated mothers. Any ambivalence for mothers about their roles at this time, according to Adrienne Rich, was based mainly on the fact that the patriarchy had, for generations, hijacked motherhood itself. As Rich wrote in 1976, "The institution of motherhood finds all mothers more or less guilty of having failed their children." She notes that this may also have been the underlying reason for the critical views many daughters involved in the movement held about their own mothers. Rich argues that motherhood could be a choice and a form of self-expression, but women had to repossess it. Rather than separating the lived reality of the two genders into opposing spheres and placing the responsibility for caring solely on the backs of females, a completely new cultural figure appeared. This, according to Ehrenreich and English, was a woman defiant, dismissive of any dictum that woman should "know her place." Feminists across the country were opting to reject all the reigning stereotypes for women, including motherhood, and challenging patriarchy in every structure of authority.

Although the pioneers of married women's employment in the 1950s and 1960s had been lower-middle-class or working-class women with high school educations, according to Coontz, it was largely upper-middle-class, college-educated women who initiated the ideological revolution of the sixties and seventies. Their demands included gender equality and the idea that paid work was an important component of life satisfaction for many women. For most of these educated women, the motivation to seek opportunities outside the home lay in the declining attraction to the life of a housewife. However, as late as 1970, cultural values seemed to die hard, with 78 percent of married women under age forty-five, according to Coontz, claiming that it was better for wives to be homemakers and for husbands to do the breadwinning. Perhaps these females still bought men's rationale that housewives were not kept housebound to exploit them but to protect them from the ravages of a cold, cruel world, although some of these women may have found the role of nurturing their children full time deeply fulfilling. Nonetheless, fear of the public sphere, which discriminated against females on multiple levels, and the safety of home apparently still held sway over the mindset of many women during this period.

In fact, it was largely economics rather than feminism that led many women to reorder their values when extensive labor force participation for mothers became an acceptable norm. For large numbers of mothers, work initially viewed as an opportunity soon became an economic necessity. In the seventies, inflation made two incomes essential for families that hoped to buy a house and all the other products promoted so aggressively by America's consumer culture. As the 1980s approached, mothers of young children faced strong incentives to work for pay. In addition to increased buying power, working mothers realized a secondary but critically important benefit from paid employment. As Ehrenreich and English put it, for the first time in history, working women could imagine that if they left home and were abandoned by their partner or widowed, they could survive and perhaps even thrive on their own. This was the scenario described by one of the mothers in the study:

> "My dad died when I was two of cancer, and my mother had dropped out of college with one semester left to marry my dad. They fell in love and got married all in three weeks during the Depression. And she's now ninety-one. This is a woman who pulled herself up by her bootstraps. She said she walked out of the hospital the night that he died with the house they had built, [and] I mean they had built it themselves with family help...and she said she didn't know what she was going to do. She was a home economics major and worked two or three jobs as I was growing up, so my older sister was really my mother. My mother is one of those women who have all sorts of one-phrase wisdom caveats. One of them is 'Don't count on a man. They're going to die, or you'll be divorced, so you have to stand on your own two feet.' She told my

sister and me that we could only go to a two- or three-year program after high school because we might not get through to the fourth year, based on her experience."

As a result, this interviewed mother went to nursing school, but at the time of the interview, her career had evolved to the point where she was serving as division director of a large health insurance corporation and was also the owner of a $45 million software firm.

The feminist movement left much work undone in terms of achieving true equality for women even as it created new opportunities for mothers. Unmooring motherhood from the tight nuclear family and gender prescriptions of the past created new paradigms for mothers in future decades. The momentum of large groups of empowered females challenging the cultural construction of motherhood continued into the 1980s, says Vandenberg-Daves, although it faced a powerful conservative backlash as the new century approached. Nonetheless, some changes from the feminist revolution would prove lasting. For example, women's age at marriage crept up, women availed themselves of effective birth control and abortion (until 2022, when this option became limited in some parts of the country), and they had fewer children. They made proactive choices regarding their families, education, and workforce participation that would have astonished their foremothers.

Many women, like myself, who lived during these years remember basking in their new-found freedom to be truly themselves for the first time in their lives. We found common bonds with women of all ages, backgrounds, and color in questioning the cultural controls and customs we no longer valued. For the first time, mothers gained access to a world previously closed off to them. All the energy once channeled toward serving others and looking and behaving in a prescribed feminine manner could finally be used for the purpose of helping females identify and realize their own dreams. For example, Ehrenreich and English state, mothers organized daycare centers and were no longer subservient either at home or at work: clerical workers joined unions, secretaries refused to accept getting chased around their desks, and stewardesses declined to offer "coffee, tea, or me" and retitled themselves flight attendants.

"POST-FEMINISM" UP TO THE INTENSIVE MOTHERHOOD MODEL

The cultural tsunami of the sixties and seventies expanded what society considered suitable life choices for women. This radically altered women's self-awareness regarding their "place" and presented women with a version of life different from what their mothers and grandmothers were permitted. For many women, this meant access to higher education, professional careers, and reproductive healthcare. The motherhood mandate of past centuries no longer held sway and meant the choice to remain childless was becoming a tolerable norm as the end of the twentieth century drew near. In addition, the script for what constituted socially acceptable motherhood was expanded, giving women greater flexibility to define mothering on their own terms. Socially constructed motherhood now encompassed working mothers, single mothers, and mothers with children born outside of wedlock or across racial lines. So although the traditional nuclear family represented by a heterosexual, married duo, each person responsible for a discrete gendered role, still held a place of honor for America's power elite, it was less a reality for a growing majority who no longer had to endure criticism and shame for the unconventional makeup of their household.

But like most seismic cultural changes that seemingly offer the promise of a better life, social, political, and economic forces over the coming decades pushed the pendulum in the opposite direction, negatively impacting the day-to-day lives of American women. The following describes the bad news as it relates to society's backlash against the progressive reforms for women during the second wave of feminism and its impact on the current institution of motherhood.

Society's failure to improve mothers' lives at the close of the twentieth century resulted in part from the fact that mothers had no voice in places where decisions about their lives were made, given that they were still living under a patriarchal system. As the ideals of the sexual revolution were operationalized, females were grossly underrepresented at the policy-making table. Earlier feminist claims that mothers were individuals in their own right, with their own needs and unique challenges, were ignored by policymakers who also downplayed or pathologized mothers' humanity by ignoring maternal emotions (including ambivalence about caregiving) and "negative" emotions they might experience in their role (such as anger, resentment, hostility, or frustration).

Exacerbating the lack of female representation in improving conditions on the home front were the sharp economic setbacks the country experienced from the late seventies to the early nineties in many regions and industries. According to Coontz, these setbacks were followed by economic recoveries that excluded many Americans and left even those who benefited from them worried about the future. Significant disparities in income across different segments of American society began to grow during this time. More families sank deeper into often irreversible poverty. Parents' fears about their children's uncertain futures set in, and even for those able to rebound financially, their quality of life worsened as their jobs became more demanding, competitive, and stressful. The seeds of today's "greedy jobs" and dramatic income inequality were planted.

As a reaction to this increasingly dire and unstable economic reality, by the eighties and nineties, a pervasive ethic of heady individualism infected the country. For significant numbers of Americans, the quest for meaning, along with a response to financial concerns, tended increasingly toward a singular focus on individualistic and materialistic goals in the marketplace and less emphasis on relationships and quality of life. Coontz notes that many of the young women of this period adopted the egalitarian goals of feminism in the workforce but ignored its emphasis on transforming social values and social constructs, including motherhood. With the gradual decline of the organized feminist movement, the notion of sharing responsibility for nurturing America's next generation was no longer a priority. The feminist idea that mothers needed equally invested partners in childcare and family management was dropped from the national dialogue. That said, many men felt that they did "help out" more at home than men of previous generations. However, according to Coontz, most fathers' failure to increase their labor at home to keep pace with mothers' increase in paid labor caused women to feel indignant when men congratulated themselves on their new domestic duties. Although modifying the American Dream to include achievement by females as well as males in the public arena was, in and of itself, a huge accomplishment, as usual, it left unanswered the central question "who will raise America's children?" And as the country's WWII-era sense of "we're all in this together" disappeared, individual families became obsessed with how their offspring would survive in an increasingly competitive world that seemed to operate according to the zero-sum paradigm that decreed progress for some must come at the expense of others.

This spirit of individualism, focusing more on personal responsibility and less on community support and collaboration, was reflected in the government's response to the cultural changes of the sixties and seventies. Although most citizens had supported the goals of the women's movement, welcoming their labor force participation, by the Reagan era in the eighties, the nation's commitment to providing policy solutions to help working mothers waned despite growing numbers of families desperately in need of two incomes. In fact, social policy began to push back against, and deliberately forestall, the normalization of maternal labor force participation.

Another major setback for mothers came about as feminist labor activists lost momentum in their efforts to set new family-friendly and equitable employment standards even as women flooded the workforce. Federal budget cuts and inaction increasingly made life harder for these women. According to Hochschild, in 1984, the Reagan administration cut federal funding for childcare by 18 percent, forcing many working mothers to leave the workforce or reduce their hours. The government's continued refusal to create meaningful legislation to ensure quality childcare led to the emergence of a largely unregulated patchwork of centers and in-home providers with high turnover rates, staffed by women who were grossly underpaid. In 1987, according to Hochschild, only 2 percent of American workplaces provided childcare, and only 3 percent subsidized off-site childcare. In addition, working mothers, both then and now, had access to fewer informal neighborhood networks of at-home parents to offer temporary childcare, and extended family support was often nonexistent.

At the same time, while both women and men faced declining real wages as the twenty-first century approached, increasing numbers of mothers found that workplace flexibility to accommodate caregiving often came at the expense of pay raises and job promotions. Today, inflexible workplaces based on the traditional model of a male employee, propped up by a full-time housewife, severely limit the revolutionary feminist ideal of equity with males in both public and private spheres.

As a result, responding to their children's needs and family emergencies remained solely mothers' concerns and, like nearly all issues related to being female, was not a topic for discussion in the world of work. In a 2011 report "Failing its Families: Lack of Paid Leave and Work-Family Supports in the US," Human Rights Watch documented that very few mothers had access to paid parental leave, subsidized childcare, or flexible work schedules, and complaining or advocating for them often had dire consequences. And this silencing and lack of support starts in utero. The burden of health issues related to pregnancy and birth is viewed as a working woman's problem and hers alone. As journalist Laura Santhanam points out in her article "It's Time to Recognize the Damage of Childbirth, Doctors and

Mothers Say," the United States has one of highest maternal mortality rates among developed countries and a healthcare system that is frequently unresponsive to painful pre- and postpartum conditions. Society in general, and employers in particular, often turn a blind eye to the physical demands of pregnancy and childbirth. Postpartum challenges and the overwhelming demands of caring for a newborn are unspoken in the public sphere. The culture promotes the message that any health issues new mothers may have need to be kept private and should be overshadowed by the happiness their newborns bring.

Even access to appropriate reproductive healthcare is a huge problem for many women, says Santhanam, considering that half of United States counties have no practicing obstetrician or gynecologist. Forty percent of pregnant women must drive thirty miles or more to the nearest delivery hospital, and nearly half rely on Medicaid for pregnancy and delivery. In some cases, an employer may be allowed to fire a woman who is unable to return to work on the employer's schedule due to her health or her newborn's, according to the US Equal Employment Opportunity Commission's "Fact Sheet: Pregnancy Discrimination in the Workplace." However, the employer does need to justify this by documenting that the woman's absence is causing a hardship for the business and that there is no reasonable accommodation that could be made to allow her to continue working.

Meanwhile, the cultural expectations of mothers, from the nineties and up to the present, have made parenting much more demanding. According to Claire Cain Miller's article "The Relentlessness of Modern Parenting," parents have greatly increased the amount of time, attention, and money they put into raising children, with mothers, who increasingly juggle jobs outside the home, spending just as much time tending their children as stay-at-home mothers did in the 1970s. Many believe that the intensity of modern-day parenting, advanced by both experts and the media, is motivated by fear—fear that children face a future with cut-throat competition over dwindling resources and will end up less well off than their parents. Because of this economic anxiety, parents feel pressure to give their children every edge possible over the competition as the gap between rich and poor drastically inflates and the cost of parental missteps balloons in the cultural mindset.

Hays coined the term "intensive parenting" in her 1998 book *The Cultural Contradictions of Motherhood* to describe this parenting style, which is still prevalent today. It primarily consists of a child-centered, expert-guided, emotionally absorbing, labor-intensive, and financially expensive parenting approach. Mothers are the ones primarily responsible for this relentless cultivation. Intensive parenting sets out ideal norms and practices for "good mothers" who must be self-sacrificing, endlessly patient, continuously emotionally available, hypervigilant about enrichment opportunities, creative, and even fun. Vandenberg-Daves claims that since the development of a unique role for mothers in children's development generations ago, the modernization of motherhood has added layers over time to the point where there seem to be a million ways to fail at this crucial job and an abundance of complex claims on women's time. Today's maternal construct continues to advance the old notion of mothers having an irreplaceable effect on children, with women's maternal sacrifices not considered sacred per se, or even valued, but deemed necessary for family survival.

Coontz adds that family life is now primarily connected to a sense that all family members are increasingly dominated by the schedules, needs, and seductions of an increasingly more competitive, aggressive, and insidious consumer culture beset by individualism and market values. Both at work and home, the pace of life seems too fast and the demands too numerous. The parents' job responsibilities are constantly colliding with family ones. The lack of time makes parents fear they are losing a struggle for the hearts and minds of their own children and allows little room for joy on their parenting journey.

This was true for many mothers in my study who stated that their daughters considered their husband the "fun" parent while they were growing up. Fathers are often more likely to be involved in parenting interactions like playing, sports, taking walks, or watching screens with their children while mothers provide the routine care like feeding, bathing, helping with homework, disciplining, doing laundry, and taking charge of healthcare appointments. These daily childcare tasks expose mothers to more disagreements and tension with their children, who frequently report liking and respecting their fathers more than their mothers. When this fatherly role is typical, what's not to like?!

Another new tension-laden responsibility for mothers is the level of parental surveillance required over outside forces that impact, and often insidiously invade, family life. Mothers need to be ever vigilant as they care for their children while facing an array of nonfamily influences, says Hulbert. Technology and screen time offer children exposure to educational and enrichment experiences that were unimaginable in the past. But on the flip side, they also make accessible a commercialized, sexualized, violent media culture that can seriously endanger young minds. Expressing this more dramatically, Ehrenreich quotes bestselling author Penelope Leach's book, *Your Baby's First Year*, which states mothers today must help kids cope with a society that is inimical to children—a cultural atmosphere universally decried as media saturated, commercialized, and sexualized to the point of being pornographic. DeGaetano is a leading expert on how to retool parenting for our new digital world. In her blog post "Screen-Free Week: And What About Next Week?" she affirms that today's culture seeks "to turn children into loyal, obedient consumers, out of touch with their personal agency and inherent creative spirits." In addition to dealing with the intrusion of harmful forces into our children's lives via screens, mothers and children must somehow function in a world perceived as unsafe for children where stories about stranger danger proliferate via a variety of anxiety-mongering media.

Given the shortcomings of the American social policy and the intransigence of traditional gender norms, striving to be the ideal American mother, especially for gifted mothers with neurodivergent children, means becoming a self-sacrificing and incredibly resourceful Supermom. Intensive parenting underscores the continuing American fixation on the "good mother" as a potential superhero, as well as her opposite, the "bad mom," responsible for nearly all of society's ills. According to Vandenberg-Daves, good mothers are supposed to do what social policy in a minimally regulated capitalist economy cannot or will not: create safe, nurturing spaces for the next generation while managing increasingly limited familial resources. America has long considered the raising and nurturing of children a private concern, sentimentalized as a labor of love. Of course, many mothers love their children and find that love rewarding and sustaining. But love does not pay bills. The state, along with many absent fathers, has abdicated responsibility to help women raise families. According to USAFacts, more than half of custodial parents do not receive the full amount of child support owed to them, and approximately 30 percent get nothing. As a result, with both society and many noncustodial fathers shirking their responsibility to care for our country's children, the burden is borne by American women alone.

The cultural discourse about good versus bad mothers has diverted attention away from society's failure to provide support for those raising the country's children. As society promoted this good mother/bad mother divide, the media attempted to spark another division between mothers, aimed at deflecting attention away from our country's failure to care for its children. Beginning in 1990, talk of supposed "mommy wars" between stay-at-home mothers and working mothers spread across the country. Many women did not fit neatly into either category or did not do so for any extended period of time, with many women moving in and out of the workforce, depending on the needs of their family. This pattern of entering and exiting the workforce was exemplified by the work histories of many mothers in my sample. Although certain divisions within the feminist movement seemed to disparage the work women did at home (most likely in their zeal to promote women's entry into the workforce), the sensational national catfight between mothers portrayed in the news made better headlines than the stark reality of mothers' difficult life choices whether working for pay or not.

The media also played up the how mothers who "chose" to work were not adequately meeting the needs of their family, according to Hochschild, again with little acknowledgement of society's role in this situation, fanning the flames of fear and guilt about how mothers in the workforce were failing on the home front. Guilt was a common emotion among working mothers as media panic about children's well-being reflected the raging ambivalence Americans experienced regarding mothers' growing labor force participation.

While some of America's youth have serious problems, the prevailing societal myth that these are the results of mothers in the workforce assumes that parents have primary control over how their children turn out. In fact, many factors affect children's development that have nothing to do with parenting choices, be they good or bad, according to Coontz. The notion that children are born like a blank slate or empty vessel (as put forth by philosopher John Locke) exaggerates the power of the parent and other outside forces as well as the malleability of the child. In fact, according to Judith Rich Harris in her controversial book *The Nurture Assumption*, parents seldom have make-or-break control over the child's growth, as parents of gifted know only too well. The drive, energy, intensity, curiosity, and overexcitability of gifted children definitely contradict the idea that they are passive receivers who must be externally motivated to learn by mothers coaxing them on a 24-7 basis.

Today's social construction of intensive motherhood deepens the commitment and raises the stakes of individual mothers' efforts. Miller states that this parenting ideal implies that mothers need to be the primary emotional connection point in their children's lives, and they must invest most of their own emotional and financial resources in their children, more or less relentlessly. Not surprisingly, a majority of mothers feel stress, exhaustion, and guilt at the demands of parenting this way, especially if they are working for pay as well. Most live in a state of anxiety, feeling that there's something wrong with them if they aren't spending more time with their children and not keeping up with work demands. Coontz holds that few women are fully self-confident in the choices they have made over the past few decades, and many agonize over whether gains in personal independence and fulfillment are worth the cost of stable interpersonal relationships. The standard for mothers in the twenty-first century—to be successful in both work and family life and selfless in their devotion to their children—demonstrates the reality that policymakers today still have little understanding of mothers and the reality of their lives. They fail to see them as fellow human beings with emotions, dreams, or needs that are much like their own. And for gifted mothers, there is little understanding of their special needs for intellectual challenge and self-actualization. The current motherhood ideal sets a standard for "good mothers" that is both crazy-making and unattainable.

THE LAST STRAW—THE COVID-19 PANDEMIC

Since America's inception, mothers have done their best to rise to the occasion. But have we been shooting ourselves in the foot with our resilience to make up for the shortfalls of a system that fails to support American families? As we've seen, policy choices regarding families, made primarily by white men of means for generations and focused on what's best for the country, have failed to establish an infrastructure to help mothers. This has forced many parents, primarily mothers, to go it alone, struggling to come up with solutions on the fly during good times and bad. Even as the rigid gender roles shifted somewhat in women's favor during the sixties and seventies, one cultural belief held strong: mothers are primarily responsible for caring for their children and handling domestic concerns, no matter what.

In early 2020, a pandemic started, throwing families into crises. As measures to combat COVID-19—a highly contagious, potentially serious, and sometimes fatal virus—were put in place by federal, state, and local governments, the burdens on mothers soared and laid bare the failures of the country's existing system to support families. The fear created by the pandemic threw daily life for nearly all Americans into a state of chaos and hurled pre-COVID-19 childcare and educational arrangements out the window.

For working mothers, the pandemic brought into even starker relief women's challenging dual roles as breadwinners and caretakers, according to journalist Sydney Ember in her *New York Times* article "What If It Never Gets Easier to Be a Working Parent?" School and daycare closures meant parents had to provide childcare twenty-four hours day as well as assist in teaching their school-aged children with limited guidance from overwhelmed teachers via the internet. In addition, parents could not turn to other informal childcare support systems like grandparents, friends, or neighbors to watch their children for fear of spreading the virus. Ember notes that women in heterosexual, dual-earner couples with young children bore the brunt of the childcare burden: "Even though the separation of the spheres of work and home had largely disintegrated (because of COVID), and men were much more likely to be physically present in their homes, we found evidence a substantial portion of couples were engaging in highly gendered strategies." As

Claire Cain Miller points out, when both parents worked from home during COVID-19, men were likelier than women to work in a home office in a separate room, while women worked at the kitchen table, which made them more accessible to their children.

COVID-19 underscored the reality for mothers that despite the dual demands of work and childcare, the buck stopped with them—there was no backup if they failed in carrying out both their work and caregiving responsibilities. And additional, labor-intensive responsibilities were necessary to keep the virus in check. Just some of these included the following: procuring masks to help stop the spread of the virus and ensuring children wore them outside the home, overseeing regular handwashing and minimizing exposure to others, taking charge of educating children due to school closures, dealing with social-emotional issues that negatively affected many children (especially gifted ones), getting COVID-19 tests for family members, caring for loved ones in quarantine, arranging vaccination shots for family members, dealing with delicate social interactions with family members and friends who had differing attitudes toward virus safety and vaccines, and self-protecting when buying food and goods for their family outside the home.

Since the pandemic began and as more parents were working from home, the work week seemed to have gotten longer as boundaries between personal and professional life dissolved. As a result, the massive increase in responsibilities for working mothers both as caregivers and paid employees meant many women internalized the pressure to be always on, and they often felt they were failing to meet expectations both as employees and on the home front. The consequence for many mothers was burnout that took a toll on their mental and physical health. This is not surprising because mothers, especially working mothers, during pre-COVID-19 days were already trying to function in an extremely demanding situation. The pandemic added a huge stressor to their already stress-filled lives.

Sadly, this untenable situation jeopardized many women's ability to stay in the workforce and resulted in a major setback for women's involvement in the public sphere. Before the pandemic hit, according to Miller in "The Pandemic Created a Child-Care Crisis. Mothers Bore the Burden," this generation of women had achieved what no other had. In the 1950s, women made up one-third of the labor force, but as of January 2019, women achieved a never-before milestone; they comprised more of the workforce than men. In addition, in her article "America Has Been Failing Mothers for a Long Time. The Pandemic Made It Clear What Needs to Happen," Lyz Lenz states that prior to the pandemic, 41 percent of mothers were the sole or primary breadwinner for their family, and an additional 23.2 percent brought home at least a quarter of their total household earnings. But as a result of COVID-19, without adequate childcare and little government support, record numbers of women had to quit paid employment. Per Lenz, "Society will call it a choice when, in reality, it's a failure of the system."

This "choice" to leave their jobs often seems a rational one, because men usually earn more, Miller notes, so if a parent needs to quit to handle family responsibilities, it makes sense for it to be the woman. And when a man becomes a father, his salary increases, while conversely, women's wages decrease after having children. Our longstanding gendered ideas of a good mother, a good father, and an ideal worker matter, says Michelle Budig, professor at University of Massachusetts, in her article "The Fatherhood Bonus and the Motherhood Penalty: Parenthood and the Gender Gap in Pay." According to Budig, "If mothers are supposed to focus on caring for children over career ambitions, they will be suspect on the job and even criticized if viewed as overly focusing on work." And even if the couple shares equal family responsibilities, employers assume all women will sacrifice work for family, meaning less pay and fewer promotions. Conversely, employers assume men become better workers after having children because of their gendered traditional role as breadwinners. Therefore, their careers are boosted by a fatherhood premium versus mothers' careers that are dinged by a motherhood penalty.

The pandemic represented the last straw for many mothers who already endured the overwhelming pressure of being both primary caregiver and paid employee. Prior to COVID-19, many mothers had learned to be entrepreneurial and creative in their attempt to carve out a career, often finding informal ways to be paid for what they did and still be the family's primary caregiver. Most had carefully planned their working lives to accommodate their children by choosing jobs or careers that offered flexibility or fewer hours, even if it meant they earned less or were overqualified, while some took the risk of starting businesses in order to schedule their work hours around family needs. But these efforts were all for naught when COVID-19 hit, destroying the fragile reality these women had pieced together to both work and adhere to society's motherhood script. As a result, women's labor force participation rate hit a thirty-three-year low in January 2021, with approximately three million women forced to quit paid employment. Meanwhile, the labor rate for males remained flat. Researchers Julie Kashen, Sarah Jane Glynn, and Amanda Novello report in their article "How COVID-19 Sent Women's Workforce Progress Backward" that by September 2020, four times as many women as men dropped out of the labor force.

For mothers who leave the labor market, according to Miller, this means more than loss of a paycheck—it's also a loss of self-determination, self-reliance, and an identity apart from being a mother. Miller states that professional women (who had invested in advanced degrees to specialize in their field and, in some cases, made names for themselves), as well as women on the opposite end of the income and job status spectrum, described devotion to their jobs. As a result, both groups grieved their loss of agency and identity as paid workers. As one mother Miller interviewed explained, "I love everything about motherhood, and yet it doesn't feel fair that I should have to sacrifice my career. I guess what I'm missing is that thing that's mine, and what that is is the little piece of my identity that's my career."

In her article "Mothers Are the Shock Absorbers of Our Society," Jessica Grose presents the case of a professional woman, forced by the pandemic to step back from her research position, who took a part-time position as a physician despite the fact that doing so may set back her research and academic career. As Grose points out, because this gifted mother is a public health researcher, this represents not only a personal loss but the loss of talent and expertise that society incurred as well. This drives home the wider impact of women's reduced career participation—the risk of mothers leaving the labor force and reducing work hours in order to assume caretaking responsibilities, which amounts to $64.5 billion per year in lost wages and economic activity, according to Kashen, Glynn, and Novello.

The childcare crisis should be a major red flag for everyone, not just parents, Brad Wilson, CEO of Care.com, says in a news release as quoted in an article by Michael Wittner. Given the extremely high cost of childcare, "Within the first five years of their child's life, parents are being forced into a financial hole that is nearly impossible to climb out of," Wilson says. "A healthy economy depends upon the ability for people to save and spend, but given the crushing weight of childcare costs, those pillars are crumbling....It is a systemic failure that will impact our nation's economic growth, and that affects us all."

In addition, America is at risk of losing senior-level women in management and leadership roles according to business and technology reporter Catherine Thorbecke in her report "1 in 4 Women Considering Leaving Workforce or Downshifting Careers because of COVID-19, Report Warns." This loss will undermine the gains women have made in recent years in achieving these positions. Thorbecke notes the key role these women leaders have played in the marketplace by advocating for gender equality and mentoring other females. The founder of Work Like a Mother, Hilary Berger, affirms that policies that provide flexibility and support for working parents are critical to attracting and retaining top talent.

In other words, we need a system that encourages and supports mothers, especially gifted mothers, in their efforts to share their talents with society at large. The pandemic has forced us to rethink the very foundation of our society: motherhood and its social construction. As we've seen, the issues for gifted mothers who choose to engage in the marketplace do not represent a new problem—we've just chosen not to acknowledge it until now. That said, as society learns to adjust and everyday life returns to some semblance of normality, working mothers fear that little will change on the home front. Ember notes that many families find themselves back in the same precarious arrangement they had before the pandemic, with the overwhelming burden still on mothers. In lieu of a social safety net for families, America defaults to its mothers. We can only hope COVID-19 exposed the vulnerability of this policy and dream that support for working mothers will emerge as one of the few positive outcomes of a truly devastating global disaster.

INTENSIVE MOTHERHOOD AND THE NEW WAR ON WOMEN

As women made some gains in the professional world over many decades, threatening the male-controlled system, the old fear-based refrain against women pursuing higher education and self-actualization outside the home returned. Cultural parenting standards continue to promote various versions of the intensive motherhood model and the nuclear family, and society's demands on working mothers continue to be unrealistic and unattainable. In addition, the unrelenting focus for government control of women's lives underscores our country's persistent refusal to consider women's humanity, needs, and worth. This ugly reality became glaringly apparent when the Supreme Court overturned Roe v. Wade, taking away women's control over their own bodies in a number of states, resulting in lifelong trauma, in some cases, and even death for women forced to live in a country where they are considered second-class citizens.

This total lack of support for women as mothers was on further display as funding for family-centered support was cut from President Biden's American Families Plan. This was the part of his proposed budget in 2022 that would have made transformative investments in our country's care infrastructure. This plan would have helped support access to childcare, early learning opportunities, funds to encourage school readiness, child tax credits, and expansion of home and community-based healthcare services as well as paid family and medical leave. A majority of American mothers and families would have benefited greatly from these programs, given their desperate need for help during even the best of times. Once again, the country failed not only to publicly acknowledge the superhuman demands required of mothers but basically "kicked women to the curb" by eliminating any proposed support for those with the critically important task of raising America's future generations.

CHAPTER 6

Gifted Motherhood's Role in the Perfect Storm

An awareness of how we arrived at society's current model for motherhood provides the context for gifted mothers to understand the obstacles they may encounter in parenting their gifted girls. This knowledge will enable them to appreciate the limitations society has placed on them, as well as their female ancestors, and to see their struggles not as personal failures but rather systemic issues related to the Perfect Storm. The cultural obstacles they may face given their gender, giftedness, and motherhood status must be "poked" as they attempt to deconstruct and reconstruct an approach to nurturing gifted females that more appropriately addresses both their unique needs and the special needs of their neurodiverse daughters.

An old college friend of mine believes that having dogs is the same as having children. She doesn't have children. As a mother and former dog owner myself, trying to underscore for her the key differences between nurturing children and caring for pets seems rather pointless. Although not as extreme, this scenario is like mothers of gifted children trying to describe the reality of their parenting lives to nonparents as well as parents of less neurodiverse offspring.

The consensus in our culture is that raising gifted children is easier because they thrive in school, and you don't have to nag them to do their homework.

Obviously, many experiences are impossible to connect with unless you've lived them. It is critical for gifted mothers to share their stories to correct the myths about the special needs of gifted parents and their offspring, primarily to garner support and resources for a demographic that has been neglected for too long. In addition, by sharing our stories and brainstorming effective parenting strategies with other gifted mothers, we can strengthen the golden thread of motherhood that binds together bright women and serves as a lifeline in staving off isolation, anxiety, and burn-out. Finally, focusing on how our culture views motherhood to include the singular issues gifted mothers face when raising gifted daughters may create the context for society to consider transforming its current motherhood model in a way that maximizes the unique potential of gifted mothers, not only to nurture the next generation of bright female minds but also to promote their ability to self-actualize.

It should be stressed that although this section describes the difficulties most gifted mothers encounter, these are often offset by the many special joys gifted daughters bring to our lives. (These will be addressed in detail in Book Three of the trilogy.) Some fundamental benefits to raising exceptionally bright girls include the following: invaluable opportunities to be challenged intellectually and emotionally, a lifelong opportunity for increased self-awareness and enlightenment, the context to understand one's own giftedness and to grow in ways never imagined, and, in most cases, providing gifted mothers with one of the most fulfilling and meaningful relationships they have ever experienced. In fact, many interviewed mothers commented that their daughters were not only their friends but their role models. As one mother shared, "My daughter was never afraid of anything. She's not afraid of life. Isn't that wonderful? I wish I was like that." A mother with an only daughter shared that her one big regret was not having "two of them." None of the forty-three gifted mothers interviewed (myself included) would have traded their exciting off-road adventure of nurturing exceptional daughters for anything. And a bonus that most of the mothers in the study appreciated was that as our daughters approached adulthood, they morphed into friends, becoming the true intellectual peers so many of us struggled throughout our lives to discover. That said, less than a handful of the study participants would describe their efforts to nurture both their own and their daughter's giftedness in contemporary society as easy or as anything most parenting experts understood.

Before delving into the unique challenges gifted women face raising gifted daughters, it's important to acknowledge that these often exist against the backdrop of the everyday realities most families struggle with. As one mother in the study put it, "I wonder how parents stay married with all the stresses they have now…of both parents having jobs, managing the household, [trying to maintain] a social life… and then having one or more children." In other words, a majority of the interviewed women faced many of the same tough issues less neurodiverse families face—giftedness serving as an additional challenge, or cherry on top, of their parenting journey.

For example, nearly half of the interviewed mothers (46 percent) described dealing with serious financial difficulties at some point. Although a few of these cases included households with two parents or families with two income earners, not surprisingly, the biggest money problems were experienced by the women who were single mothers. In *The Lenses of Gender,* Bem notes that women are often awarded little in the way of financial support if they divorce, resulting in a serious decline in the quality of life both for themselves and their children. Sadly, according to the US Census Bureau, only 43.5 percent of custodial parents receive the full amount of child support. The stories of the mothers in the study whose partners abandoned their family were heartbreaking and reinforced the fact that there is often no "village" for women who are solely responsible for raising their children. In one instance, the husband left when the mother was pregnant and had an eighteen-month-old daughter. Displaying incredible resilience, this young mother started back to college, worked three jobs, and lived on a farm with another single mother so they could share childcare responsibilities. Another husband left behind two toddlers and no money. This mother stated that her firstborn was a very difficult baby who had extreme allergies and never slept, was always active, and screamed most of the time. This mother described being constantly exhausted, struggling for years just to feed her family while working entry-level jobs. She said, "I was only getting paid $3.56 an hour and trying to support two kids. So we were living in a slum…There were mice running between the walls and everything really…roaches in my breakfast cereal, in the drawers. It was just a terrible place. The kids called it the 'bug house.' They were afraid to go pee at night, because they would crunch on the bugs."

Financial constraints for families with special needs children, including those who are gifted, impact not only a mother's ability to meet the basic needs of her children but also her ability to access resources. If these services are unavailable within the public school system, or if for some red tape reason their daughter isn't considered eligible, many families pay out of pocket for them. Failing that, they live with the sad reality that they are unable to provide their children the help they need. The high cost of evaluation, testing, therapies, medications, tutoring, homeschooling, transportation, and taking time off work to take their gifted daughter to and from these resources can be insurmountable. And families living in rural areas are often faced with the frustrating situation where no educational resources (public or private) are available even if they manage to scrape together the money to access them.

One of the mothers in the study shared how her parents (her gifted daughter's maternal grandparents) struggled to find a good educational fit for her as a gifted child in a rural community.

> "When I got to sixth grade, I started failing my classes. I was getting Cs and Ds and just doing very poorly in general. My parents, who recognized that I was smart, knew that there was no reason for that to be happening. They decided that they were going to try to send me to the school district next to ours. We were in a small, rural district, but the next district over was bigger and had a full-time gifted program. So my parents, with great sacrifice to themselves…The first thing they tried was renting an apartment. My mom moved with me to

the city so I could attend the gifted program, and that worked for a while, but evidently the program decided that they wouldn't allow people [whose permanent residence was] outside the city to attend. So my parents moved to a house in town, and my whole family lived there except for my older siblings, who stayed out at the farm. But after a year, they stopped renting this house, and we moved back out to the farm. The [gifted] program then allowed me to attend as long as my parents paid tuition. And when I turned fifteen, they bought me a car so I could drive to school on a school permit."

This woman's childhood experience of switching to a gifted program had a huge positive impact on her.

"I remember very clearly when I switched to the full-time gifted program, because it felt as if my mind was waking up. It's like I had been in a deep slumber. To this day I remember some of the things I learned that year. I learned about number bases in math, and it was just fascinating to me. It's still a passion of mine—different number bases. I count my laps when I'm swimming in base twelve and do fractions in base twelve, which is an interesting experience."

Although 53 percent of the sampled mothers faced serious challenges related to their daughter's biological fathers, only 26 percent of these marriages resulted in divorce (eight of these women eventually remarried). Some of the more common problems mentioned with their partners included substance abuse and domestic violence. In other cases, the fathers abandoned the family, had a fixed approach to parenting and/or giftedness, had a sexist view of raising girls, or had mental or physical health issues. Nearly half volunteered that their partner was not as involved in parenting as they were, while nearly one-fourth felt that their daughter's father represented a negative factor in their daughters' lives. One mother shared,

> "My husband doesn't understand why I am under so much stress. He downplays it and minimizes it, making me feel like I am crazy. Stress drives me to have my own meltdowns, which I am not proud of...He viewed my exhaustion and struggles with my daughter as evidence that I hadn't established authority and effective routines and that I was being 'that mom' about her schooling...and that our daughter just needed to learn how to adapt."

Another mother described her co-parenting situation this way: "He did not participate in childcare, and I was glad. He was truly mean—extremely critical, always right, and swore at me as his mode of relating."

Although most of the study mothers stressed the importance of extended family members while their daughters were growing up, especially the positive role model provided by their daughters' maternal grandmother, a number of women dealt with extended family members who were less than helpful and who frequently undermined the mother's position as the primary caregiver. A variety of scenarios were shared that reflected the different approaches to parenting between mothers and extended family members. In most cases, this appeared to demonstrate their family members' lack of knowledge about giftedness. Specifically, some questioned whether it was "normal" for a child to be learning advanced material, wondered if she was missing out on her childhood, and/or strongly suggested that the parents "just let her be a kid."

Others family members expressed concern about their granddaughter's overexcitability, stating that "kids don't have anxiety" or "she's too sensitive." Other extended family members claimed, "You must be one of those helicopter parents," "If she's so smart, she should be able to figure it out by herself," "She's driven because she feels pressure," and "She'll be fine. Just leave her alone, and she'll find the cure for cancer one day." A few grandparents believed in following rigid gender scripts and had strong opinions about "appropriate" careers for females. In one case, the mother's father-in-law was a principal of an elementary school and strongly opposed to homeschooling. This mother commented, "I don't think he approved of the Montessori school our daughter attended either." But despite this strong resistance, this mother forged ahead to do what she thought best.

Nearly one-third of the interviewed mothers shared that they faced significant work stress and professional challenges while raising their girls. Roughly this same number described dealing with major health issues that, in some cases, required hospitalization, an inability to function for long periods, and the need for significant lifestyle changes. One of these women was diagnosed with advanced cancer when her daughter was a preteen and, sadly, died shortly after being interviewed. In another case, a single mother with four children was confined to a full body cast for months, which required her oldest daughter to care not only for her mother but also for her siblings with a bit of support from a friendly neighbor.

Four women mentioned serious challenges related to ongoing conflict between their children that, in one instance, resulted in the adult daughter sharing painful details of how her brother had, unknown to her mother at the time, abused her throughout her childhood. When her daughter informed her of this years later, this mother deeply apologized to her daughter for not protecting her and carried a lot of guilt for not realizing the severity of her son's aggression while her daughter was growing up.

Like many women today, caring for elderly parents was an additional responsibility for some mothers in the study. Many also mentioned feeling pressure to volunteer in their daughter's school and their extracurricular activities or live with the guilt of not doing their fair share.

Nearly half of the families moved during their daughters' school-age years, with most of these relocations occurring during elementary school. The reasons were varied but mainly included the father's reassignment by the military or for the father's job. However, some moved to be closer to extended family, to live in a community with better schools, or, in a few instances, for the family to experience a different culture abroad.

A number of women mentioned spending considerable time and effort to support their husband's business. The seemingly high number of fathers in the sample who were entrepreneurs may be related to the fact that, as the mothers claimed, many were exceptionally gifted and driven, and as a result, they chose to be their own boss. In these families, the mothers often served as part-time employees in the family business, assumed a much greater share of childcare duties, and held down the fort during the father's (sometimes quite lengthy) business trips.

The overriding reality was that nearly all of the interviewed mothers were the primary caregiver for their daughters. They were the parent who stood at the front of the line to address whatever issues arose. They were keenly aware that if they didn't look out for their children, there was a good chance many of their daughter's needs might fall through the cracks. This often unspoken parenting reality represents a heavy emotional burden and psychic drain for mothers of both neurotypical and neurodiverse children, requiring them to be hypervigilant and ready to respond to their children's needs whenever they arise. But for gifted women raising a gifted daughter, the stress and ongoing demands of this situation are heightened by the special (and frequently unacknowledged) challenges they face both outside and within the family as they attempt to address their own exceptionality.

THE OVERWHELMING ROLE OF NURTURING IN GENERAL

The pioneer of gifted education and a brilliant voice in the world of gifted, Roeper gave us a powerful insight into the critical role primary caregivers play in their offspring's life (whether they are gifted or neurotypical). This role is rarely acknowledged, valued, or publicly rewarded. Roeper notes in *The "I" of the Beholder* that our society lacks a fundamental understanding of the human soul (the Self), its basic needs, and how it develops. Every individual's unique Self is complex, has its own inner agenda and passions, and exhibits conscious and unconscious reactions, drives, feelings, and anxieties. Sadly, an individual's agenda is often in conflict with the goals of society, which, not surprisingly, tries to mold its members toward meeting the society's needs and purposes.

Because the impact of the outside world often represents an overwhelming obstacle to the growth and development of the Self, the need for the love, protection, and intervention of the primary caregiver is critical. Roeper shared her young client's description of this predicament: "There's a whole world inside of me that doesn't match with the world outside, and that is why I am having trouble." The delicate balance between the child's inner and outer worlds must be mediated by empathic interactions with the primary caregiver who offers a lifeline to the child. This determines her future emotional, intellectual, and physical growth and development. The child's relationship with her primary caregiver is central to nurturing her unique Self and represents the prototype for the child of all future relationships.

What an awesome responsibility for mothers! Realistically, however, the Self within each mother has its own conscious and unconscious needs, which impacts to some degree her vital bond with her child as the mother tries to address both her child's needs and her own. As Roeper notes, the less cluttered with other forces the relationship remains between the child and caregiver, the freer the child will be to blossom: "to possess some inner control and become capable of confronting [her] chaotic internal and external worlds without panicking." The task of the child is to develop emotional trust and the emotional, intellectual, and physical skills to enable her to gain some control over her vulnerability and empower her to thrive in a less-than-supportive environment. The challenge for the mother is to facilitate this development while attempting to nurture her own Self. This is a very delicate balance and a daunting task.

What drives the mother, in an ideal scenario, to take on this decades-long struggle is her proactive decision to love her child. A character in Gabrielle Zevin's book *Tomorrow, and Tomorrow, and Tomorrow* presents a beautiful description of love: "And what is love in the end? Except the irrational desire to put evolutionary competitiveness aside in order to ease someone else's journey through life?" As mentioned, bell hooks provides another insight regarding this emotion, often difficult to describe, in her book *All about Love: New Visions*. She stresses that love is not a noun but a verb and, as such, implies choice. Mothers who choose to love their children mix ingredients—care, affection, recognition, respect, commitment, trust, and honest and open communication—in their ongoing interactions with their offspring. hooks states that care is a dimension of love but that giving care does not mean the caregivers are necessarily loving. Like Roeper's vision, hooks views a life force ("some of us call it soul") that, when nurtured with love, enhances our capacity to be more fully self-actualized and able to engage in communion with the world around us.

It is often thought that love is critical to the survival of our species. Cheryl Strayed emphasizes its importance in her book *Tiny Beautiful Things: Advice from Dear Sugar*: "Love is our essential nutrient. Without it, life has little meaning. It's the best thing we have to give and the most valuable thing we receive. It's worthy of all the hullabaloo." Let's hope that primary caregivers continue to undertake all the hullabaloo for the sake of society's future generations.

STRESSES RELATED TO MOTHERING GIFTED CHILDREN

Gifted children, according to Roeper, have a stronger inner agenda and more intense drives, feelings, and anxieties than nongifted children, and they tend to be more physically and emotionally sensitive. As a result of their intense agenda and highly attuned senses, their experience of the world creates an expanded reality, bringing an extreme global awareness. The resulting impact on the daily life of these individuals (who make up 2–5 percent of the population) often goes unacknowledged by a society that views giftedness as simply influencing intellectual abilities rather than every aspect of a gifted individual's existence. Basically, the other 95 percent of people think gifted folks are "just smarter."

Therefore, the mother of a gifted child has a more daunting mission than most. She is charged with nurturing the growth of her child's unique, quivering mind, body, and spirit and sustaining her child's precious life force in a world that does not understand the essence of her child's exceptionality and offers minimal resources to support mother and child in this difficult undertaking. And on top of this, there can be the added struggle of nurturing twice-exceptional children. One interviewed mother described feeling overwhelmed by the task: "There's this tremendous responsibility knowing that you've been given such a gift and that you really need to be a super-good parent to this exceptional child…And you know we're not. We're human, and we make huge mistakes."

An additional challenge for a number of mothers in the study was having to nurture two or more gifted children who presented with very dissimilar personalities, talents, and strengths. This often required the mother to develop parenting strategies best suited for each child, which, in some families, resulted in fierce competition between siblings. One mother described her four gifted children as being "incredibly competitive. You could never just do a jigsaw puzzle. It was always a big race to see who could get the most pieces in and who was doing what piece. Card games were competitive. All the board games were competitive games. It's just the way they are—the girls just as much as the boys."

Another mother shared how having a gifted older sister created a tough childhood for her younger daughter, who felt like she could never keep up. She described the challenges related to nurturing two very diverse daughters:

> "Kids are born with their own personalities, and I don't think you can ignore that as a variable as well as birth order. Because my younger daughter was born second, she was always behind—always! My older daughter advanced so quickly. I actually think that they're equivalent in intelligence [their Stanford Binet L-M scores were within one point of each other], but my younger daughter always felt that she…never could measure up to her sister, and when you're little, you can't understand that that's perfectly normal. If she had had a younger sibling, I think she would have felt better about it, but as the younger of two, she just always felt [behind]. Even though she went to gymnastics, she never stuck with it, because my older daughter was better. And she also had much more separation anxiety than my older daughter…and was a lot more emotional. In fact, I was feeling for a long time that I kind of neglected my older daughter because my younger daughter [was more needy]. My husband couldn't help, because that type of emotional personality was not his thing. So basically, he was in charge of my older daughter, and I was in charge of my younger

daughter, because he couldn't take that kind of emotional dependency. So my older daughter and I kind of grew apart a little bit, and my younger daughter was more my charge."

Society's message that to be considered "good mothers," women must "stay in their lane" (as prescribed by cultural mores, parenting experts, educators, and peers) is difficult if not impossible for parents of gifted. Many describe their experiences of nurturing their neurodiverse offspring as "off-roading"—to meet their child's special needs, the normal parenting approach simply doesn't work, and they have to forge their own path. Not surprisingly, because a high number of parents of gifted children are themselves gifted, this demand to think outside the box may come rather naturally, given that social conventions and scripts didn't fit for them growing up either. In addition, as gifted individuals who have experienced the world in a unique way all their lives, they may have developed an intuitive feeling for the limits of typicality.

In addition to being more aware of the limitations of socially constructed parenting conventions, many gifted mothers at some point start to appreciate the unique parenting challenges that raising a gifted child provides. These challenges can satisfy their inherent craving for stimulating, thought-provoking experiences. (That said, it may take years or decades to develop this perspective, and it may emerge only after one's gifted offspring have left the nest!) Rather than viewing these challenges as obstacles, gifted mothers eventually value the long-term benefits they reap from them: to learn, grow, and deepen their own self-awareness. For gifted mothers and their children, as we shall see, such adversity often breeds clarity, growth, and transformation.

Roeper stresses that much is asked of mothers of these very intense, sensitive, and hyperaware children whose gaze can penetrate our very souls. These children constantly wonder if our intentions are honorable in terms of their emotional and physical survival in an often hostile world. In *Raising Gifted Kids,* Dr. Barbara Klein adds to this by describing the difficulty mothers of gifted face in dealing with their child's intensity, demanding-ness, smartness, perfectionism, and persistence as well as their constant love of debate and frequent negotiation about what they will or won't do. And, unfortunately, because their view of the world is so much broader and insightful than average, many gifted children experience existential crises and overwhelming distress regarding world affairs. Obviously, this further complicates the gifted mother's painstaking efforts to respond to her child's emotional needs.

If the mother finds that her efforts don't seem to be working or meeting her child's expectations, she may begin to feel inadequate, guilty, and frustrated. But Roeper underscores that these mothers need to understand that they are not doing anything wrong or harmful long term and that the key parenting element most needed by the gifted child is their emotional connection to their mother. And in *The "I" of the Beholder,* she reassures parents that as gifted children grow, in most cases, they "will find ways to protect and soothe themselves" and learn to develop the emotional skills necessary to cope with their own uniqueness, intensity, and sensitivity. But Roeper appreciates that this is not a quick, easy process for either the mother or her child.

Stories shared by the mothers describing the details of this "not easy" process of raising their gifted child wove a common thread through the study. Mothers frequently mentioned the exhausting demands they faced in dealing with their daughters' general day-to-day behavior as well as their social-emotional ups and downs, not to mention trying to get their special needs met in a world not set up to address them. As Roeper explains, "When any child's inner agenda is interrupted, disregarded, or denied, conflict emerges....Much of what we interpret as negative or pathological is simply the expanded awareness that can result from giftedness. If their behavior becomes a disturbance, it has to be dealt with, but it's important not to pathologize it." It's hard to fit an exceptionally square peg into a round hole, and our culture often perceives this to be a mother's main job.

One mother described picking her daughter up from school after work at which point her daughter would immediately talk, animatedly and incessantly, all the way home and beyond. "When we got home after school and teaching, I would run to the bathroom, and my daughter would be in the other room still talking nonstop to me through the door the whole time, saying, 'Mommy, this is what happened, and then this is what she said, and then...' And I'd say, 'Okay, okay.'" Mothers described similar scenarios in many of the interviews about their daughters desperately needing to share the details of their day with an intellectual peer—i.e., their gifted mothers—after spending the day among more neurotypical age cohorts.

Many women also highlighted their daughters' lack of sleep from birth. "From the time she was little, she would not sleep. My daughter told me that sleeping was just not fun. 'Oh, Mom, there was always something else to learn about and something to do.'" Sleeping appeared to be a waste of time for many of these young, high-energy, neurodiverse brains that craved stimulation. In addition, some individuals just physically don't require the seven to eight hours that most need. Some daughters struggled to sleep due to their constant rumination about stresses and concerns (typically existential and on a global scale). One mother mentioned that her two daughters often couldn't fall asleep because of ongoing angst related to climate change. She would sometimes find them fast asleep in the morning cuddled together with their pillows and blankets outside her bedroom door. In *Untamed*, Doyle provides an excellent description of her gifted daughter's sleep trials that began in kindergarten when the teacher discussed how polar bears were losing their homes and food sources because the icecaps were melting. Doyle describes tiptoeing out of her daughter's bedroom one night, hoping against hope that she had finally fallen asleep, when her daughter asked her to wait, saying, "Mommy, I just can't stop thinking: It's the polar bears now. But nobody cares. So next, it's gonna be us."

As many of the gifted children in the study ventured off to school, their families were forced to deal with new emotional upheavals on the home front. This was especially true for mothers with twice-exceptional offspring. One mother shared a very heartbreaking account; her daughter would cry for about forty-five minutes each morning before school, come home later, and again break down in tears. After fighting the school to have her tested, her gifted daughter was finally diagnosed with high-functioning autism. This mother stated that it was devastating to see her daughter suffering and not knowing the cause. She initially couldn't understand why her daughter couldn't just adjust to the routine of school.

A number of mothers in the study stressed their children's incredibly high energy level and drive coupled with insatiable curiosity. One described having to call the information desk at the local university library (before the Google search days) on numerous occasions, seeking answers to her two young, gifted daughters' many questions about science and medical advances. Another mother gave a colorful description of dinnertime for a family with six bright children. She stated that the whole family would be

> "sitting around the table at dinnertime where my husband, and I would do the whole grilling thing with each child about his or her day…But it was always interesting how we'd have these conversations that ended up being pretty scientific or mathematical, and again I think that's because we both had PhDs in engineering. I don't know…we're actually a weird family! But I think it was a good thing. Somebody would be jumping up to grab the encyclopedia or dictionary on occasion or scribbling on the back of an envelope, trying to figure something out. All of the kids would be engaged despite the significant age span, so they would have different levels of input…I think that they learned early that family time was important…We'd have a little guy in a highchair while we were talking about Mars rovers. But they all seemed to be part of the conversation."

Fortunately, keeping up with the exceptional liveliness, vigor, and life force of their gifted child is possible in many families because it's matched by the high energy level of gifted parents. For gifted women looking for adventure and challenge, parenting a gifted daughter will more than fit the bill. But another common characteristic of gifted children frequently provides an unexpected challenge. Just as parents begin to feel comfortable with their parenting approach, they'll often find their child advancing (sometimes overnight and to unimagined new heights) to a developmental level that requires completely new parenting strategies. And progress in one area may happen while the parents are simultaneously experiencing their child regressing in others. This atypical (or asynchronous) developmental path can catch a mother off-guard and obligate her to live in a state of constant flux and uncertainty. According to Widawsky, asynchronous development "means the gifted individual is likely to mature faster in some ways, and slower in others. In the area of their gifts, they may be years *ahead* of their peers, while simultaneously lagging years *behind* in other areas, particularly in the emotional realm." This often leads those unfamiliar with giftedness to judge the mother's parenting skills and assign pathology to the child's behavior—for example, others fail to understand why a child may be speaking like an adult but throwing tantrums like a baby. In *The Gifted Parenting Journey,* Post notes that the NAGC considers asynchronous development to be a hallmark of giftedness, representing a mismatch between cognitive, emotional, and physical development. Post shares Tolan's claim in her article "Giftedness as Asynchronous Development" that this developmental trajectory for gifted children is outside of norms from infancy onward. "They reach recognized milestones of development on a schedule that is unique to them, putting them out of sync with society's expectations. In addition, they may be out of sync internally, with cognitive, social, and emotional development on separate and sometimes quite different timetables." Tolan believes that this can frequently cloud diagnosing giftedness in many children, especially with twice-exceptional children.

Brilliant diarist and gifted woman Anais Nin provides an insightful description of the asynchronous development that our gifted offspring experience: "We do not grow absolutely, chronologically. We grow sometimes in one dimension, and not in another; unevenly. We grow partially. We are relative. We are mature in one realm, childish in another. The past, present, and future mingle and pull us backward, forward or fix us in the present. We are made of layers, cells, constellations."

Sadly, the task of dealing with asynchronicity, along with the additional parenting challenges faced by gifted mothers, is compounded by the many conflicting cultural messages and values that mothers of gifted children feel pressured to impart to their offspring. Some of these include the following:

- "Don't be cocky about your giftedness or act like you're special, but at the same time, be proud of being gifted."
- "Use the gifts bestowed upon you to change the world, cure cancer, and solve social ills, but don't think of this as your gifted burden."
- "Do things well, but at the same time, don't be a perfectionist."
- "Compete with yourself and not with others, even though we live in an increasingly competitive society."

- "Be caring and empathetic, but don't get overwhelmed by the needs of others or ruminate about world problems and suffering."
- "Think deep thoughts, figure out what's meaningful to you, but don't get frustrated, overwhelmed, or depressed."
- "Work hard to succeed, but find time for fun and self-care."
- "Follow your passion, but best if it's something marketable (like STEM careers) in today's economy."
- "Make friends, but be yourself, and don't dumb yourself down."
- "Be independent, but at the same time, stay safe (and maintain family ties!)."
- "Don't avoid challenges—embrace struggle—but try not to fail."

Many gifted mothers often find themselves wasting precious energy and feeling anxious when constantly trying to live up to cultural parenting standards that conflict with their value system and don't fit with their day-to-day parenting reality. They may often wonder "What's wrong with me?" and "What's wrong with my child?" This internal chaos began early for one mother who was interviewed. She described how it began one morning at a gathering for new parents:

> "I noticed the difference when [my gifted daughter] was an infant, because a lot of people mentioned to

me that they could put their babies down on a mat, and the baby could sit there and play by themselves for hours on end and ooh and ahh and coo…But never in my life was I able to let my daughter just play on a mat by herself. I thought there was something wrong with me—this kid would simply not lie and coo on a mat, so I was sure there was something wrong with what I was doing."

Kochis notes in her article "It's Not Just in Your Head: Self-Care for Moms of Gifted Children" that parenting a gifted child is exhausting and can take an emotional toll. Although these challenges are akin to challenges faced by parents of special needs children, raising gifted children can be an especially lonely vocation because of the cultural assumption that having a gifted child makes parenting a piece of cake. This warped social misperception makes parents of gifted wonder if it's all in our heads. As Kochis points out,

> Who's going to believe your 11-year-old just learned how to tie her shoes or ride a bike when she's been reading Tolkien since four? Who's going to believe you've backed out of a social obligation because it's windy out and the 7-year-old refuses to leave the house? Who's going to believe you don't have a single sleeper, even though each child is out of diapers and can solve mathematical equations like a pro?

As Kochis succinctly puts it, "The internal struggle of gifted parenting lies in the disparity between social perception and the reality we face every day. Gifted kids are supposed to be easy...But while our children are indeed wonderful, there's a lot most people don't understand."

For her PhD thesis in clinical psychology, "Dwelling on the Right Side of the Curve: An Exploration of the Psychological Wellbeing of Parents of Gifted Children," Natalie Rimlinger evaluated whether parents of gifted do in fact have a quantifiable and significantly elevated level of stress. Her findings were more striking than anticipated. The stress level of parents of gifted children was similar to another parent group whose struggles are widely acknowledged: those with developmentally delayed children and those with children with psychological issues pronounced enough to necessitate professional help. Therefore, Rimlinger concluded we need to broaden the definition of gifted so that it encompasses social, emotional, and intellectual characteristics and correct society's widespread belief that a child's advanced intellect paves a smooth road for their progress throughout childhood. While it's hard to feel reinforced in your efforts as a mother if your child's needs are out of the ordinary, it's all the more stressful if no one believes you need support. Rimlinger's study provides a much-needed message for mothers of gifted children that it's not just their imagination—raising a gifted child is challenging.

STRESSES RELATED TO NURTURING FEMALE GIFTEDNESS

Nurturing gifted daughters requires mothers to extend themselves beyond what is required for raising gifted sons. The extra dimension stems largely from the cultural limitations placed on females in general and bright females in particular. Gifted mothers have had to confront the impact of patriarchy and the pervasiveness of male domination in our culture throughout their lives. But this battle becomes even more emotionally fraught when mothers experience their daughters confronting many of the same limitations they faced growing up.

One of the offshoots of patriarchy in our society is the cultural script for a "good" daughter that sets up an obvious mismatch between what the script means and the key characteristics of gifted girls. The stereotype of a "good" daughter is mother's little helper (and later on, her spouse's helper)—obedient, passive, appropriate, sweet, and definitely not "sassy." She is expected to be totally focused on helping her mother in her socially determined primary role of caring for others. But gifted children are often intense, energetic, creative, determined, driven, spirited souls. These qualities will enable them to self-actualize in adulthood but make it impossible for gifted girls to mesh well with this "good daughter" script. And trying to force girls to embody this script disempowers them and often hurts their connection to the family. As a result, the gifted mother's challenge to try to squeeze her gifted girl into the good daughter mold is frequently as impossible as forcing her to fit into a typical classroom designed for neurotypical students.

For the gifted mother of such an empowered gifted daughter, dealing with life's day-to-day realities, including meeting her unique needs to self-actualize as well as those of other family members while staying within the outermost lines of society's dictates, can be exhausting. Often, gifted mothers are at their wit's end, wanting more than anything to embolden their gifted girls and nurture their spirits but finding themselves secretly and guiltily hoping that their daughter, as several interviewed mothers confessed, could go with the flow for once and "just be normal."

In addition to the "good" daughter script, the patriarchy in our culture negatively impacts the mother/daughter relationship on a more insidious level. As mother/daughter relationship therapist Rosijke Hasseldine points out in her book *The Mother-Daughter Puzzle: A New Generational Understanding of the Mother-Daughter Relationship*, mothers and daughters don't relate within a cultural vacuum. While this relationship is central to females understanding and valuing themselves, Hasseldine stresses that our patriarchal society sets mothers and daughters up for conflict with its restrictive gender roles and the expectation that women should sacrifice their needs. This not only shapes how mothers and daughters view themselves and each other but impacts their interaction as well. Because popular wisdom tells mothers that they are supposed to be close with their daughters and that motherhood represents a blissful bond between two individuals, when conflict occurs between the mother and her daughter, mothers often internalize this as a personal failure. Mothers then search for answers, frequently blaming themselves, hormones, or different or similar personality traits for their relationship difficulties. They rarely consider the larger multigenerational and sociocultural contexts that negatively impact their lives.

When the unique characteristics of gifted are added to this mix, the stress for gifted mothers and their gifted daughters can become overwhelming. Nearly half of the fifty-eight gifted daughters in the study experienced mental health issues at some point during their childhood. And for more than one-third, the issues were significant enough that they received therapy (and, in a few cases, inpatient treatment). These mothers described their daughters' struggles growing up to include depression, rage/anger, severe mood swings, dysfunctional perfectionism, ideational and anxiety disorders, self-harm, and eating disorders. Kerr notes that these issues are especially true for highly gifted females, who are not as likely to seem well-adjusted: "There is some evidence that the brighter the girl, the more likely she may not choose to please. Some highly gifted girls choose social isolation over conformity if none of their true interests coincide with those of peers." For some mothers, learning about how their highly gifted daughter's uniqueness will require them to struggle and blaze their own trail can be anxiety provoking. This makes sense, given parents' instinctive fear of the unknown and concern for our daughters' happiness and safety. This was the case for one of the mothers in the study. "We met Barbara Kerr… and attended one of her lectures…It was helpful although some things were hard to hear. You know, things like 'highly gifted girls may not find a suitable husband' or 'they may marry somebody who's a lot older.' Just when you hear that maybe your kid is not going to follow a normal path, it's a little disconcerting."

Another mother described life with her gifted teen who dressed like a Goth and became very rebellious. Their daughter's appearance and attitude worried both of her parents until a helpful counselor put it into perspective. The mother shared,

> "I was working, so my daughter had to transfer buses after school in the area at the time where a lot of homeless teens lived. And she met some of them… Being as bright as she was, she could see the dead-endedness of these kids' lives who had dropped out of society and moved away from their homes, with

some of them coming from really horrific situations. But she became kind of entangled with them. She didn't leave home, but she did start wanting to be with them more and more. She started dressing… They had this way of dressing in extremely ragged clothes and heavy black makeup—a lot of black and stuff like that. And she was just a mess…Years later I was at…this is kind of an aside…I was at a big shopping mall—a very upscale, popular shopping mall. And I saw this woman getting out of a car with her daughter who was every bit as much of a mess as our daughter had been if not more. The daughter just looked awful while the mom was just dressed to the T. And they both walked into the mall, and I thought, *There goes a good mother!*…Anyway, we tried to get our daughter into counseling with us, because we knew that there was something wrong— something very wrong—and she would *not* go. She said, 'You can drag me physically into the car. You're stronger than I am between the two of you, but I won't get out of the car. And if you drag me in there, which you're capable of doing, I won't say anything.' And we knew that this was absolutely true. There was no way she would do it. So we went and talked to the counselor by ourselves who had worked with a lot of teenagers and homeless teenagers, so she knew the scene and she knew what was going on, and she asked us several questions that kind of put it all into perspective, bless her heart. 'Well, is she failing her classes at school?' 'She failed PE.' 'Well, that's no biggie, is it?' 'No.' 'Is she into drugs?' 'No.' 'Alcohol?' 'No.' 'Ever gotten pregnant?' 'No.' And then she just looked at us. And this just took the panic that we were feeling and sent it dropping through the floor, and it was like, 'Okay, now we can work with her and figure out what to do.' So we went through some very stormy years with her, but she pulled herself out of it...We really thought that if we blocked her, she would run away from home...She was just super rebellious. But...we're just the best of friends now."

Another interviewed mother echoed these sentiments. She shared that she secretly always wanted her daughter to be that "preppy" kind of kid: "So we are just hysterical when our daughter was an adolescent, because at our local [wealthy, suburban] high school she was Miss Weirdo—out of the box—and I was going nuts trying to make her into a J. Crew/Gap/Brooks Brother kid." This mother stated that she's finally gotten to the point where she accepts her daughter for who she is: "I just learned. I guess I realized that there are other things more important in life."

Another key characteristic many mothers brought up during the interviews was the strong need their gifted daughters had to feel in control and in charge. For many, this tendency to demand to "do it myself!" became evident at a very early age, which required extreme patience as the mothers watched their offspring struggle to do something that would take much less time if they could just step in and help. And in later years, this forced many of the mothers, despite their fears, to let their daughters go.

One often unforeseen outgrowth of this early independent streak was that many of these gifted girls bristled at cultural constraints that didn't make sense to them, left home earlier than expected, and boldly followed dreams that took them far afield. Nearly 75 percent of the mothers interviewed stated that their adult daughters were living far from home while pursuing their passions. Most daughters lived in a different state, several in another country. One mother expressed her wish that she had had more children like her daughter, because now that her daughter had moved away, this mother missed her a lot. As another mother whose daughter graduated high school early put it, "She just grew up too fast!" Gifted girls may push for the increased independence of going to boarding school or studying abroad and, in many cases, after completing the standard thirteen years of school faster than "normal," be ready to start college early. Fifteen of the fifty-eight daughters graduated high school early, and three went to boarding school for high school. Several mothers shared that they were wistful about "losing" their children earlier than expected. In one case, the daughter skipped kindergarten, studied abroad junior year in high school when she was fifteen, graduated at sixteen, went to college and graduate school in another part of the country, and is a college professor, living with her child in a different country. For this mother whose daughter is an only child, "losing her daughter" earlier than expected and now being so far away from her and her only grandchild has been very difficult.

Often, the fact that our gifted daughters don't follow the "normal" developmental path or prioritize being close to family over following their passions can translate into their pursuing very different paths as adults. This sometimes forces us, their mothers, to face family scenarios radically different from those depicted by Norman Rockwell. This applied to one interviewed mother's experience. "When our daughter was less than a year old, I went to pick her up at the Church's Mother's Day Out program, and they couldn't find her. Turns out she was crawling across the lawn towards the street. If I had been wise then, I would have known that this was who she is in terms of risk taking and not letting grass grow under her feet." When her daughter started middle school, this mother shared that her daughter decided "that she was not going to play the school game anymore. We'd make her do her homework, and she'd walk out the door with it in the morning but wouldn't turn it in." Her daughter would say, "Oh, I'll do it!" but she just wouldn't hand it in. "It just got to be such a battle." At this point, her daughter started seeing a therapist. Her parents did too, but eventually they ended up going to a tough love group, at which point their daughter started running away. According to her mother,

> "Luckily, she had one friend who she maintained contact with from grade school through college who always knew where our daughter was, and the friend's mother would call and tell me. So I always had a vague notion of where she was, but it was still really terrifying…She would come home after a week or two. A week after she turned eighteen, our daughter took off with two disreputable-looking boys in an old station wagon to start her new life in [another part of the country]. She had been working at a movie theater and saved $1,000. The three of them stayed in a motel, but she blew through her money in a little over a week and struggled to find work. Finally, she took her letter of recommendation from the movie theater job and got a job at

another theater. But after two days, she called and asked us to send her money for a plane ticket. She said, 'I want to come home and start college. There has to be more to life than sweeping up popcorn'... In hindsight, that's the best thing she ever did."

In *Transitions: Making Sense of Life's Changes*, William Bridges describes the emotional impact on parents as their offspring reach different milestones. He points out that loss is the first part of any transition process and that even good changes begin with having to let go of something. Parents are forced to face the fact that the old reality is gone, often when a new one is not yet viable. These transitions are exciting but at the same time contain elements of fear. Amy Joyce expresses the emotions surrounding these changes very powerfully in her article "Parenting: We Celebrate Growth, and Mourn Little Losses Along the Way":

> "We mostly don't know which moment will be the last of whatever that stage of childhood is...I've thought a lot lately about all the evenings and weekends we have spent over the years on the Little League field...So when the last at bat happened, the tears welled. Because, as with most things related to raising kids, it's another little loss. A tiny grief. A reminder that parenting, which is made up of moment after moment of guiding, teaching, and raising our children is also, therefore, essentially made up of moment after moment of letting go. We lose a little every time our child grows, each time they graduate to whatever is next. Each moment they become a little more independent, which is also, ironically, what we strive for as parents."

One of the study mothers lived through high drama related to her daughter's independent streak. Her daughter needed to break away and affirm her own values, and she chose to share this rebellion with their whole community. The mother, who can laugh about it now, described what happened: "The end of our daughter's sophomore year in high school we wanted her to...she had a bat mitzvah in Israel, and we wanted her to be confirmed, which is like another two years of studying [at the synagogue]. But she hated that idea, and she wasn't friends with any of those kids, and at the end of the two-year program, most of those kids go to Israel, but she didn't want to do that."

Her daughter had claimed, "I've been to Israel. My brother was there. I had my bat mitzvah there. I'll do this program for you, but I want to go on a different trip afterwards."

This mother continued:

> "So my husband said, 'Okay. Where do you want to go?' Our daughter replied, 'I want to go to Tibet and Nepal.' She had read a lot about Buddhism, and that's where she wanted to go. And my husband, who was also interested in that as well, said, 'Okay. Let her.' So I found the Cadillac of trips, and she went off to Tibet and Nepal for seven weeks and comes home [just before she turned sixteen] and announced, 'I have something to tell you.' And I thought, *Oh my God, she's pregnant!* But no, she wasn't pregnant. She said, 'I have converted to Buddhism.' Well, now that I've read more and understand more about Buddhism than I did then, I don't care, but then, she pushed my buttons, and I went

berserk! Then she was interviewed for the school newspaper, because who goes to Tibet and Nepal from our local high school? Not too many. And the article that came out was 'My mother forced Judaism down my throat like spinach.' And many other superlatives like that. So everybody in [our town] saw it. And it was just horrible, horrible, horrible."

Developmental, physical, and hormonal issues for both mothers and daughters are also key factors in family dynamics. These issues are exacerbated by the intensity and sensitivities related to female giftedness. As gifted daughters enter puberty, new fears related to pregnancy, sexual harassment, and assault creep into parents' psyches. The emotional and physical ups and downs of both the menstrual cycle and menopause influence the family's day-to-day reality as well. For daughters, Kerr points out that "soon after the onset of puberty….gifted girls seem to undergo great change, a restructuring of personality that is far more extreme than the change occurring in average girls." There is an abrupt change in gifted girls' interests that Kerr attributes to the change in society's attitudes toward her, going from encouraging and rewarding her intellectual achievement to focusing instead on her attractiveness to boys and her "likeability." Parents begin to worry about these issues, according to Kerr, because they only want her to be happy, and social happiness does not come to girls who are different.

A MOTHER IN THE STUDY SHARED SOME OF HER FAMILY'S struggles related to physical changes for both mother and daughter:

"As a young child, the biggest challenges with my daughter were definitely health issues. She was born coughing. She was tested for cystic fibrosis twice, and then we found out it was asthma. And I really think it was the asthma medications that eventually caused her seizure when she was four… Then later on, my daughter and I had a very, very rough relationship when she was in middle school. We fought a lot and said very angry things to each other…This was especially hard because here I had this daughter who, I thought, was going to make up for issues that I had had in my family growing up…About this time, she had just come off the antiseizure medication and was starting her period, so there were lots of chemical changes going on for her. I think there's so much related to physical stressors that we don't really acknowledge.…And I think that part of my significant chemical sensitivity issues, which I was going through at this same time, were related to perimenopause. This resulted in me being completely off kilter with lots of tachycardia and arrhythmia."

One of the interviewed daughters mentioned that her mother recently shared how she had suffered from postpartum depression after the birth of her half-siblings. This daughter's response to her mother was, "Well, why didn't you get some treatment for that? Because it really did affect my childhood during that time." Some of the likely reasons that this mother failed to get help were apparent from hearing the mother's story about the family's situation during this period: their lack of money, the mother's need to work full time to support her family of five while her husband attended medical school, and again, the cultural message for mothers to focus on meeting the needs of the family while denying their own. And perhaps "back in the day," going to therapists just wasn't considered "normal," given the historical cultural stigma associated with seeking mental health treatment. Although this stigma has diminished, it hasn't disappeared and, sadly, may still represent a barrier to treatment for some in need.

Because mothers are assigned the role of enforcing what society considers appropriate, gifted women are forced to balance opposing cultural dictates as parents while, at the same time, cultivating their daughters' gifted potential. Some of the conflicting cultural messages communicated to gifted mothers, who are then pressured to somehow magically get their gifted daughters to comply, include:

- Socialize your daughter (encourage her to conform to customs and traditions that frequently limit female potential), but at the same time, nurture her giftedness and uniqueness

- Protect your daughter's voice; allow her to speak her mind but to do so politely, observing the cultural limits for female assertiveness

- Help your daughter be "successful" as defined by the culture (go to top schools, achieve financial success and status), but make sure she's "happy" and well-adjusted

- Promote the cultural myth that she can easily have a stellar career and, when the time is "right," effortlessly be a good wife (supportive, fun, attractive, slim, a "tiger in the bedroom") and a "good" mother

- Encourage her to challenge the status quo and question authority figures that limit her potential but in a nonthreatening, "feminine" manner

- Be concerned about her personal hygiene and appearance, but don't foster her obsession with looks or encourage her to present herself in an overly sexualized way

- Ensure her safety (and in our culture, it's safer to be invisible, inconsequential, silent, and go with the flow), but at same time push her to self-actualize and take risks

- Encourage her to have "no fear," but make sure she's aware of the dangers females face in today's society

- Give your gifted daughter the message that she can do anything, but help her have realistic expectations about what she can accomplish within the limits of our patriarchal system

CHAPTER 7

Challenges within the Family

Another important aspect for gifted mothers parenting gifted daughters relates to challenges within the family. Much of the advice and discussion in the gifted world about parenting assumes the relationship between parents and their gifted child is unidirectional—how we as parents impact our child. This conversation typically focuses on how mothers can best nurture their child's gifts. It appears that like most contexts females find themselves in, mothers in the gifted world have become invisible—who we uniquely are, what we need, how parenting neurodivergent children impacts us, and how this influences the relationship with our gifted offspring is rarely considered.

But motherhood is a complex, constantly evolving relationship between two unique individuals, especially when giftedness and femaleness are thrown into the mix. Because mother/child interactions are reciprocal, equal focus on nurturing female giftedness should be given to addressing the gifted mother's special characteristics and needs as well as figuring out more about the part these play in her parenting. Again, this is important, given the studies like the one by Dr. Dimitrios Papadopoulos and published by Multidisciplinary Digital Publishing Institute that show

"Parenting a gifted child is a journey with unique experiences...[that] typically raise concerns, influence decisions, and exacerbate stress and anxiety...Enhancing the caregiving capacity of family members—by reducing the stress associated with their parenting and caregiving roles—can have a powerful impact on the course of giftedness." These studies highlight how the bond between the mother and her gifted child is intimately tied to nurturing the child's intelligence and crucial for brain growth, and, not surprisingly, it plays a key role in how the gifted mother herself self-actualizes.

So how does our own neurodiversity influence how we mother, for better or for worse? What part do our gifted characteristics like intensity, high energy, drive, overexcitability, perfectionism, social-emotional quirks, and possibly twice exceptionality, just to name a few, play into our interactions with our gifted daughters? Is our intensity spilling over into how we approach parenting? How emotionally draining is it for a gifted woman to have a daughter and feel like her heart is walking around outside her body, to feel so deeply as only one with overexcitabilities can do? How do our experiences growing up as gifted females in a male-oriented culture impact who we have become and, hence, how we parent? The synergy between "quiveringly alive" gifted mothers and their gifted daughters with similar temperaments is often palpable—dynamic, intense, powerful, and at times even explosive. Attempting to understand the dynamics of this unique bond is key to both the growth of gifted mothers and gifted daughters. As gifted mother Ginny Kochis so wisely noted in her blog post cited above about self-care, "And then there's me, just as sensitive and anxious and headstrong as they are, wondering how the heck I'm still standing, and how much longer that's going to last."

Psychologist Alice Miller cautions in *The Drama of the Gifted Child: The Search for the True Self* that frequently a child's very gifts, like her intensity and curiosity, will confront her mother with issues that she herself had tried to repress while growing up by blending in and following society's rules, regulations, and limitations. This awareness may lead to cognitive dissonance for the mother who is proud of her daughter's giftedness but finds herself, often subconsciously, trying to tamp down or even destroy what's best and truest in her daughter. This was an ongoing issue for one of the mothers in the study whose family embraced more traditional values, which her daughter openly rebelled against. During the interview, in response to my statement that she had apparently raised a very direct, authentic, and strong-willed daughter, this gifted woman honestly replied half in jest, "Well, I didn't mean to!"

Other scars from our past may create fears as we raise our gifted girls, causing us to put up obstacles or restrictions on their growth and risk taking. This abundance of caution may harm the mother/daughter relationship in the long run. In these situations, we may rationalize our behavior, telling our daughters that we're protecting them by enforcing cultural norms and values when really we are protecting ourselves from our own complex feelings of self-betrayal and loss that result from our compliance and desire to please others rather than ourselves.

Our gifted daughters' drive to be "all they can be" may scare us, because they are unwilling to knuckle under in situations like we did. We worry about what they may face as they venture more and more outside the protective walls of their families, fearful of how their giftedness and gender will be dealt with in the outside world. Watching them mature with our increasing awareness of the limitations society will place on them as gifted females reminds us of what we've been forced to shut down or abandon in ourselves to fit in and survive. We cheer them on but often with our hearts in our throats and some feelings of regret.

One mother in the study demonstrated the importance of a gifted mother's self-awareness of her past and the need for her to deal with her own gifted characteristics and challenges. This brave woman shared a very sensitive and painful story about how her inability to know and value who she is devolved to the point where it almost blew up her family.

> "I can't say it was all a bed of roses. I will tell you, quite honestly, that there was a time when I did not live at home. I moved out. We were having a lot of difficulty. It was during her senior year [in high school]. We had let our daughter get a little too much power in the house…and I was having a lot of problems letting her go and not being all-encompassing. So for everybody's mental health, I moved out for about nine months. I moved out in October, and my daughter and I did not speak until December, and this was just very briefly…Finally, in May, my daughter called, I was living in an apartment not too far from where we lived, and said, 'How about if we go to Disneyland for the weekend, just the two of us?' And we had a fabulous time."

This mother explained that she found another place to live because she wanted her daughter to stay at home and in her surroundings, especially for her senior year.

"Everybody needed to own up to what they had done, and I just said, 'I can't seem to let go.' And maybe it was because she was an only child—because maybe you're putting all your eggs in one basket kind of thing. But I had a very difficult time letting go. And she had a lot of power…and she knew it because she was bright enough and could manipulate the situation. She didn't like that either, because it made her very uncomfortable. We all went to therapy. But in hindsight, I felt it was the best…it probably was the best thing that any of us had ever done…I got help from a therapist and did a lot of work on my own—and did a lot of crying. I was living by myself for the first time in my life, and it was a big lesson for me and made me feel good about myself. I went right from college into marriage, which is what you were supposed to do in those days!…I finally decided that I had to let go. I had to let my daughter live her life, and I couldn't live my life through her. I had my own friends and I had value, and it wasn't associated with her. It was about me and who I was. So I learned, and I'm still learning. You think you're all alone and that nobody else is having any problems. Everybody else seems fine. But I've subsequently learned that this ain't the truth, and anybody who says that everything's perfect is not being honest…I used to have a friend who would say, 'Everything in my life is perfect.' But she'd wear a neck brace half the year, so you're thinking, *Something's wrong here.* Raising a gifted daughter is challenging and exhausting, and sometimes you can't get a perspective on anything because you're in the middle of it. You can't distance yourself from what's going on…Raising kids is so difficult, but then, on top of this, raising kids who are so bright adds this extra piece to it. They aren't always pliable, and they don't always say yes to things…And they can outthink you!"

With the birth of her gifted daughter, a woman goes from being a gifted female with all that that entails to additionally being an individual primarily responsible for helping her bright girl thrive against all odds in our culture. Many gifted women find that the coping skills they developed over the years to thrive in academia and the work world are no longer applicable as they take on a new role as mothers requiring totally different skills that are undervalued, unacknowledged, and unappreciated by the larger culture and for which many of them are wholly unprepared.

Having a newborn gifted infant placed in your arms, immediately following the major changes involved in pregnancy and giving birth, demands that new mothers get up to speed immediately and serve as the primary (most likely nursing) caregivers to intense, sleep-adverse, sensitive creatures on a 24-7 basis. In addition, the cultural myth that these women will find inherent joy in motherhood sets them up with the unrealistic expectation that this baby will make them happy. This false emotional narrative, along with the overwhelming physical changes and demands of their new motherhood situation, can spark a variety of emotional conflicts for gifted women. For many, this often includes triggering unpleasant memories of growing up as gifted girls that imbued in them a general sense that the world is unsupportive and even unsafe.

When mothers reflect on painful memories of the challenging times they suffered related to giftedness, it adds an additional layer of stress to that which most neurotypical mothers feel. Gifted mothers worry about their ability to provide a more nurturing and less traumatic childhood for their bright daughters than the one they experienced. These concerns, along with the gifted mother's deep-seated drive to self-actualize and be as successful a parent as she has been in her past endeavors, make the milestone of welcoming a gifted daughter into her life one of the most dramatic changes she's ever experienced. On top of this, caring for a child who rarely sleeps, is highly sensitive and intense, and is constantly driven and curious rubs up against the same qualities in her very intense, sensitive, sleep-deprived, driven mother. On every level, for many gifted women, giving birth to a bright daughter truly rocks their world.

Many of the past traumas gifted mothers are anxious for their girls to avoid are related to their experience of feeling different all their lives and not understanding why. As Willem Kuipers points out in *Enjoying the Gift of Being Uncommon: Extra Intelligent, Intense, and Effective,* many gifted adults most likely were able to develop various coping mechanisms to deal with these painful, chronic, and unpredictable scenarios of feeling "other" but with varying degrees of success. In most cases, gifted mothers have also developed a variety of coping mechanisms to survive as smart females in various sexist environments. Most likely, these represent both effective and dysfunctional ways to get their unique needs met in a patriarchal culture that tries to keep gifted women "in their place."

When a gifted mother witnesses her daughter confronting similar challenges and experiencing the same anxiety, angst, and fear she went through, the mother's long-repressed feelings of hatred for the world's injustice may be triggered. This may trigger self-hatred as she feels, once again, powerless to change these experiences for her daughter. In these situations, the mother's knee-jerk and very human reaction is to jump in and fix problems to ensure that her daughter learns from the bad choices the mother made in similar past situations. Dweck's term for this, "struggle theft," aptly describes how our well-intentioned desire to be protective may actually harm our gifted daughters by depriving them of the growth and learning that comes from developing their own uniquely suited coping mechanisms and strategies. But like most issues related to nurturing female giftedness, this is complicated. Especially when gifted girls are younger, we do at times need to advocate for them to ensure their special needs are met and model how this is done. Navigating this minefield of when it's best to advocate versus allowing our daughters to figure it out for themselves is challenging, especially as both our daughters' reactions and the situations they find themselves in are probably different in many ways from our own.

When a gifted mother does choose to advocate for her daughter, Kuipers notes that a surprising number of these women often find themselves putting in tremendous effort to assist their child's high potential without ever acknowledging their own. But as Kuipers puts it, the penny can drop when observing their gifted daughter, causing the parent to wonder about her own different traits and quirks—what do they remind the mother of, and what do they portend for their daughter's future? For mothers unaware of their exceptional intelligence, witnessing how their daughter's giftedness is manifested can spark the mother's recognition and acknowledgment of her own high intelligence. Helpful family members or friends sometimes then reinforce this awareness, says Kuipers, when they point out, "Oh, you were just the same way at her age."

A number of gifted mothers in the study were unaware, or unsure, of their own giftedness. These mothers often suggested that their daughter's giftedness came from their father and tended to downplay, despite all evidence to the contrary, their own exceptionality. In their article "Parents of the Extraordinarily Gifted," Linda Silverman and Kathi Kearney posit that these women's tendency to credit their offspring's smarts to their partner's genetic endowment and to deny their own may be due to their socialized understanding of giftedness as achievement in the public arena. And again, using this metric, the paucity of eminent women in our culture, especially for those with children, reinforces this limited perspective.

There are a number of other reasons gifted mothers might downplay their brilliance. Some mothers may have suffered from indifference or neglect, growing up in situations where caregivers failed to appreciate and nurture their potential. Or they may have been bored and overlooked in schools that refused to challenge them until college when academics become more difficult, and they began to think if they had to work hard to succeed, they probably weren't that smart after all. Another contributing factor may be that they were bullied or struggled to find true peers throughout their childhood to the point that they weighed the pros and cons of embracing who they truly were and decided it simply wasn't worth it to be smart. Finally, for some, growing up with what one daughter termed the "gifted burden" of others' high expectations, and failing to meet these unrealistic goals, they concluded that they were never really that bright to begin with. As a result, many gifted females carry hidden scars from their childhood as they assume the primary role of raising another gifted female. These scars potentially prevent them from being able to create the context in which both they and their daughters can flourish.

Because women face pressure to conform to gender roles that deny female intelligence and to repress and even lie about their personal emotions and needs, their opportunity to self-actualize is often thwarted. Sadly, even the brilliant, gifted guru Annemarie Roeper experienced this, writing: "Many of my emotions have been covered up. I lacked permission to express them, or rather I feared that they would be unwelcome in their intensity." The sexist socialization many gifted mothers have experienced growing up frequently alienates them from their true feelings as well as a sense of self-awareness about their own high potential, often leaving them insecure about who they truly are and what they want. As such, these gifted mothers may find themselves constantly repressing emotions that society has deemed "bad" for females and especially for mothers—anger, rage, intensity, anxiety, sensitivity, envy, and yearning. This repression leads to unexamined lives not worth living, as Socrates put it. This represents a huge loss not only for these women themselves but also for society and their gifted daughters.

The heavy cultural burden placed on mothers to be the cornerstone of their family reinforces this repression of feelings and needs. Mothers are expected to provide a strong foundation for their households and serve as the support beam of their gifted daughter's lives. The motherhood script requires gifted females to be devoid of weakness and to prioritize other family members' needs and success above her own. In her article "When I Replaced Strength with Vulnerability, I Grew Closer to My Daughters," Emilie Smith comments, "I can't remember a time that my mother cried… My mother is a loving woman in her own way. I think she's just gotten really, really good at hiding her emotions under a front of strength. I've often taken that road, too, of holding onto my emotions and burying them, allowing only my strength to show."

THIS CULTURALLY INSTILLED VALUE OF FEMALE STRENGTH and service also demands that mothers pull more than their fair share of the domestic weight, performing more day-to-day services than other family members and doing work that has much less status and requires less mental aptitude than many assignments in the workplace. While the other family members observe this scenario, they naturally assume it means the mother is better suited to these menial activities and must enjoy doing them. In many families, as author Kelly Corrigan put it in *The Middle Place*, Dad is the glitter while Mom is the glue.

Unlike gifted women who are encouraged to repress or deny their high intelligence, fathers are frequently emboldened to proudly embrace and assert their brilliance. Other family members often comply with this narrative by supporting the family myth that the father is in fact the exceptionally smart one in the household. Sadly, the message our daughters take away from this may lead to repressing or denying their own giftedness and having less respect and appreciation for their gifted mothers as well as mothers in general, viewing any woman in the motherhood role as less than. However, one very aware interviewed daughter slowly came to realize and appreciate her mother's exceptional intelligence:

> "One of the things that's most precious to me about my mother is how she thinks about other people and how she brings a softness and a consideration… I also value my mother's love of culture. My mother is an incredibly cultured and widely engaged person, while my father, like many men, tends to be mono-focused…So I think the combination of her empathy and her willingness to help others and her ability to be in tune with the larger culture—that has evened me out and softened me in a way that if I had been entirely my father's daughter, I think I'd be even more insufferable than I am now…I've been reading Carol Gilligan's stuff…and she posits a hypothetical about a man breaking into a pharmacy. And men tend to say 'right and wrong' or see the scenario as 'black and white,' while women tend to equivocate. But what they are really doing is weighing both sides of the argument and looking much more deeply at possible reasons and ramifications for what's happening. So what they are doing is looking at all sorts of possible relationships and explanations…which seems much smarter…but it does take longer. And I look at my mom's processing of information versus my dad's. My dad is very quick, while my mom's processing takes longer, which then leads him to be impatient with her, but I actually believe her processing is much deeper."

Fortunately, a number of the interviewed mothers also eventually came to the realization that they too were highly intelligent. As one mother asserted, "Turns out, I'm smart too!" Without this self-awareness and self-acceptance, a gifted mother may turn to her daughter to help in healing past wounds related to denial or repression of her abilities. As one mother shared, "I eventually learned not to lean on my daughter for the emotional support I needed" to deal with the challenges this mother had faced trying to self-actualize in a male-dominated academic field. "I came to realize that I was the mom, and it was my job to give my daughter support…Not the other way around." Interestingly, this daughter eventually went on to get a PhD in a STEM field, which her mother had been unable to achieve due to a lack of support (from both her male dissertation advisor and her husband) and the fact that circumstances required the family to live in a small community that offered few educational opportunities in her field.

When mothers discover and come to terms with their own giftedness (and twice exceptionality, if applicable) so late in their lives, it begs the question: Would their lives have been richer or more enhanced if they had been aware of their giftedness much earlier? Or if they lived in an environment where their exceptional minds were valued and nurtured? How much potential has been lost because so many brilliant females have been unable to maximize their gifts? And how can we encourage our gifted daughters to embrace their giftedness and be proud of who they are if we don't acknowledge and appreciate our own?

In addition to embracing their own giftedness, it is critically important for gifted mothers to grasp everything that accompanies high intelligence in order to understand the part these can play in their relationship with their daughters.

Hopefully this understanding can also allow gifted mothers to cut themselves some slack. The typical strong emotions, overexcitabilities, perfectionism, and intensity gifted females bring to motherhood can at times collide head on with the greater-than-average parenting challenges they may face. For many, dealing with these characteristics—along with issues related to possibly being twice exceptional as well as changes in hormonal levels related to female reproductive issues—can result in higher emotional levels of anger, stress, depression, and anxiety than most neurotypical mothers experience. Raising incredibly smart girls and rarely getting a reprieve from the intensity represents a very real daily struggle. A few of the interviewed mothers shared that they often got through times of stress with the mantra, "When they go off to college, I'll get a break." (Ah, if only this were true!)

In her article "I'm a Parenting Perfectionist and It's Going to Be the Death of Me," Tonilyn Hornung shares similar concerns, noting her overwhelming feeling from the get-go that her baby deserved her unmitigated best. But as time went on, she became aware that her inner perfectionist was pushing her toward maximum exhaustion. "Instead of taking moments alone to rest, I'll choose to organize so I can feel accomplished about *something*...If I give up on being there for my family and instead work on being there for myself, I'll be abandoning the motherly post I promised to keep." She eventually realized that being a perfectionist could have its positive points but also kept her isolated from even her own family. "I miss out on fun times with family... My inner push for perfection stops a great deal of joy."

For many gifted women with a history of achievement, acknowledging that they are struggling as parents or sharing their distress about handling this overly demanding role creates a place most don't want to go. One of the mothers in the study who benefited from counseling when her daughter was older stated that her therapist strongly believed that parents of gifted, even more than their children, need to receive counseling to work through their own issues, because a lot of buttons get pushed raising their offspring. Sometimes these well-meaning mothers can even make things worse than they already are for gifted girls in our society. The mother stated, "For me, I feel like I grew up along with my gifted daughter…because I don't think I grew up in the way I could have or should have as a gifted child…And I don't know what this has really done to my daughter in the long run."

In some cases, the gifted mother may come to the realization that she and her daughter have very different personality traits and that their unique combinations of talent and temperament do not make for easy living. The particular way these mothers and daughters are knit together, each having unique quirks and complexities related to their neurodiversity, may over time become quite tangled. Kuipers notes that two exceptionally bright individuals in a relationship can be widely different in the makeup of their intelligence and the diversity of ways in which each of them may excel. This complicates a correct estimation of the other's extra intelligence and creates interpersonal conflicts stemming from the mothers' and daughters' different strengths and ways of looking at the world. That said, Kuipers does, fortunately, suggest that this bond can also be heightened to some extent by shared gifted characteristics such as mutual intensity, complexity, and drive.

For a few of the interviewed mothers, learning that their daughters were highly or profoundly gifted was a bit off-putting and scary. For some, their daughters' giftedness triggered feelings related to imposter syndrome. Having primary responsibility for nurturing a daughter who was even more of an outlier than her gifted mother often instilled fear of not being up to the task. Some mothers were uncertain how a daughter with this "off the charts" level of intelligence would fare throughout her life. Another difficulty for some mothers in the study was realizing that their daughter excelled in areas that they themselves found challenging or had failed in. One such mother, who excelled in social sciences both in school and in her career, realized as her daughter approached middle school that she was brilliant in math and computer science. This was shocking to this mother who shared that she herself had flunked remedial math her freshman year in college. Along these lines, another mother commented that her husband (who was a successful athlete both in college and in his career) came to the realization very early on "that our daughter was going to be on the opposite end when it came to body smarts. But fortunately, he was appreciative of what she was capable of doing academically and came to embrace the fact that her smarts were very different than his type of smart."

Not surprisingly, gifted daughters may exhibit very different temperaments from their mothers, which can interact with their parents' idiosyncrasies in a variety of complex and unpredictable ways. As Elizabeth Strout puts it in her novel *The Burgess Boys,* "We are all mythologies… We are all mysteries." In many cases, trying to peel back the layers of our bright daughter's very complex personalities is a never-ending challenge. As one mother shared, taking the Myers-Briggs Type Indicator assessment along with her husband and daughter revealed significant differences in terms of their preferences, needs, and values.

> "We were able to see that we each shared one or two preferences from the four main categories, but none of us were the exact match on the possible sixteen distinctive personality types. This helped us understand why our daughter's lifestyle preference was more spur of the moment, whereas we liked to plan everything out. It was funny because once on a vacation when she was young, she said, 'Can't we ever just wake up in the morning and decide then what we want do?'"

Several mothers struggled to deal with criticism from their daughters who, at times, appeared to enjoy taking their mothers down a few notches. And while all the interviewed mothers seemed to prioritize creating a context for their daughters to feel comfortable "in their own skin" and to be authentic, in some instances, this was not reciprocated by their daughters, which left these mothers feeling like they were walking on eggshells around them. For gifted women who may have struggled throughout their lives to be able to be genuine and to freely express their values and opinions, experiencing this same situation within their own families represented quite a hardship. Sadly, in a few cases, the love a mother had for her daughter was not always reciprocated. In our culture, a mother's love is expected to be unconditional, whereas this is not an expectation we place on our children, although we certainly hope they will love us in return.

But Ruth Whippman, in her article "Can We Really Love Our Children Unconditionally?" believes that a mother's unconditional love for her child is a cultural myth and another unrealistic demand placed on mothers with some sexism buried in it. According to Whippman, "The nagging sense that this emotional requirement is both essential to everyone else's well-being yet impossible to achieve in practice certainly seems to be drawn from the file labeled 'Unachievable Expectations Placed Mainly on Women.'" She goes on to note that psychoanalyst Erich Fromm distinguished the unwavering, selfless love of a mother from the inherently more conditional love of a father, whose love needs to be "earned" with good behavior and success.

Miller comments in *The Drama of the Gifted Child*, "As adults we don't need unconditional love…This is a childhood need." It was apparent in the hours-long interviews that the forty-three mothers in the study did love their daughters unconditionally, at least while they were growing up. However, one very honest mother, when asked what she loved most about her adult daughter, paused for several minutes and asked if we could come back to that. As the interview progressed, it became clear that key personality differences between herself and her daughter, the drama she had lived through during her daughter's childhood, and the rejection she had experienced by her gifted daughter since adolescence made it extremely difficult for this mother to feel unconditional love for her adult child. They still maintained a relationship, but this mother would not describe it as close. This sentiment was echoed by several other mothers in the study.

Differences in the way mothers and daughters approached cultural conventions and scripts also led to some relationship problems. One mother discussed how her daughter's approach to dealing with reality was in direct conflict with her own. She lamented,

> "My daughter's greatest passion in life is being *honest*. She doesn't do well with people who aren't just 'in your face' blatantly frank…and I'm not a person like that…My daughter wants everything out in the open, and too bad if it hurts your feelings…And I think my daughter thought I was wrong because I wasn't mirroring her [approach]…In my family of origin, it was always 'Oh no, we've got to be careful about this' and "Don't say that!'…Lots of secrets, and my daughter's just the opposite…My daughter was born into an extended family on both sides where females were supposed to take a subordinate role, although her mother didn't quite do that, but in the rest of my family and in my husband's family for sure…I wouldn't say females are second-class citizens, but it kind of gets to that point…But my daughter's always just blazed her own trail and made things happen."

The daughter now lives in another country and with "a sweet, darling man who told me, 'You know she carries you around in her head all the time, and she's always arguing with you.' I thought that was pretty depressing."

One of the interviewed daughters gave another example of personality differences between gifted mothers and daughters. In this case, it seemed that the mother could be described as an empath (who, according to psychologist Deirdre Lovecky, is an individual who feels things incredibly deeply to the point she can become overwhelmed). This trait may cause others to be reluctant to share their problems with the empath because of the strong emotional reaction it can trigger. As a result, this daughter often felt robbed of her own feelings, which tended to negatively impact their mother/daughter relationship. I would also note that this interaction may sometimes flip the parent/child dynamic to one where the child feels the need to take care of the mother. The interviewed daughter mentioned in this scenario described the impact this had on her relationship with her mother, stating that she rarely turned to her mother for help when she was emotionally upset: "I mean she's helpful in practical ways but not…if my world is falling apart, she's not the person I'm going to call. It would be too hard for her, and she gets very emotional. And I want somebody to problem solve or just listen. But her problem solving would be caught up in all this emotion, which I don't deal with very well. That kind of support I don't need."

In *Bad Mother: A Chronicle of Maternal Crimes, Minor Calamities, and Occasional Moments of Grace*, Ayelet Waldman asserts how our lack of awareness and acceptance of our daughter's uniqueness and differences from our own can create pain and anxiety. This discomfort stems from a mother trying to be the perfect parent based on preconceived notions of what that means from her own past:

> The thing is my fantasies about being a parent always involved fighting for my unpopular child, doing for her what my own parents couldn't do for me when I was a girl…There's only one problem. My children are nothing like me…Your job is to parent your child's needs, given the particulars of

his or her own life and nature. It's hard to separate your remembered childhood and its emotional legacy from the childhoods that are being lived out in your house by your children. If you're lucky, your children will help you make that distinction…You want to protect them, but sometimes what you have to protect them from is the ongoing avalanche of your own childhood—crashing on you like a hail of dodgeballs.

But, conversely, a mother in the study noted that having strong similarities with a gifted daughter may also present a challenge. For example, one of her bright daughters closely mirrored her mother's tendency to be anxious, worry, ruminate, and to be empathetic, almost to a fault. As a result, when a difficult situation arose, the anxiety and stress level for both mother and daughter could reach dysfunctional levels. For example, when the daughter would turn to her mother with a problem, together they would work themselves up into an emotional tailspin trying to resolve the situation, often leaving both feeling spent, angst-ridden, and depressed. And because mothers tend to be hypercritical of themselves, in situations like this where the mother and daughter share many personality characteristics, the mother may tend to be as highly critical of her doppelganger of a daughter as she is of herself.

However, another mother who tended to worry a lot shared that her daughter had a very different personality and was much more cerebral, pragmatic, and rational. When her daughter sometimes found herself in difficult straits, she eventually resolved most of these problems on her own rather than turning to her mother for advice or support. Consequently, this daughter's "don't worry, be happy" approach basically enabled her mother to fret about her much less. While raising a child who was so much her opposite possibly minimized a tight emotional mother/daughter bond, it also showed the mother the value of an entirely different but equally effective approach to life. Experiencing this was enlightening and transformational, according to this mother. In this respect, it seems the gifted daughter most unlike us, who constantly nudges us to grow and view the world through a different lens, can serve as a valuable role model.

CHAPTER 8

Challenges outside the Family

Most gifted women have been highly successful in many areas before becoming a parent and often find the birth of their first child a rude awakening. Their gifted personhood and identity are overshadowed by their new role for which they are, most likely, unprepared. As new mothers, every interaction with their child is judged by both the gifted women themselves and the whole wide world. Venturing outside the home, they become vulnerable to many folks who seem to hold strong beliefs about the right way to parent and the right way for children (especially daughters) to behave. As Dr. Deborah Tannen notes in *You Just Don't Understand: Women and Men in Conversation*, mothers are the family members most likely to be targets of the world's disapproval, hostility, or aggression, because many in our culture feel far more comfortable expressing disapproval to women they don't know than to men. This results in a difficult situation for many gifted women: the sense that they're just not measuring up.

As Dr. Stephanie Pace Marshall points out in *The Power to Transform: Leadership That Brings Learning and Schooling to Life*, the guiding metaphor for raising the next generation in our culture is based on rigid conceptions of the world as a machine, which views children as mechanical systems, with the goal of fitting all of them into the "normal" child mold: "This worldview and its illusions of predictability, precise measurability, and external controllability continue to influence almost every dimension of our culture." This mechanistic approach often fails to consider the unique individuality and potential of each child and focuses on getting all children to achieve developmental milestones within a set time frame, adhere to social norms, and conform to societal expectations. Within this framework, mothers are tasked to be on the lookout for any deviations from what's considered appropriate and quickly fix these "problems." One can see how difficult, if not impossible, this task is for mothers with neurodivergent offspring who, like their gifted mothers, are outliers. As such, schools and mainstream society try to fit these square pegs into round holes with little to no understanding or appreciation for who they truly are and what is lost in the process. Variability among people in our culture is, sadly, often viewed as a disorder rather than something to be celebrated.

Kochis struggled under the weight of others' opinions and notes that it began to insidiously impact her relationship with her gifted children. Kochis shares, "Sometimes it feels like the person your neurodiverse child is—his sense of humor, his wit, his intellect—is all but eclipsed by other people's perceptions. When will they see how smart she is? When will they stop prefacing conversation with 'She's so brilliant, but…' It's easy to let the fear of other people's attitudes become a wedge between you and your kids." Marshall explains this happens because society is not set up to embrace all aspects of our children because of its simplistic and mechanistic perspective that discounts the whole child along with the holistic experience of parenting the child. One of the interviewed mothers in the study questioned the value of society's rigid standard that discriminates against outliers: "Why does everyone want your gifted daughter to be 'normal'? If you think that 'normal' on a scale from zero to one hundred is about fifty—why do we want everyone to be a fifty? What's so great about being normal?"

In a January 2013 interview with Michael F. Shaughnessy, Ruf notes the additional challenge for mothers with more than one gifted child and, therefore, more than one mystery to solve. Ruf states: "I have three grown sons, and all of them are very smart, but they are still quite different from each other. As they started school, I learned that they each had different needs, different ways of coping with what they encountered in school, and they require different kinds of attention and support both at home and at school."

But while gifted mothers feel coerced to make their gifted daughters fit in, at the same time society holds extremely high career expectations for their offspring. Consequently, the stakes are often higher than anything a gifted mother has experienced in the past—to socialize a small human in such a way that the child will behave "normally" while, at the same time, nurture her high potential so she will go on to achieve exceptionally or eminently great things. In this respect, the "gifted burden" of the gifted child is also placed upon her mother. Karen Maezen Miller addressed this pressure as the key speaker at the Mothers' Symposium at Stanford University in 2009. She touched a nerve with many of the women in attendance when she shared that shortly after her daughter was born, the one word that stuck in her mind was "Stanford." The mothers in the audience responded with nervous laughter—we all knew only too well what she meant. She went on to say that for her, like most mothers today, her biggest challenge was how to get her daughter—this little organic creature with a mind of her own—from here to there. This is what we believe our job is: to manage an outcome, nurturing our children from where they currently are (not quite "good enough") and from where we are as their mother ("not quite good enough") to an ideal (gaining admission to a top university) so they can go on to change the world.

Maezen Miller went on to note that this parenting predicament is exacerbated for gifted women by other factors unique to their situation. Not only does their internalized goal of ensuring that their daughters, like themselves, succeed at an exceptionally high level, but their situation is made even more intense because of their own high cognitive abilities that crave intellectual stimulation. On top of this, given the mothers' own distinctive gifted personality characteristics (like intensity, sensitivity, and drive), one discovers the perfect recipe for a parenting experience very different from the norm and for which there is no guidebook. As Kochis expresses it with the title of her blog, raising exceptional kids is "Not So Formulaic."

VENTURING INTO THE WORLD OF SCHOOL

The vision of the preferred future many mothers raising gifted daughters hope for their daughters in our educational system is offered by Fiedler and Nauta. They describe a state of being called "flow," which was defined by psychologist Mihaly Csikszentmihalyi in 1975. In flow, students are completely involved in an activity for its own sake. According to Fiedler and Nauta, during flow, ego falls away, time flies, every action, movement, and thought follows inevitably from the previous one, your whole being is involved, and you're using your skills to the utmost. In flow, high levels of skills are used simultaneously with high levels of challenge. Unfortunately, this ideal learning environment is rare in our schools, and only a small number of the fifty-eight gifted daughters in the study sample were lucky enough to experience flow during their many years in school.

ONE OF THE MOTHERS IN THE STUDY GAVE AN EXAMPLE of a very less-than-ideal situation for gifted daughters as they venture outside the family. When her daughter started school, this mother realized that the rigid school curriculum in their rural town was a complete mismatch for her daughter. Sadly, their idyllic family life turned into chaos due to the ongoing conflict between the school and their daughter, with the parents caught in the middle. After ten years, the parents finally decided to remove themselves from the battle, which had been emotionally draining for the whole family. They allowed their daughter to try to figure out the school situation on her own and deal with whatever consequences the system deemed appropriate. Fortunately, during this daughter's second college attempt, this very bright young female was able to rediscover her passion for learning and went on to earn a PhD, resulting in a successful career. As her mother put it,

> "Our daughter was very verbal and precocious at a young age and often, as a toddler, would entertain our fellow graduate students at parties we hosted. She wanted to learn everything…And it was hugely fun until she went to school…She was placed in

the first grade, skipping kindergarten. She wanted to do her own thing in school and couldn't get her act together to do what teachers wanted her to do. She was in the school's gifted pull-out program, but it was 'crappy'—and just mostly busy work. As a result, our daughter perceived this program as basically punitive, because she had to make up the classwork she had missed when she was pulled out of her mainstream class as homework and would then not turn it in—she was highly disorganized."

This mother was angry at the school's perspective regarding what was happening: "If she was underachieving, it couldn't be anything they were doing, and the fact that school was so freaking boring and homework was so unbelievably meaningless…No, they claimed, it had to be that there was something wrong with our daughter…Sadly, up until the start of school, our daughter was one hundred percent the most delightful person on earth."

Unfortunately, many gifted mothers and daughters are confronted with this sad reality when their gifted child enters the school system. A powerful synopsis of this situation was provided by one of the interviewed women in the study:

> "How do you take a child with great potential and throw them into a system where every word used to describe that child is negative and the child is getting signals, not just from the other children but from the adults as well, that something is wrong with them because they are who they are? To me, the child who survives that system with any sense of

integration about their brain and wholeness about who they are is a miracle child."

However, it is important to step back and widen our lens before delving into the various challenges gifted daughters face in the educational system. Appreciating the fact that many of these challenges stem from failures within the system itself prevents us from falling into the trap of blaming individuals who are merely trying to function as best they can within a dysfunctional system. It's a very common knee-jerk response to resort to bashing teachers or administrators as we witness our daughters struggling and, conversely, for educators to get into the habit of parent-bashing. But it furthers the mission of both parents and teachers to be aware that they share the common, worthwhile goal of educating children and that most obstacles to achieving this are often the result of flaws within the educational system rather than of individuals struggling within it. I am the mother of an adult daughter who has taught math in the public school system in an underserved community for nineteen years. As such, I have had the opportunity to understand many of the daily challenges teachers face working in understaffed, underresourced, underpaid, demanding positions. Rather than providing the additional resources and training necessary to meet the special needs of both students and teachers, the burden is placed on the gifted students, their parents, and their teachers to try to compensate for and overcome the major deficits in the system itself. Both mothers and teachers are given little status, support, resources, and validation. This is further evidence of how little our society values those in need of care and the caring positions held mostly by females.

ONE TYPICAL (AND INEFFECTIVE) STRATEGY TO SUPPOSedly support gifted students in the classroom that is imposed by the system on teachers and gifted children is "differentiation." In her blog post "Why Differentiated Instruction Fails Gifted Children," Post states that advocates of differentiation have not supplied data showing the educational benefits of heterogeneous classrooms for gifted children, and in fact most studies support the merits of the opposite approach: ability grouping for these students. And differentiation requires Herculean effort on the part of teachers who are already overwhelmed with large class sizes and myriad responsibilities above and beyond teaching. Specifically, with differentiated classrooms, teachers must create a variety of different lesson plans each night to address the wide range of learning needs in their classroom. This approach leads to additional stress and burnout for educators who already have way too much on their plate and often falls far short of its goal.

ANOTHER HARSH REALITY FOR GIFTED MOTHERS IN advocating for their daughters is the open-endedness of the situation. Because their daughters' academic needs are constantly changing (as are grades, teachers, and peers), their learning environment must be constantly monitored to ensure they are being challenged appropriately. The need for relentless vigilance throughout our gifted daughters' schooling years can take a toll. As one mother put it: "Uncertainty constitutes the landmass of a gifted mother's parenting journey."

The majority of gifted mothers interviewed described the considerable amounts of time, resources, and energy they invested in trying to help their gifted daughters survive in the absence of challenging learning environments. Sadly, most eventually realized that, as Post points out, it's hard for parents to compensate entirely for the hours their children lose in school. As a last resort, a number of the sampled mothers transferred their daughters to different schools in the hope that they would eventually find one where their daughters would thrive. It appears that many mothers today raising neurodiverse children are experiencing similar issues, but they are tending to resort to homeschooling as a more viable option.

EXAMPLES OF THE MEASURES THE MOTHERS IN THE study undertook to ensure that the curiosity, drive, and fire in their daughters' bellies for intellectual stimulation was not extinguished include the following:

- One gifted mother noted that she became a very strong advocate for her daughter over the years and eventually supported her daughter's decision to drop out of middle school to homeschool herself, because she was more than capable of meeting her own educational needs at that point. This mother's main driving force in fighting for her daughter's educational needs was simply put: "I didn't want my daughter to lose her passion for learning." She added, "The interesting thing about supporting my daughter's decision to homeschool herself was that I had other parents tell me I was abusing my child by not allowing her to have the typical high school experience."

- Another mother shared the personal pain she experienced for several years related to the enormous amount of effort and ugly politics that she faced in starting a gifted school for her daughters.

- Because of the lack of resources in their very rural area, another mother was forced to endure a long, painful legal due process battle that enabled her daughter to finally attend the gifted program in a nearby district.

- One mother who worked in her daughter's school district fought to get her daughter reinstated into the gifted seminar program when she started middle school, causing her career as a school administrator to suffer. She commented, "I was always pleasant and always nice, but I was firm."

- One of the gifted daughters was finally diagnosed as autistic at thirteen after her mother overcame numerous hurdles to have her evaluated, stating, "Her pediatrician refused to see it." This mother stressed that she fought a lot of battles for her daughter "pretty much alone," and after her daughter's diagnosis, it took more than three years for the district to finally make special provisions for her.

- One mother with seven children shared, "We planned for four. But you know how all the birth control packets say ninety-eight percent or ninety-nine percent effective, and you wonder about that other percentage? That's us!" She stated that she led "a lot of parent-teacher organizations and things, which I hated doing. I didn't do the social stuff very well, but we had a lot of issues with the school district and politicking with the unions and the parents, and apparently it turned out that was something I'm good at." This mother said she would intervene among the principal, the parents, and the teachers and "help them all talk to each other." And she mentioned in passing that she also ended up volunteering on field trips and in classrooms that her own children were not in simply because there was such a need.

- Another gifted mother shared how she came to the conclusion that the educational system would be a very poor fit for her daughter. Despite painful criticism from members of her synagogue, this mother ended up leaving her career in medicine to homeschool her profoundly gifted daughter from kindergarten until she started community college as a preteen.

- One of the mothers gave this overview of trying to fit her highly gifted daughter into a rigid school system:

"The most challenging time as a parent began when my daughter started school…So initially, there's great happiness and a little bit of pride [when you learn your daughter's highly gifted], and then I found out about the battles that I had to fight…I remember feeling like we need to get a handle on this. So we took [her] to be tested privately by a wonderful psychologist who stated, 'If your daughter was as deviant on the other side of normal as she is on the gifted side, she'd be confined to a crib the rest of her life.' That was a stunning thing to hear."

This mother added:

"With my daughter, I just felt like I was banging my head against the wall, dealing with the school district. I always pushed for what was the best for her. I'm sure I was known as the pushiest mother in the school, but I just got to the point that I didn't care…I wanted her to be challenged, and I knew that she wasn't especially. I actually got so frustrated I went back and got a master's in gifted education so I would have some credibility. But it was painful dealing with the school."

"I remember one conference with the school counselor that was just horrible. My daughter had a gifted teacher in high school, who was a saint, who went to the conference with me. After the conference, I was real teary, and he asked why, and I replied, 'I'm just so weary from fighting this battle.' He said…I'm going to cry thinking about this…'Did you ever think that God gave you a child like your daughter because he thought you could handle it?' But there were many times I thought, *Oh, I would give anything to have a* normal *kid!*"

GIFTED MOTHERS' INTERACTIONS WITH INDIVIDUALS OUTSIDE THE FAMILY

When gifted mothers confront the difficult reality they and their gifted daughters face outside the safe confines of home, another challenge awaits them. When attempting to speak openly about our gifted daughters—discussing their unique behaviors, their special educational needs, or pride in their accomplishments—we fear not only being shunned personally but also negatively impacting our daughter's already tenuous social status and reputation. If a gifted daughter is an outcast, given her atypical intelligence, if her mother speaks up, she may compound this situation by drawing attention to the fact that her daughter has special needs. This may create a situation where both mother and daughter are viewed with mixed reactions—as lesser than, because they're misfits, but also with envy because of the myth that for gifted students, the world is their oyster and their high intelligence level puts them at the head of the pack in our increasingly competitive culture.

For parents of children further down the IQ scale who may be grieving over the obstacles they perceive their children will face in our culture, talking about issues related to our gifted daughters can be taboo. Most people don't see giftedness as a special learning need but rather as a ticket to ensuring future value or success. People think it's easier for parents of gifted, so when we are looking for support, others think we are bragging. They are typically unaware of the other characteristics related to giftedness that can make parenting these children difficult. And even if you keep your parenting struggles to yourself, just being identified as the parent of a gifted child makes you more likely to be on the receiving end of completely unwarranted hostility.

The general sentiment is "so what's the problem again with being too smart?"

Who then can these gifted women turn to outside of their family? Who can they rely on for support during tough times or celebrate with during good times? In many instances, these mothers pick up on cues from friends as well as parents of their daughter's cohorts that it's not appropriate to talk about their daughter's giftedness. Jill Williford Wurman, director of research and development at the Grayson School for Gifted, captures this reality in her article "Warning: Parenting a Gifted Child May Be Hazardous to Your (Mental) Health," stating that being unable to connect with other parents to either commiserate or celebrate can be terribly isolating. She describes the situation:

> "Relating a story about how impossible it is to keep your voracious reader's brain fed may sound to the parent of a reluctant reader like someone singing the blues by crooning lyrics like: "Woe is me—my diamond shoes are too tight."....Similarly, if your child is performing exceptionally well at school.... but...is deeply unhappy and disengaging more and more from school, even excellent grades don't quell your fears about what to do for them. Unless you're living this story, it's nearly impossible to convey that without sounding whiny...While it's hard to feel supported in your efforts as a mother or father if your child's needs are out of the ordinary, it's all the more stressful if no one believes you."

In addition, because gifted children display more outside-the-box traits the further they are from the average IQ range, mothers of profoundly gifted children may find little in common with mothers of more mildly or moderately gifted children. Parents of highly and profoundly gifted children have difficulty describing how different the needs of their exceptional children are without others thinking that they're boasting or that their girls are pathological. As we know, gifted individuals themselves are a highly diverse lot.

Kim Hildenbrand succinctly expresses something that most likely all mothers of gifted would like the world to know. In her article "My Son Is a 'Gifted Child.' Here's Why Raising Him Has Been Anything But Easy," she declares, "The thing is, none of us chose this." She adds, "When a friend told me her daughter missed the cutoff for the gifted program by a few points, it was all I could do not to say 'Lucky you!'" This sentiment contradicts the prevalent cultural assumption that parents of gifted children intentionally pressure them to be exceptionally smart and are, for the most part, tiger moms who push, prep, and hothouse their children to become the best and brightest. Nothing could be further from the truth in most cases. As Post states in her blog post "Is It All Right to Feel Proud of Your Gifted Child?": "Most [parents] stand back in puzzled wonderment as their [gifted] child dives into interests and passions, with little input on their part. In fact, many struggle to keep up with their whirlwind children." One of the mothers in the study echoed this sentiment. At a kindergarten teacher's urging, she had her firstborn tested and learned his IQ was 158 and he was reading at the eleventh-grade level. This mother shared, "It was scary, and I didn't want that…I then went on to spend two decades being viewed as one of those pushy moms…I repeatedly defended myself, 'I have roller blades on, trying to keep up with these kids. My one goal is for them [her son and gifted daughter] to just have one day when they are happy.'"

Trying to break down these barriers to connect with others outside the family involves risks: sharing our parenting reality, expressing our deepest feelings and concerns about parenting gifted girls, speaking up, and asking for help. When we attempt to do this, it can feel like we're letting go of our rung on the societal ladder that promises a safe haven for us and our children if we just go along with the status quo and try to act "normal." Letting go of this ladder means plummeting toward the unknown. Post acknowledges this and reflects that it's incredibly hard as parents of gifted when we feel we can't openly express our reactions and must squelch expressions of pride or joy in our child's achievement. For gifted mothers, this is merely a continuation of the cultural message they have been forced to live with since childhood: remain silent and mask who they truly are. Their posture can be described as "defensive silence" that involves striving to avoid conflict and to not be portrayed as bragging because our daughters happened to inherit high IQs. However, this silence only serves to distance us from making authentic connections and reinforces our feelings of being alienated and weird. When we observe everyone else (often more neurotypical folks) going along with the accepted cultural norms that seem to work just fine for them, we just assume we should too. This is why in part so many of us gifted mothers decide it's best to keep our authentic selves, unique needs, and exceptional potential, as well as those of our daughters, hidden while feeling shame and personal failure for not speaking up and expressing our truth.

One of the interviewed mothers shared this deeply personal account that provides insight into the comfort level gifted mothers feel at home versus in the outside world: "I don't like the spotlight at all. I enjoy teaching, because I actually have a role that I know I can do and enjoy performing if I can get out of being who I am and be this role instead. I can be Dr. [mother's last name]." When her daughter was little, this mother shared that she thoroughly enjoyed joking around with her and doing a lot of dancing and acting together: "I was comfortable—I didn't have to think, *Oh, now I have to put on this role,* because you can do things with your kids that you can't do with anybody else, because they just accept you. You are you."

BLAMING THE VICTIM

Experiencing the many pitfalls society places in the path of our gifted daughters as they develop can have a devastating impact on these very vulnerable and extremely sensitive children. A number of the fifty-eight sampled daughters fell victim to these. Unfortunately, their emotional reactions to the challenges they confronted sometimes resulted in them resorting to dysfunctional fixes. This behavior took the form of self-mutilation, eating disorders, depression, suicidal ideation, anxiety attacks, assuming fake personas, dropping out, dumbing down, running away, and/or substance abuse in an attempt to minimize their pain and suffering.

A number of mothers in the study shared heartbreaking scenarios, describing incredibly tough times during which their daughters began to self-destruct. In most cases, this behavior resulted from their girls' hostile school experiences, but a variety of other compounding stressors may have played a part as well. (It should be underscored that all these daughters eventually flourished, and how this came about, with the love and support of their amazing mothers, will be described in Book Two of this trilogy.) Some of these stories include one of the sampled gifted daughters becoming extremely withdrawn and uncommunicative during middle school when she began cutting herself. Her mother stated that it felt like a death in their family—"our lively, curious, happy little girl seemed to totally change overnight." Another mother disclosed that her middle school daughter was hospitalized for anorexia and that "going through this with our daughter was like living a nightmare." A third sampled mother discovered that her daughter had a serious writing disability in elementary school, and, unfortunately, the family was forced to move the next year for her father's job, which meant her daughter had to leave behind her best friend. Two years later, this bright girl was hospitalized for depression and bulimia. One of the interviewed mothers was forced to quit her job to be home when her thirteen-year-old daughter got out of school because she would melt when she walked through the door and cry for hours; this mother felt it was important for her to be home to comfort her and help her through this. Finally, one of the sampled daughters, despite being accelerated two grades, still greatly outpaced the classroom curriculum and could not relate to her neurotypical peers. When she started pulling her hair out, this bright girl was diagnosed with trichotillomania in fifth grade.

Other gifted mothers in the study described incidents where their girls acted out, mainly due to the incongruity between who their gifted daughters were and the mold society was trying to force them into. One gifted girl became extremely rebellious in middle school and maintained this stance throughout her college years. In high school, she frequently stayed out all night and was generally irresponsible despite every measure her parents resorted to in their efforts to turn this situation around. Another daughter struggled in school as a twice-exceptional student and started partying on a major scale when she went to college. Her parents and the gifted girl herself decided she should drop out of the expensive, private university in which she was enrolled. She then went to the community college near home, working part time and going to therapy. In high school, another daughter became involved with a group of homeless teens and wanted to hang out with them more and more. Her mother shared, "We were terrified she would run away. She seemed that angry and rebellious. Those adolescent years were very, very difficult." Finally, a group of sampled daughters could be described as "drop outs" (another pejorative label). One of the mothers stated that this was "the worst thing that could happen—when she dropped out of school… My mind started thinking about all the worst possibilities like my daughter's going to be a welfare mom. I thought I lost her, I really did." Fortunately, all of the "dropouts" in the sample eventually returned to school, graduated from college, and are successfully pursuing their passions. Another label applied to gifted females who, despite turbulent school histories, go on to excel is "late bloomers." But again, this is most likely a misnomer for those bright minds who, trapped in an educational system designed for more neurotypical brains, are finally fortunate enough to find themselves in learning or work environments where they can maximize their true potential.

And to make matters worse, those responsible for creating the context for these dysfunctional behaviors often tend to essentially blame the victim (and/or her mother) for her own suffering, thus making a bad situation even more traumatizing for mothers and daughters. It's heart-wrenching for gifted mothers to see our brilliant daughters doing so poorly when we know, in our souls, that they are capable and driven to achieve so much more. Then to be told it's our daughter's fault (and in many cases, our fault too) is like rubbing salt in a wound.

This gaslighting often occurs to gifted students who act out. A variety of negative labels are commonly applied to this group. These students are termed "disruptive" if they simply are bored and/or "underachievers" if they fail to measure up to the higher expectations placed on them. Interestingly, some in the gifted community have flipped this paradigm by using the label of "selective consumers" to denote those gifted students who refuse to engage in rote, meaningless tasks. Other bright girls are labeled "misfits" or diagnosed as "having poor emotional/social skills" if they have trouble connecting with more neurotypical age mates. Others who are grade accelerated are commonly labeled "immature" when in fact they literally are younger and less advanced in some areas of development than their classmates but require the intellectual challenge provided by skipping several grades ahead. Asynchronicity also leads to this kind of mislabeling.

FINDING A "SURE SHELTER" FRIEND

Another major challenge for gifted mothers involves supporting their daughters in their struggle to find and connect with true peers. Silverman writes in *Counselling the Gifted and Talented*, "When gifted children are asked what they most desire, the answer is often 'a friend.' The children's experience of school is completely colored by the presence or absence of relationships with peers." Sadly, finding and making friends is not easy for many gifted children and becomes even more of a challenge as a child moves up the IQ scale. This is not surprising given the fact that only a very small percentage of children are gifted, and even fewer are in the highly gifted category. This makes slim pickings in terms of finding a true peer, especially in a traditional classroom setting,

Wurman points out in "Beyond Playdates: Finding Gifted Friends" that parents of gifted children often have to go the extra mile to help their offspring find friends, given that like-minded peers are few and far between. She goes on to quote Dr. Dan Peters, cofounder and executive director of the Summit Center (from the Menda blog, "Friendship 101" by Van Gemert and Bear), who asserts that "Kids need to be mirrored—they need someone else who gets them, who values them, and who enjoys them for who they are." Typical social challenges for gifted children include their asynchronocity, which may result in social immaturity, their overexcitabilities, their possible twice exceptionality, and their general gifted characteristics like deep moral concerns, perfectionism, high energy, and drive. In addition, Wurman cites Ashley Freeborn, a counselor at Grayson School, who believes that gifted children are often "thirsty" for friends. "In a terrible irony, this very thirst can be off-putting to others who don't live emotional lives that are quite so intense. Gifted children…may be so thrilled at the very idea of making a friend at all that they throw themselves into the relationship wholeheartedly, which might be understandably overwhelming to another child." This can be disconcerting to potential friends who begin to view the high-energy gifted girl as "more" or, sadly, just too much. As Wurman puts it, "A gifted child often seeks not a buddy but a soulmate—and nothing short of that will do."

Dr. Miraca Gross also observed that gifted children's friendships are especially intense. This finding is based on her study of seven hundred children with a range of abilities, ages five to twelve, described in her article "Play Partner or Sure Shelter: What Gifted Children Look for in Friendship." Gross found that children's conceptions of friendship progress through a developmental hierarchy as they age. These stages, as described by Gross, include children's expectations of friendship as well as their beliefs about friendship. These expectations and beliefs become increasingly more sophisticated as they progress up the ladder:

Stage 1: "Play partner": In the earliest stage of friendship…a friend is seen as someone who engages the child in play and permits the child to use or borrow her playthings.

Stage 2: "People to chat to": The sharing of interests becomes an important element in friendship choice. Conversations between "friends" are no longer related simply to the game or activity in which the children are directly engaged.

Stage 3: "Help and encouragement": At this stage, the friend is seen as someone who will offer help, support, or encouragement. However, the advantages of friendship flow in one direction; the child does not yet see herself as having the obligation to provide help or support in return.

Stage 4: "Intimacy/empathy": The child now realizes that in friendship, the need and obligation to give comfort and support flows both ways, and giving affection, as well as receiving it, becomes an important element in the relationship. This stage sees a deepening of intimacy, an emotional sharing, and bonding.

Stage 5: "The sure shelter": At this stage, friendship is perceived as a deep and lasting relationship of trust, fidelity, and unconditional acceptance. Per Gross, "As a highly gifted 12-year-old boy described it: 'A real friend is a place you go to when you need to take off the masks…You can take off your camouflage with a real friend and still feel safe.'"

A key finding of Gross's study was that it showed what children look for in friends is dictated not so much by their chronological age as it is by their mental age. The gifted children in the sample were found to be substantially farther along this hierarchy than their age cohorts of average ability. For example, they were seeking friends with whom they could develop close and trusting relationships at ages when their more neurotypical age peers were looking for play partners. In addition, at all levels of ability and at all ages, girls were, on average, significantly further along the developmental scale of friendship conceptions than boys. The data suggest that a gifted girl may not only be seeking the intellectual compatibility of a mental age peer but may also be searching for a friend whose conceptions and expectations of friendship are similar to her own. Gross concludes that it's no wonder gifted children encounter difficulties with socialization. There is little common ground between a six-year-old girl seeking "sure shelter" in a friend and an age-peer looking for a "play partner." Sadly, gifted children often become acutely aware very early on that they seem to be looking for very different things in friendship than their age peers and that these things are not easily found.

For smart little girls, the whole matter of friendship is puzzling, according to Barbara Kerr and Robyn McKay in *Smart Girls in the 21st Century: Understanding Talented Girls and Women*. The bright girl quickly realizes that the other kids her age aren't reading at her level and often don't seem to understand the rules of even simple games, according to the authors, and she may get tired of her strenuous efforts to teach them how to have fun. And not only do the hobbies and interests of gifted children (determined by their stage of cognitive development as well as what they're looking for in a friend) set them apart, but their more highly developed sense of humor makes it difficult for them to find peers who chuckle at the same things. Their often mature sense of humor can sometimes be problematic, as Gross pointed out in a 2006 seminar: "If you are five and into puns and your classmates have no idea what you are talking about or finding funny, this can lead to loneliness…It's difficult to bond in friendship with people we can't laugh with!"

Most of us choose friends based on our similarities—gifted children do the same. They gravitate toward those who share a similar level of intellectual and emotional development. Ironically, Gross states these gifted students, who don't easily form friendships with more neurotypical age peers, are sometimes mistakenly labeled "emotionally immature" when just the opposite is true. Often, solitary play for a gifted girl simply underscores the fact that she has no peers who share her interests and ability level rather than indicating social maladjustment or peer rejection. Again, this highlights the importance of looking at systemic problems rather than blaming the victim.

In fact, some gifted children can grow to feel very lonely in school systems that place students with age cohorts rather than combining age groups. This dysfunctional environment not only negatively impacts their relationships with peers, but perhaps more importantly, it can be a huge blow to their social-emotional development and have a lifelong negative impact. In her interview with Michael F. Shaughnessy, Ruf explained the critical need for gifted children to spend time together:

> When any child gets to spend the majority of his or her time among true peers, social and emotional needs are more likely to be met. It is when we do not fit in with the group we spend the majority of our time with that we can feel awkward, lonely, and generally out of sorts. So…which do I feel is primary—the social, emotional, or cognitive needs of the gifted? I'd have to say finding true peer groups will lead to meeting all three needs.

Although many younger gifted children may be proud and grateful that they are bright, they eventually may come to realize that being bright, along with the other characteristics that often accompany giftedness, alienates them from their peers. As Gross notes, the attraction of the camaraderie and acceptance by their peer group may prove too hard to resist, especially if the gifted girl has struggled with finding friends and yearns to fit in. For her, academics and being her authentic self may start to take a back seat as she faces an uneasy compromise between her interests, drive, and high potential and a burning desire to be accepted by the group. As Dr. James Webb and fellow authors note in *A Parent's Guide to Gifted Children*, in an ideal world, "a child will find peers who will not force her to choose between the need for affiliation and the need for achievement."

However, other gifted children may be less willing, or less able, to compromise themselves and their abilities for the sake of acceptance by the group. These children often become "loners," preferring to invent solitary intellectual games or pursue academic interests on their own. Because they find little interest in peer interactions, they concentrate on gaining knowledge and academic achievement. This occurs, most likely, at the cost of developing social-emotional skills. A significant number of gifted children tend to be more introverted than their more neurotypical peers, so making the choice to prioritize intellectual pursuits over socializing with others may come more naturally, although this may still result in them feeling lonely and isolated. But as Gross found, because a characteristic of highly gifted children is their preference for the company of only a few close friends rather than large, looser groups or "surface" relationships, this probably makes this choice less difficult. In addition, having just a few friends and more alone time appears to be important to many gifted children, because it creates the context for them to concentrate on developing their ideas and abilities. As Kerr found, gifted girls, who later became eminent as adults, share a common trait: they all seem to need large amounts of alone time to read or think or follow other pursuits.

However, their daughters' choice to spend time alone and have only one or two friends (or in some cases, no friends) can be hard for some mothers of gifted girls who feel it's important for their daughters to develop connections with people outside their family, learn to get along with others, and basically have some fun. It's understandable that these mothers want their daughters to be well liked (or, truthfully, loved by others as much as they love their girls), but when our daughters approach adolescence, going along with their peers may not always be a good thing. And for some bright girls, growing more conscious of and feeling pressured by peer influences may create internal conflict. One of the interviewed mothers stated that both she and her daughter agreed that, in hindsight, it was best that she was not close friends with any of her high school peers. They felt that because most of the students at her school were involved in drugs and other self-destructive behaviors, the daughter's choice to stay isolated from this negative culture was best, although this resulted in several lonely years for the daughter.

For many gifted children, who are hyperaware of their surroundings, trying to make sense of the different, and sometimes contradictory, social messages they experience growing up can be extremely confusing. As Barbara Clark notes in *Growing Up Gifted: Developing the Potential of Children at School and at Home,*

> Young children may start out to become what their parents value. When they begin school, they must shift to their teachers' values. How closely the values of parents and teachers are aligned will determine the energy that must be expended. Later, students discover peer values. For example, a gifted girl may discover that, if she wishes to be considered feminine and gain acceptance, the perfect papers required by parents and teachers become a liability. The challenge of inquiry into unusual subjects becomes less rewarding. Again, peer values may cause a re-ordering of accepted parental and teacher values. In either case, students may decide to use their giftedness to appear not at all gifted.

As children approach middle school, gifted boys' popularity increases while gifted girls become the least popular. Given this reality, masking their giftedness is not an uncommon strategy for gifted girls. A number of mothers echoed this sad truth. One shared, "My daughter doesn't speak up, because she knows the other kids don't understand what she's talking about. She feels weird—lonely and misunderstood—while the other students think she feels better than they are. She wishes she could just be 'normal.'"

Because our culture prizes conformity, the situation for a bright girl frequently becomes increasingly problematic as she progresses through school. If she has been a high academic achiever in the early elementary grades, these accomplishments are often viewed by peers as threatening in the upper grades. Not only does her academic success underscore the relative weakness and inadequacy of those who are not performing at this level, but as we've seen, being an exceptionally smart female of any age is frowned on in our culture in general. As stated in *A Parent's Guide to Gifted Children*, "To be popular, girls 'should' be nice, sensitive, friendly, passive rather than aggressive, compliant, pretty in the sense of having well-groomed hair and stylish clothes, and not too bright. Notice how many of these qualifications are irrelevant to academic success or even run counter to those characteristics shared by eminent women." The focus on maintaining the "right" appearance means that girls must allocate lots of time, resources, and energy to pursuits contrary to maximizing their potential. This may be one reason a number of daughters in my study chose to hang out with boys, who tended to share similar values. Given the gendered socialization for boys, focused more on competition, risk taking, achievement, and being more agentic, these gifted girls may have felt they had more in common with them.

In the absence of gifted peers, Post states on her blog, *Gifted Challenges,* (in an article titled "Welcome to Gifted Parenting, A checklist of emotions"), that the self-doubt and insecurity of gifted are often fueled by an excruciating awareness of their differences and compounded by sometimes painful experiences with ostracism and bullying. Post goes on to note that, despite many achievements, "some gifted adults bear the burdens of their childhood scars. The years of outlier status and difficulty relating to peers take a toll…Many still feel like misfits." The flip side of this kind of toll was described by a mother in the study—her middle school peer group chose to bully other girls in their class. Wanting to fit in, she went along with this but has lived to deeply regret her behavior.

According to *A Parent's Guide to Gifted Children,* many successful gifted adults mention that they did not have a true peer group until late in life. Although a number of daughters in my sample were able to find a social comfort zone when they went off to college, some continued to struggle socially into adulthood. This was the case for one of the interviewed daughters. However, with a family of her own, she found a new source of social connections, of sorts, with a few other mothers:

> "The transition to motherhood was actually really good for me, because for so long I hadn't really had friends. And I still struggle with the friend thing. I still feel different. It's a struggle because I have such unique children, especially my oldest. Some people just can't handle that…It's a challenge. It's hard to

find people who can just accept us…So I'm still struggling with the friendship thing. But I have to say that when I became a mom that was just a huge introduction to the world of women, which I had been without for many years. So for me it was a new thing! You've got a common ground. Whereas before that, as an engineer and PhD candidate, it wasn't as much…there wasn't as much common ground. And there just weren't that many women. And I wanted to talk about science and weather and weird things…[laughing]. So it was hard to find… When I was younger, I just felt like I was missing something. Like I needed those friends and 'Oh, I'm lonely. I miss that.' And I'm to the place now where I'm good. Come or go…people come in and out of my life, and I'm grateful when they're here. And I don't need…I'm not feeling that need anymore. I don't know if that's good or bad."

She shared that having a large family was part of this: "That was a big part of the reason I really wanted…I really wanted three. Four was a surprise, and five was a shock. But I thought, *What a gift for each other*.…I want them to have people they relate to that get them their whole life, because I just don't think you can replace that."

THE SOCIAL CHALLENGES GIFTED GIRLS FACE PUT AN added burden on gifted mothers and their daughters to work harder and dig deeper to find meaningful connections outside the family. They must ferret out intellectual peers, activities, learning environments, and resources to provide mental stimulation, meaningful conversation, and creative outlets. The more gifted the child, the greater the challenge. During the elementary school years, mothers and their daughters slowly realize the need to look beyond cultural boundaries for "appropriate" friends, searching beyond chronological age limits, socioeconomic status differences, and, with the internet, beyond the limits of geography. In many cases, according to psychologist Maureen Neihart in her article "Finding True Peers," gifted children are similar in cognitive and social development to children two to four years older. Or they find companions of the opposite sex. One of the profoundly gifted daughters in the sample enjoyed sitting with a brilliant, elderly gentleman in her neighborhood on his front porch and having deep conversations with him on her way home from school.

Some environments, apart from one-on-one interactions with peers, may provide a proxy for "sure shelter" companionship, as a number of daughters discovered. One mother commented that her daughter frequently self-isolated in the school library, which underscores how many gifted girls identify closely with characters in books. (Judith Wynn Halsted's *Some of My Best Friends Are Books* contains an annotated bibliography of more than three hundred books recommended for gifted students.) Another mother noted that her daughter sought refuge during her free periods in high school in the art studio, under the guidance of an understanding art teacher. Many interviewed mothers mentioned their daughters' involvement in organized activities like drama, marching band, and sports teams. These provided social opportunities but in very structured settings, where everyone was focused on the same goal and the gifted girls felt accepted and part of the group.

Webb and his coauthors point out that trying to keep an eye on how their gifted child is doing socially while not interfering too much can be a delicate balance for parents. This is especially true for an extroverted mother who may prioritize having many close friends and worry when her more introverted daughter chooses to have only one. Because our culture prioritizes social skills and extroversion, it creates the context for those who prefer to keep more to themselves to often feel less than. A mother's efforts to mold her daughter's behavior in a way that will make her daughter more popular and socially accepted typically come from a good place—she understands the hurt of being unpopular in our society and wants her child to be happy and feel accepted.

But even more introverted mothers may struggle in this area. For those who experienced being lonely and rejected gifted as a child, seeing their daughter going through the same thing can be painful. Unfortunately, this may cause a maternal overreaction that, rather than helping, may make the gifted daughter feel more like a misfit and loser, exacerbating the problem.

CHAPTER 9

Challenges Finding Professional Support

While in the throes of dealing with these parenting challenges, some gifted mothers decide to turn to professionals for help. Nearly half of the mothers in my study shared that they had received some form of counseling or therapy over the course of their parenting journey, and more than a third of their daughters did as well. Most mothers who reach out for professional help are concerned about whether what their daughter is experiencing is "normal." Should she be assessed, and if so, what does that involve? They may worry about whether they should change their parenting approach or tweak something in their daughter's environment like schools or peers. Or they wonder if their daughter would benefit from some type of medication.

Webb and his coauthors advise that a parent should seek professional assessment and guidance if a problem such as anxiety, sadness, depression, or poor interpersonal relations continues for longer than a few weeks. However, reaching out for professional help is not always easy. It can take time, money, effort, and courage. For starters, a gifted mother needs to have some clarity regarding who will be the focus of this help or, in other words, who the primary client is. This client may be the mother, her daughter, both the mother and daughter, or the whole family, although this may fluctuate over time. Having some vision about what the mother hopes professional intervention will accomplish is also important. Psychologist Dr. Aimee Yermish's blog, *da Vinci Learning Center*, contains her article "Clues on Finding a Therapist for a Gifted Client." It states that the goal of professional help is not "to get our kids (or us!) to act like everyone else. The goal is to help us figure out who we are and how to act like *ourselves*, just in an adaptive way."

Figuring out how to get started and who to turn to is often the first piece of the puzzle. Doing some quick and dirty information gathering on your chosen search engine about the issues of concern and the treatment options may help to increase your knowledge base—with the understanding, of course, that everything on the internet needs to be taken with a grain of salt and the source evaluated.

Targeting which type of specialist can best address the presenting problem may be difficult, but informally surveying the parents of your gifted daughter's peers, teachers, and any gifted specialist in her school or school district for recommendations may yield some results. However, in many cases, mothers reach out initially to their daughter's pediatrician. Ideally, the mother can work together with the pediatrician to zero in on the specific area of concern and determine if this issue would benefit from professional intervention. If specialized care is deemed necessary, the pediatrician may attempt to provide this directly or recommend another healthcare provider like a counselor, psychologist, psychiatrist, occupational therapist, speech-language therapist, educational psychologist, and/or neurologist. In *Parenting Gifted Children: The Authoritative Guide from the*

National Association for Gifted Children, Edward Amend and Richard Clouse point out that engaging your child's physician is often beneficial given that they can interact with educators and other health professionals, which may be necessary to obtain appropriate educational or professional services.

But a note of caution is in order when turning to your daughter's physician. Amend and Clouse state that most physicians, unfortunately, receive little if any training on the needs of gifted and may need direction and assistance to understand the situation. Often you, the parent, are in the best position to provide that information. In her article "The Misunderstood Face of Giftedness," Dr. Marianne Kuzujanakis quotes Dr. William Smith, the former dean of the Menninger School of Psychiatry, who cautions, "Giftedness can be confused with some psychiatric disorders, obscure other disorders, and it often needs to be included in treatment planning." Kuzujanakis goes on to state, "Pediatric primary care physicians diagnose psychiatric conditions and prescribe psychotropic medicine, but rarely feel adequately prepared by their training to do so."

As evidenced by this warning, whether the pediatrician herself tries to address the presenting problem or recommends another professional better suited in the area, it is critical to ensure that the chosen expert is aware of and understands the complexities of giftedness. And finally, it's important to ensure that this individual is the right fit (personalitywise, valueswise, and perhaps even sense of humorwise) for the gifted mother, daughter, and/or family.

In some cases, having your daughter assessed by a professional can provide valuable information. Webb states that a thorough professional assessment focusing on the child may take several hours, spanning two to three appointments, to obtain an accurate assessment of the child and her environment, costing between $400 and $1,500 (in 2005). This fee can be higher depending on the location as well as the amount and type of testing recommended. Adding to this the burden of scheduling appointments, arranging transportation to and from the professional's office, taking time off work and from a busy school schedule, and the psychic energy needed to motivate yourself or your daughter to go to the session, it becomes obvious that getting help from experts sounds a lot easier than it may be in reality.

However, some of these may be mitigated through counseling/therapy sessions via the internet. Finally, another hurdle to reaching out for help is the strong disincentive for most gifted mothers to openly admit they are struggling. Their fear of being blamed, judged, and labeled a "bad mother" can trigger a gifted woman's lifelong history of being misunderstood and maybe labeled as pathological or weird. Up to this point in her life, her attempts to admit she is having a problem or voicing a need may not have been successful in improving her situation, and going outside the safe haven of her family involves a huge risk. The courage needed to speak up and try to connect with a stranger to help her and/or her daughter deal with her deepest emotions and personal issues can, sadly, be beyond the capabilities of some gifted females. Several of the interviewed daughters in the study mentioned that they would have benefited from professional help growing up but that this simply wasn't something that was done in their family.

However, overcoming these hurdles often proves extremely beneficial. As pointed out in *A Parent's Guide to Gifted Children*, the benefit of finding a supportive professional can often be worthwhile: "In the end, you may find a professional who not only understands the needs of gifted children but who also knows the needs of your family. A good therapist is a resource that does not end. This professional can become a guide, advocate, and anchor point for you and your family well into the future." And given the myriad challenges gifted women with gifted daughters face, having an advocate in your corner over the course of your parenting journey may be worth overcoming all the challenges involved in finding them.

A PROFESSIONAL KNOWLEDGEABLE ABOUT GIFTED

Sadly, some gifted females may find themselves at psychological risk when seeking therapeutic help. Like the typical "good parent/normal child" development models that don't apply to neurodiverse mothers nurturing neurodiverse daughters, most typical treatment models don't apply to gifted mothers and their daughters. This is especially true for twice-exceptional individuals and those at the very upper ends of the IQ scale. The need for modifications in counseling and therapy for gifted was underscored by the Columbus Group: "The uniqueness of the gifted renders them particularly vulnerable and requires modifications in parenting, teaching and counseling in order for them to develop optimally."

Helping a gifted individual increase their self-awareness by identifying their unique way of perceiving and experiencing reality, with the goal of enabling them to best use this knowledge to optimize their environment, requires the expertise of a professional who understands and appreciates their exceptional worldview and, ideally, is gifted themselves. Unfortunately, it can be difficult to find a professional knowledgeable about giftedness (although the websites of organizations serving the gifted may list such experts, most stress that they have not vetted them). As Webb notes, few mental health professionals have received special training in the social-emotional needs of gifted individuals and often assume that being gifted is only an asset, never a liability. And for those who do have some knowledge about this unique population, the little training they do have about giftedness is often full of misconceptions.

As a result, professionals unfamiliar with issues related to giftedness may diagnose as dysfunctional those characteristics typically associated with high potential. This situation may put their gifted clients at greater risk, thereby exacerbating the situation they were seeking help to correct. Tolan, a member of the Columbus group, commented to Michael Piechowski, as noted in his book *Mellow Out, They Say. If I Only Could,* that some of the very greatest gifts bring an inevitable downside that you cannot "cure" without curing the gift at the same time. Therefore, it's critical to find experts who will not view gifted behaviors as necessarily representing behavioral disorders and will place them within a wider, more informed context. And not only does misdiagnosis (sometimes accompanied by medication) often make a bad situation worse (as therapist Lynne Azpeitia and Mary Rocamora point out in their article "Misdiagnosis of the Gifted"), but "there is the danger that the wonderful inner fury of the gifted process will be neutralized, thus minimalizing the potential for a life of accomplishment and fulfillment. As a result, those who have the most to offer society are the least likely to get their therapeutic needs met." And this applies to both gifted mothers and their daughters.

For example, Azpeitia and Rocamora mention that the inner conflict many gifted individuals experience may actually represent a first step in developmental progress rather than a degenerative indication of dysfunction. This inner conflict often drives the gifted client to higher levels of personality growth than her more neurotypical peers. The psychologist and psychiatrist Kazimierz Dabrowski initially described the steps that this inner conflict, or existential depression, follow in achieving greater personality development. Webb elucidated his theory in his article "Dabrowski's Theory and Existential Depression in Gifted Children and Adults," which opens with a quote from Woody Allen: "It's very hard to keep your spirits up. You've got to keep selling yourself a bill of goods, and some people are better at lying to themselves than others. If you face reality too much, it kills you." Individuals with high potential are frequently less able to lie to themselves and just accept reality as it is, which is necessary to lead a life of quiet desperation like the masses. Instead, they often reject the socially constructed life scripted for them and seize the opportunity to design and control their own destiny. Ideally, they do so with the guidance and support of loved ones and, if needed, a therapist who understands what they are going through. As Webb cautions, "the experience of existential depression can challenge an individual's very survival and represents both a great challenge and at the same time an opportunity…an experience leading to personality growth."

Other common behaviors related to giftedness that may be misdiagnosed as pathological include ADHD, Oppositional Defiant Disorder, mood disorders, sleep disorders, and OCD, to name a few. Kuzujanakis says, "Normal giftedness can be easily confused with a diagnosable mental disorder. Gifted kids may talk a lot, have high levels of energy, and be impulsive or inattentive or distractible in some settings—similar to symptoms of ADHD. It's not unusual for gifted kids to struggle socially, have meltdowns over minor issues, or have unusual all-consuming interests—all pointing to an inappropriate diagnosis of autism." Additionally, Webb and his coauthors name multiple personality disorder as a behavior associated with giftedness that might be misdiagnosed, stating that anecdotal evidence shows that the two are related. As discussed, one of the daughters in the study adopted a highly constructed different personality on two separate occasions (most likely in environments where she felt uncomfortable), but, fortunately, her mother was gifted and a psychologist herself and didn't rush to diagnose these incidents as pathological.

However, giftedness may in fact coexist in some cases with behavior problems, pathologies, and/or disabilities (as evidenced in twice-exceptional individuals.) As a result, misdiagnosis of gifted individuals is common and can take two different paths. Professionals may diagnose normal gifted behavior as pathological or actual behavior problems as giftedness. Therefore, some gifted may be erroneously labeled and medicated for mental health disorders they do not have while others go undiagnosed and untreated for learning or mental disorders they do have. Because giftedness plays such a major role in the diagnostic process, the need for an expert knowledgeable in giftedness is critical in ensuring that they will do no harm. Kuzujanakis quotes Dr. Jack Wiggins, former president of the American Psychological Association: "This is a widespread and serious problem—the wasting of lives from the misdiagnosis of gifted children and adults and the inappropriate treatment that often follows."

SEARCHING FOR A GOOD FIT

Determining if you, your daughter, and/or your family will be the primary client is important when searching for professional help, because some experts specialize in working with individuals (and even different age groups), couples, or families. If the mother is seeking help for herself, the right expert for best meeting her needs may be very different from one who would best work with her gifted daughter. For example, one interviewed mother shared that the therapist she found for her teen daughter, who was experiencing depression, proved to be an excellent fit for her daughter and mentored her for years, while the mother felt that she and the therapist never quite clicked.

Finding the right expert for you and your family typically involves screening the resources available. Online sessions can play a role for those who live in rural communities. Starting this search with the understanding that interviewing several different professionals to ensure they have the necessary expertise and personality to best address your needs helps ward off the feeling that you must just go with the first one you contact. In other words, mothers have every right to shop around and be assertive about choosing the expert who best meets their criteria. Professionals are people with different personalities, values, experiences, educations, backgrounds, senses of humor, and preferred parenting approaches. Some mothers find that it may take interviewing a handful of different professionals to find the right one. And even after one is selected, Webb states that the counseling or therapy process should be started on a trial basis, because sometimes a very competent professional may simply have a personal style that doesn't fit.

Yermish cautions that when interviewing prospective providers to assess their expertise related to giftedness, "Pay attention not just to the content of the responses, but also to the nonverbal signals and your gut feeling about how they're responding to the notion. If you feel like you're getting a dismissive or hostile reaction, *go somewhere else* and don't feel bad about it." She adds, "Anyone who frames giftedness as being part of the problem, anyone who defines the intensity and drive and perceptiveness and differentness and postformal reasoning as 'the thing that's wrong with you', leave and don't look back."

THE COMMON "BLAME MOM" REACTION

As gifted mothers know only too well, life with their gifted daughters can be both exhilarating and exhausting, triggering reactions that we're not so proud of and sometimes causing the mother/daughter relationship to suffer. Some of our gifted daughters' behaviors as well as our own—like being intense and strong willed, questioning everything constantly, being extremely sensitive, and going nonstop—can be challenging to live with and, at times, lead to power struggles, arguments, tantrums, and withdrawal.

If a professional working with the family is aware of the impact a gifted daughter's behavior can have on the mother/daughter relationship as well as within the family in general, this helps to avoid the typical knee-jerk reaction many experts may have about the cause of problems in the family dynamics, which is frequently "blaming Mom." Starting in the later part of the twentieth century, mental health professionals have made progress, slowly veering away from solely blaming mothers for their children's atypical behaviors, and they now tend to consider other factors like genetics that might be at play. Sadly, the scientific advance of considering genetic causes came too late to refute the cruel "refrigerator mother" theory (prominent in the 1950-1970s), also known as Bettelheim's theory of autism. Bettelheim asserted the cause of autism for the children on his caseload was a lack of maternal warmth. It's heartbreaking to imagine how devastating this misdiagnosis was to the women involved.

In his article "Are Parents Always to Blame? A Therapist Answers," Michael Bader notes that "many a mother has had to bear the terrible weight of unfounded self-blame and doubt about her role in producing a child who is schizophrenic or autistic. It's only in recent years that the biologic underpinnings of these and other mental afflictions have been discovered." Today, it is widely accepted that children are born with certain temperamental tendencies and personality characteristics, and in many cases, their nature trumps their nurture. But Bader goes on to question why some therapists continue to blame parents, especially mothers, for what's wrong. He holds that this posture reflects a sexist bias in psychology and, as we've seen, also in our culture. Bader states, "Since Dr. Spock's famous books…we've been led to believe that parents—and mothers in particular—have an almost omnipotent power and responsibility for raising either healthy or unhealthy children, and the load of guilt and blame suffered by parents as a result has been unwarranted and unfair."

And because gifted mothers often exhibit unique characteristics themselves, they are especially vulnerable as targets for parent blaming if their gifted tendencies are mislabeled as pathological and negatively impacting their parenting. Yermish points out that being misunderstood by experts is not just a problem for our gifted children:

"Gifted adults *also* struggle to make sense of ourselves in a world that often isn't even remotely a good fit. Giftedness isn't just a school-bound phenomenon, and it doesn't expire upon graduation—we are who we are across domains and throughout the lifespan."

Cultural myths about motherhood are prevalent in the mental health field. Experts often hold strong beliefs about what being a "good" mother entails even though there are lots of contradictory professional opinions about what parents should and should not do. This begs the question: why blame mothers if most experts themselves can't agree? And this is especially true as it relates to parenting a child who is atypical, in which case a typical "good" parenting model certainly doesn't apply. This was the situation for one of the women in the study. The mother described mentioning to a psychologist that when her gifted daughter was in elementary school, she seemed to be thriving and never complained about not being challenged, to which the expert replied, "Well, this speaks to the poor quality of your relationship." However, when this mother asked her adult daughter about this years later, the daughter shared that she never questioned her elementary school curriculum because she simply didn't know there was an alternative. A similar account was presented by another interviewed mother (herself a therapist) whose daughter only mentioned that "she was sick of pretending that school stuff didn't matter to her" during her senior year in high school. As this mother put it, "I hadn't realized that this had been an issue…I hadn't realized that it had been that level of problem for her." The insight this mother gave regarding why this occurred was that it was "really hard sometimes to know what's going on with our gifted daughters, because they do such a good job of protecting people around them." As these cases show, an awareness of giftedness and all that it entails can often help experts make more informed assessments of mother/daughter dynamics rather than jump to the conclusion that Mom was asleep on the job.

Sadly, when professionals disempower gifted mothers, fail to listen to their needs, and focus on blaming them, it can be traumatizing. This underscores the critical need to find a professional who can appreciate and point out their parenting strengths while collaborating with them to design better parenting strategies. Unfortunately, gaslighting gifted mothers may sometimes be the last resort too many professionals turn to when they realize that their traditional treatment approach is not working.

ATYPICAL TREATMENT APPROACHES FOR ATYPICAL CLIENTS

Parents (well, probably most potential clients, actually) sometimes approach experts with the expectation that they have some magic that will immediately solve the presenting problem. But like with most things, progress takes time, every family represents a unique living system, and every individual within the family is complicated, especially those who are neurodiverse. Therefore, any expert will need an appropriate amount of time to best discern the nuanced dynamics of the situation, requiring patience on the part of everyone involved. This is easier said than done for many gifted parents, however, given the high cost of treatment and the deep yearning of the mother, daughter, and family to heal the emotional pain they may be experiencing ASAP.

One key for experts working with gifted clients that greatly facilitates the therapeutic process is understanding and embracing the active participation of the gifted mother (and gifted daughter, if applicable and age appropriate), viewing them as an invaluable resource in working together to meet their stated goals. Webb and his coauthors of *A Parent's Guide to Gifted Children* stress that the relationship between professional and client "is very important and contributes to a positive outcome. Psychologists who work well with gifted children and adults tend to be flexible, open to questions, smart, creative, resilient, and skilled in avoiding power struggles." Gifted clients benefit from professionals like these who employ a collaborative treatment approach as opposed to a more directive one in which the expert hands down diagnoses and treatment suggestions based solely on his or her own wisdom. The traditional, directive therapeutic style failed miserably with one of the interviewed daughters dealing with trichotillomania. Her psychiatrist recommended that her mother hold her down and force her to look at her bare scalp in a mirror to see the harm caused by her anxiety disorder. Needless to say, according to the daughter, this strategy not only failed but further traumatized both mother and daughter.

Webb and his coauthors state when counseling services are being considered, the discussion should start with a clear understanding between the expert and mother, addressing the mother's questions, clarifying the relevant issues, and outlining the desired goals. They go on to note that if it's determined that therapy is needed for the gifted child, the parents should insist that the counselor or therapist meet with them and their child at least once for every three or four times the child is seen.

Yermish underscores that during this initial interview, when sharing your experiences related to giftedness, it's important that the professional "seems to have some level of personal empathy with those experiences—they don't necessarily have to have had them themselves, but it helps if they're close enough that they didn't experience their own intelligence as always a positive thing." Yermish adds that, ideally, the professional needs to be pretty smart: "When you're trying to figure out who you are and how you're going to exist in the world, you don't want to have to wait around for the therapist to catch up, or to feel like you're doing all the work yourself." After the initial meeting, when you leave, you should feel like you've been heard and understood and that you and the professional have reached a mutually agreed-upon approach to the process.

In her article "Successful Coaching and Psychotherapy for Multi-Talented Gifted and Creative Adults," Azpeitia details why a collaborative therapeutic approach is critical with gifted clients. She states that because gifted individuals are typically independent thinkers who maintain an internal locus of control, they tend to not automatically adopt or rely on the opinions of authority figures for direction or instruction. Although they may respect the professional's insights, they also value their own, so any suggestion or recommendation by the expert will be thoroughly evaluated before they choose to apply it to their situation. There is no greater gift a therapist can give than working together with a gifted individual. Azpeitia says,

> A therapist or coach who acknowledges and supports a gifted client's intuitions, perceptions and thoughts is important because the majority of gifted adults live much of their daily lives without anyone who can share or understand what they are seeing,

thinking or experiencing…Whenever a therapist or coach is able to consistently relate to a gifted client and his or her point of view, there's a turning point in the client's sense of aloneness and alienation. The experience of being supported and understood facilitates a gifted person's acceptance of self and his or her talents and abilities, which, in turn, frees the gifted adult to focus on utilizing her talents and abilities in new and different ways.

Azpeitia goes on to note that enabling a gifted client to see the way others view the world in order to connect with them (not conform to them) is an important step in helping her develop the skills necessary to assess situations correctly and to communicate and interact in her own best interests. She adds that this empowers gifted individuals to understand how to live a life with less stress, strain, or struggle. What an invaluable outcome this is for gifted mothers and daughters, and it certainly validates the fact that the risk they took to reach out for help was well worth it.

CHAPTER 10

Self-Actualizing for Gifted Mothers in the Perfect Storm

For gifted mothers, as a gifted female in an anti-intellectual culture and in a patriarchal country founded on the idea that women were less than where, as a woman, and especially as a mother, you're treated like a second-class citizen in the work world, and where the 24-7 role of nurturing your offspring (that you consider more important than anything you've ever done) is devalued (especially in light of your high potential) both in terms of status and monetary rewards, learning to love yourself and self-actualize in the middle of this Perfect Storm is quite an achievement. In fact, it's a miracle.

Society has historically framed self-actualization using criteria based on a male-dominated culture and a capitalistic system that equates success with how much money or fame one receives. "Getting ahead" is idolized. In this context, self-actualization is often unattainable and, in some cases, undesirable for bright women raising children. Today, American women of working age are the most educated ever (especially true for gifted females like the fifty-eight daughters in my study). But the current traditional career paradigm fails to provide the necessary infrastructure to support them, which makes it nearly impossible for most females, especially mothers, to apply their gifts and educational achievements optimally in the public sphere. While the financial returns and status for most jobs requiring advanced degrees such as positions in STEM fields, finance, law, management, and consulting have increased, so have the demands on employees to work long, inflexible hours. Many of these so-called "greedy professions" are described by Dr. Claudia Goldin as high-paying, high-pressure roles in fields like finance, management, law, and academia that demand workers be available at unusual times outside their contracted hours. They require that all professional employees, including nonparents and parents, be available round the clock. Parents can be on call at work only if someone is on call at home. In most families, this person is the mother. This explains in part why America has one of the lowest labor force participation rates for college-educated women and why women do not fare well in the race for eminence, according to "A Feminine Perspective of Giftedness" by Linda Silverman and Nancy B. Miller.

Silverman and Miller go on to note that eminence is a masculine concept rooted in hierarchical, patriarchal value structures of power and competition. Men control the designation of eminence and decide who will or will not be publicly recognized. Based on these metrics, society has yet to recognize the enormous contribution made by mothers who devote so much of themselves to the care and development of their children. "Success" in the public arena (where females must create ways to graft female functions onto traditionally male structures) comes at too high a price for many gifted mothers. This is because these mothers face ever-increasing career demands as well as the rising norms of intensive mothering, which requires keeping both themselves and their neurodiverse offspring functioning at their maximum level. As a result, many women are unable to achieve acclaim in their professional field because the main focus of their talents is on caregiving. Working alongside their male cohorts (who often have female partners at home, cheering them on and propping them up) while performing the equally demanding work of social reproduction that includes childbearing, childcare, housework, and the many other forms of labor required to create and sustain human life is like competing with one hand tied behind their back.

To thrive in both spheres requires total commitment to both roles. This is rarely possible even for highly gifted individuals, male or female. For gifted mothers, attempting to achieve their promise, using our current patriarchal definition of success and within the constraints of our patriarchal structure, is very similar to the analogy Tolan uses to describe the situation of a highly gifted child in our educational system—it's like putting a cheetah in a cage, limiting her freedom, choices, and ability to thrive. For many gifted women, the reality is that if they want to get to the top in their career (expending extra energy to overcome the misogyny in many workplaces), they should not have a family. Or if they choose to have a family, they must tamp down their ambition (or at least put it on the shelf for a decade or two). They often find that the trophies awarded at work, or the flow provided by a challenging job in their field of interest, simply are not worth the price both they and their children must pay on the home front. But this decision can be a painful one for gifted mothers who, unlike fathers, given our culture, do not have the privilege to procreate unhindered.

Anne-Marie Slaughter came to this decision after almost two years into her job as the first woman director of policy planning at the State Department. She realized that her desire to be with her family rather than away from home five days a week and that juggling high-level government work with the needs of two teenage boys was not possible. In her article "Why Women Still Can't Have It All," she asserts,

> The minute I found myself in a job that is typical for the vast majority of working women (and men), working long hours on someone else's schedule, I could no longer be both the parent and the professional I wanted to be....I realized what should have perhaps been obvious: having it all, at least for me, depended almost entirely on what type of job I had. The flip side is the harder truth: having it all was not possible in many types of jobs, including high government office—at least not for very long.

Another option, which many mothers in my study chose, is for gifted mothers to free themselves by creating a new script that is more flexible, organic, and fulfilling. One of the interviewed daughters was a mother of gifted eleven-year-old twins. She was financially fortunate enough to be able to achieve her wish to be a full-time mother until her children were in school. She was then given an alternative to the greedy position she held as an attorney pre-kids. She stated,

> "A lot changed when I had the kids and I asked, at that time, to go part time. I was an in-house counsel. I liked it but…I liked the more routine aspects of it,

but then when it got really challenging, it was less fun, and I didn't really like the real, real long hours, because I like my time at home. So when the kids came and I asked to go part time and they said no, I think it was pretty easy for me to say, 'Well, I'm having two babies at once. I'm just going to take a break.' And I really enjoyed those years with them a lot—so much. And I just started back…I'm just starting my third year, so I started a couple years ago, and I found this incredible situation of some buddies who were in law school with me. I ran into one of them at a swim meet, and they said, 'What are you doing?' And I said, 'Well, you know, every once in a while, I'll do a little part-time or freelance stuff if someone needs a lease looked at or something, but the problem is that I really cherish the time with my children and I really like summers off.' And these guys said, 'Oh, we need so much help. If you would just come and work for us fifteen or twenty hours a week during the school year, that would be great, and you could take summers and vacations off when they're off.' So I can't have a more ideal job. Although it definitely makes me feel like I'm a little bit more scattered at home and I'm a little bit more scattered at work, but not like someone who's working full time and year-round."

RUMINATIONS OF GIFTED MOTHERS REGARDING SELF-ACTUALIZATION

All gifted mothers are unique. They have distinct natures, personalities, and patterns of neurodiversity as well as variations in childhood histories, socialization, role models, and access to resources. Therefore, it's difficult, if not foolish, to try to identify the shared inner workings of their psyches. That said, a number of thought patterns related to the challenges of self-actualization for the forty-three gifted mothers in my study emerged as common themes.

One of these patterns that the gifted women were socialized to believe was related to the cultural notion that it's only by maximizing their potential in the public sphere that a gifted female can garner eminence, self-respect, and meaning as well give back for their exceptional abilities. Novelist Eleanor Catton's character in *Birnam Wood* provides a rather crass but apt description of the mental pressure society places on individuals to self-actualize, which, I believe, is exacerbated for gifted individuals:

> Every little thing now has to be about maximizing your potential and perfecting yourself...It has to be about your authentic journey towards physical and psychological perfection...Everything's a game, and if you want to win the game then you're going to have to optimize yourself, and actualize yourself, and utilize yourself...and, God forbid, that you should have an actual human experience of frailty or mortality or limitation or humanity—those are just distractions, obstacles, defects, They're inconveniences in the face of our curated, bespoke, freely f___ing chosen authentic existence, and we can never quite decide if we're the consumers of our lives or the products of them.

However, this internalized cultural message (to optimize your talents to win at all costs in the public sphere) shifted for many gifted females in my study when they had children. The new world of parenthood created the context to, as Rumi put it, "Sell your cleverness and buy bewilderment" and offered benefits (as well as limitations!) dramatically different from anything the gifted females had experienced in the public sphere. Like the gifted mothers Reis describes in her research, the mothers in my study stressed that despite all the challenges involved, they highly valued having children and shared that, in hindsight, they viewed it as the one achievement they were most proud of. But emotionally, there were times when these gifted mothers were torn between these two opposing and equally enticing frameworks of meaning without an internal script on how to survive juggling both.

If a gifted mother does attempt to maintain her career, she may find herself demonized for being ambitious, coldhearted, and self-interested for prioritizing her professional needs over her family's. This psychic conflict between career and family frequently results in many women ruminating about how the more time spent with their children means less time available to maximize their potential. And, conversely, time spent working leaves many worrying about how their children are faring in their absence.

In her article "The Special Challenges of Highly Intelligent and Talented Women Who Are Moms," Dr. Belinda Seiger presents the profile of gifted mothers who possess, as she puts it, the "rage to achieve." These mothers are motivated for the most part by a love of learning rather than financial gains or status. Seiger describes their never-ending passion to learn, create, and be intellectually productive as a constant in their daily lives even while raising children. Seiger shares that the gifted women she worked with in therapy described facing many moments of frustration when the demands of family and their need for intellectual immersion collided. One client labeled this drive to learn and to know as the need to feed her lion—she said, "if you don't feed the lion, it roars and makes itself known, for sure!" According to Seiger, if a gifted mother tries to repress key facets of her personality like her intensity, energy, curiosity, and high intellectual ability to focus solely on her family, this may lead to depression, anxiety, and feelings of being unfulfilled emotionally and intellectually. Not being emotionally and intellectually fulfilled, she underscores, can leave a gifted mother feeling "like I have lost myself."

Conversely, some bright women. whose lives prior to motherhood were heavily dependent on intellectual success for a sense of self, both in academia and professionally, may find a different type of internal lion to feed when they become parents. Before parenthood, they may have had limited awareness or experience in terms of finding deep emotional purpose in their lives. The joy in filling this void (or feeding her soul, if you will) related to authentically connecting to and nurturing another human being might both surprise and fulfill them in ways they'd never before imagined. As de Marneffe so poignantly states, "In our unfolding relationship with our baby or child, we sense an integration among the various registers of our experience: the yearning for closeness…the aspiration to reach the depth beneath the surface, to be, as Robert Frost put it, 'tripped into the boundless.'" Being immersed in a collaborative, caring, communal, and loving environment—as opposed to the more transactional, competitive, and every-man-for-himself reality of the work world—and watching her offspring thrive, in large part because of her care, can be a novel and immensely rewarding experience for a mother. This was true for one mother in my study. A highly successful physician and entrepreneur before having her daughter later in life, she decided to leave her career and found deep meaning (as well as intellectual challenge) in raising her profoundly gifted child.

Sadly, most of us as gifted women have learned to suppress our conflicted emotions about motherhood, because we don't feel that it's socially acceptable to acknowledge that we suffer. We deny or downplay what this inner struggle is doing to us and endure way more than we should. As psychologist Madeline Levine points out in *The Price of Privilege: How Parental Pressure and Material Advantage Are Creating a Generation of Disconnected and Unhappy Kids*, mothers in our culture are not allowed to be vulnerable—at least not publicly. "Vulnerability is a kind of admission—of hurt feelings, neediness, things not going well…In public we shine and so do our children." She states that often we hide our wounds and focus on presenting a "perfect" and formidable front. But as psychologist Susan David stressed in her TED Talk, "Research on emotional suppression shows that when emotions are pushed aside or ignored, they get stronger. Like that delicious chocolate cake in the refrigerator. The more you try to ignore it, the greater its hold on you. You might think you're in control of unwanted emotions when you ignore them, but in fact they control you. Internal pain always comes out. Always. And who pays the price? We do. Our children, our colleagues, our communities."

The fact that so many gifted mothers and their families not only survive but thrive in today's society is a testament to their resilience, adaptability, and, truthfully, their heroism.

Jane Caro comments in her book, *Accidental Feminists,* that what strikes her about women and their history is just how damn sane we have managed to stay. I strongly share this reaction after getting to know the gifted women in my study.

OBSTACLES TO SELF-ACTUALIZING FOR WOMEN IN MY STUDY

Like the wide variety in parenting approaches and strategies found in the study sample, the challenges the forty-three mothers faced in terms of self-actualizing were quite diverse as well. Every woman in the sample had unique skills, educational backgrounds, drives, career dreams, role models, access to resources, and career histories and obstacles when they first became mothers. As a result, they exhibited a range of approaches to maximizing their potential in the work world while raising their girls. From a handful who worked full time without skipping a beat in their professional careers over the course of their parenting journey and another few who made caregiving their full-time occupation to the majority who fell somewhere in between, each sampled mother had a unique narrative about self-actualizing while parenting her neurodiverse offspring.

Not surprisingly, the handful of sampled women who worked nonstop over the course of their entire parenting journey turned to extended family, nannies, childcare workers, and/or partners to meet their children's needs in their absence. These exceptionally energetic women were able to maintain demanding careers because a highly functional support system was available. One mother in my study was a partner in a law firm and returned to her career shortly after the birth of her firstborn. She shared,

"Our childcare provider took care of my daughters from the time they were born, and they formed a very strong bond with her. She would wait on them hand and foot and was very devoted to them. When our second daughter was born, I did take six months of maternity leave but still kept the childcare provider. I kind of used that period to spend more time with my first daughter, who had been very sick since birth…I am convinced that my working was a very positive thing in their lives, in part because of the modeling but even more because I did not turn my intensity on them. I believe that this freed them up to become who they uniquely are and that my imprint would have been stronger than optimum if they had been the focus of my life sans work."

This same mother went on to state that in addition to a nanny, her husband's involvement was also key to enabling their two-career household: "I am sure my working prompted my husband of necessity to be more involved in parenting than he would otherwise have been…My husband took the kids to school each day and has always taken their calls or otherwise interrupted his work life to put them first when they wanted or needed that."

Of course, despite their support systems, most of these mothers could not delegate all their domestic responsibilities. Despite their full-time careers, they were often the parent in charge of supervising the care providers and making other care arrangements if the situation changed. They were the on-call parent in case of emergencies and the parent in charge of ensuring that the household ran smoothly in their absence. In a few of these cases, these women were also the main breadwinner in the household.

Only five of the gifted women in the study were full-time mothers for the entire time their children were growing up. However, in addition to serving as primary caregivers, they were very actively involved in homeschooling, advocacy, and/or volunteering while raising their daughters. In many cases, this included starting gifted schools or programs or supporting education in a variety of other positions, like PTA president, or heading up associations for gifted children. One mother pursued a career for two decades only after her third child was nearly ready for college. This mother shared that her plan all along had been to be a full-time mother until her three children were raised. However, she was offered a great job during her last child's soccer game his senior year by another mother she had known for years, and it was too good to refuse. Her husband encouraged her to pursue it and assumed responsibility as the primary caregiver for their son until he graduated from high school a few months later. This enabled this mother to embark on a new career, traveling globally and loving every minute of it for more than twenty years.

These five mothers embraced full-time parenting as their form of self-actualization. For the most part, they were situated well enough financially to be free from the pressure to earn money to help pay the bills while they were full-time mothers or had decided jointly with their partners to make the financial sacrifices necessary to refrain from income-producing work. In her article "A Stay-at-Home Parent Is Not a 'Luxury,'" Allison B. Carter addressed this latter group and shared that saying it's a "luxury" that she can be a stay-at-home-mom is upsetting:

What goads me are the financial and lifestyle implications this statement carries. Yes, it is absolutely true, my husband and I are lucky that he has been able to secure and keep a job that can pay for all of us to live. I am aware that there are many families who require a dual income to sustain their basic needs....But the fact we can afford for me to stay home is the result of conscious decisions and choices, not luxury...Ours aren't the choices for everyone. But can we agree that, for many of us, they are choices that are made possible by conscious sacrifices, not wealth? There are so many different options for parents. A happy family...is one that makes the choices that work for them and respects the choices made by others.

One interviewed full-time mother described the factors relevant to her chosen role:

"We had our first daughter and made a very conscious choice that I would be a stay-at-home mother, because we believed in raising our own kids...So I actually did work [as noted in other parts of the interview, leading major advocacy and volunteer efforts and homeschooling her daughter for middle school] but wasn't paid for it in addition to raising the girls. When we decided to have kids, we knew that we wanted one of us to be a stay-at-home parent...and it was obviously going to be me, because he had a career in which he could make enough money to support the family and he has the personality—I mean he would *have* to be out working...So we made a conscious choice that I would stay at home at least for a while and he would work."

De Marneffe claims that often a woman's wish to care for her children is something she feels both hesitant to admit and called to defend. She goes on to note that current society has created a minefield where we step gingerly around our own feelings and those of others, balancing self-revelation and self-concealment in an effort to respect others' choices, maintain friendships, and not offend. "There is an intransigent insistence that something is lacking in women who spend their time mothering....Fear that their agency, power, prestige, and their very identities are at stake...In the current milieu, women rarely perceive their desire to care for their children as intellectually respectable and that makes it less emotionally intelligible as well."

For the rest of the sample (77 percent), the gifted mothers intermittently pursued income-producing work, either part time or full time, while raising their offspring. This involved moving in and out of jobs depending upon the needs of various family members, financial problems, career opportunities that popped up, and/or available childcare providers. Many of these gifted mothers had little to no consistent childcare support and lacked the fantasized "village" society gives lip service to. As a result, they were compelled to prioritize caring for loved ones over their careers and frequently had to prioritize the demands of their partner's career as well.

A number of the gifted mothers in these families faced economic situations that necessitated finding some type of income-producing work in a nongreedy profession. Ideally this work held some meaning for them (although one mother mentioned doing factory work to support her family while her husband was in medical school), but it often wasn't necessarily their "dream" job. But fortunately, for many of the women in this group, their intermittent involvement in the career world eventually morphed into a professional life that they found fulfilling and at the same time offered flexibility. This allowed them to straddle the public and private spheres while meeting the special needs of their gifted children. One of the interviewed mothers in this group described her career journey: "I wasn't working when I had all seven children. I was working but not in the traditional sense of the word—outside the home." But she stated,

> "I did work when I had just two of them, lecturing at a university in my husband's country for a while but decided I couldn't do that and worry about babysitting, because we couldn't get into the daycare center. So I quit and then taught at a high school, and then I just decided to get daycare qualifications and provide daycare at home, which was fine. Then we moved back to the States. I look back on it, and I had a lot of fun doing it."

This mother, who earned a PhD in behavioral science before having children, returned to work when her children were in middle school and high school. She worked full time in a learning disabilities program, which she enjoyed because it was relevant to her educational background and professional interests.

Studies have documented the challenges faced by gifted mothers who try to find some balance between working outside the home as a professional while also serving as the primary caregiver. The findings from this research demonstrate that mothers in fields like STEM and other "greedy" professional careers frequently lack flexible hours and are eventually forced to adjust their careers. One of the gifted daughters in my study, who was a lawyer on the partner track for a large law firm, had an aha moment when she realized that the overwhelming demands of her job were incompatible with her desired motherhood role. This incident occurred shortly after becoming a parent. After finishing up her work for the day at 7:00 p.m., she looked forward to going home to her baby daughter. However, at the last minute, she was given a huge legal brief that needed to be reviewed by the next morning. Eventually, she made the decision to abandon her dream of becoming a partner and find a more flexible and personally meaningful job, using her legal knowledge to help nonprofit organizations while still making it home in time for family dinner.

The group of mothers who moved in and out of the public sphere while raising their children faced other challenges to self-actualization. In one instance, a mother's gifted daughter became depressed in middle school and began cutting herself. At this point, her mother decided to stop working to provide her daughter with more emotional support. Another mother quit her teaching position to be home after her daughter started having anxiety attacks when she arrived home and her mother was still at school. In another family, the mother took a break from working full time when they started having trouble with their son, who eventually went to a therapeutic boarding school. She then switched to part-time work as a consultant because her daughter was still in school and "I wanted to be around" for her. But when her daughter turned sixteen and needed more independence, she told her mother, "Get full-time work and leave me alone—I can drive." Finally, a mother of fourteen-year-old profoundly gifted twin girls quit working outside the home to homeschool them. She said, "They need lots of special attention."

In addition to these issues, a significant number of daughters and/or their siblings suffered from physical problems that required these mothers to either cut back at work or quit. These included seizure disorders, congenital hip dysplasia, migraines, addiction, disabling accidents, chronic health concerns, severe allergies, and a brain disorder that required surgery.

Other obstacles that interrupted income-producing work for these women were their own health-related issues. One mother was teaching full time until her back deteriorated and she was put in a full body cast. A single mother developed a severe autoimmune problem that forced her to leave a "good job." Another mother was diagnosed with a serious chronic autoimmune disorder:

> "They diagnosed me with lupus when my daughter was little, and I'd been in the hospital for quite a long time, and I remember her coming to visit one day with the whole family. And I told her. 'Now, you listen to Grandma [who was caring for her daughter while she was in the hospital]. You be good and do that.' And that little stinker put her hand up to her forehead, saluting, and said, 'Yes, boss! Yes, boss!' She was just a little more than two, but she knew exactly what I was saying…That's how she was all throughout her life."

This mother realized at this point that she needed to prioritize self-care and find work that allowed for this so she could survive and raise her daughter but could also help support the family. Another mother experienced so much stress after deciding to leave her husband that she went into early menopause and had to take a medical leave from teaching school. One last example is a mother who suffered two heart attacks in her early fifties. She shared, "I'm a Type A personality, and unfortunately it works against me. I just always wanted to do and go and be." She said about her second heart attack:

> "I had bypass surgery. I was in and out of the hospital a lot for over ten years. Then two years ago, I went through breast cancer surgery and radiation… For someone like me who's Type A and likes to be in control of her own life…with cancer, I had no control. I've had to learn to let go and 'Okay, I can't control it, so let's just carry on, and if it hits again, we'll deal with it.' So it's a mental thing…I've realized, though, that it's much harder for men accepting a heart condition than for women. I think men feel like they're finished. 'I can't work anymore.' They feel helpless, whereas a woman comes home, and she's still got to do the cooking and the laundry and…There's no break for a woman. I'm sorry, but she's just got to carry on, whereas for a man—when he gets home, he gets babied by his wife… and apparently, they have a lot more psychological problems adjusting after a heart attack."

An example of every cloud having a silver lining!

The sampled women who lived with a partner while raising their children were frequently faced with the need to support their husband's or partner's career, which impacted their own efforts to self-actualize. In many instances, this involved providing significant in-kind support to help their partner run their own businesses. Not surprisingly, many of these partners were also gifted and, as such, tended to be more entrepreneurial and preferred to be their own boss. And their venture typically became the "family business" that benefited from the help given by the gifted mothers. As one of these mothers stated, "Supporting my husband's business is a lot of work." In addition, many of the interviewed mothers were required to uproot their families quite often when their spouse was transferred or needed to relocate his company to a more friendly business environment. A significant number of the women also faced long periods when their partners traveled for work or were assigned to military locations where families were not permitted, which resulted in the women serving as both mother and father while holding down a job. Fortunately, about half of the mothers in this category stated that their partners were very supportive when available, and several mentioned having the support of informal networks (relatives, neighbors, babysitters) that could step in when needed. That said, being in a household where life revolved primarily around the father's career typically meant the mother and children needed to adjust their daily lives, and find their own identities, within these more limited parameters.

Other women in the sample faced different challenges related to their daughter's father. More than one-fourth of the women who worked at some point while raising their daughters experienced problematic situations with their partners that forced them to remain in or reenter the workforce. In several cases, these mothers left abusive partners, taking their children with them, which made them the sole support of their families. Another mother left her alcoholic partner who never expressed any interest in his children: "He didn't have enough money to drive to see his children… So the first year, I was driving them to meet him twice a month. Then it got down to once a month and then every other. As the kids got older, it was harder and harder to get him to send the child support check. Then he completely pretty much disappeared." Two other sampled mothers were abandoned by their partners while their children were toddlers, leaving them and their offspring in dire financial straits. Sadly, it took these mothers, who had no college degrees at the time, years to pull their families out of poverty. One of these women, who remarried, chose to support her second husband in medical school, doing substitute teaching and short-term factory jobs, to provide for their family. Another mother mentioned that her family needed her help as well as her daughter's to survive financially.

> "We were struggling when we raised our daughter… We worked for every penny. We had our own business at one time [a small shop], and our daughter used to come and help out after school…It's so funny…When she was only fourteen, she could take money at the register and help the customers and talk to them like crazy. But my idea of having her come to the shop was to help me clean the inventory, dust, or take stock, but, oh no! My husband called her the counter queen. She wanted to stand there and take the money while Mom kept cleaning."

Finally, one gifted woman shared, "I did know that if I didn't work, I would go absolutely mad!" But in hindsight, she regretted working such long hours when her children were adolescents. She started out working six hours a day, but it became eight and eventually morphed into ten. "We were very understaffed, and I would just stay until the work got done. I was wearing too many hats at the same time at the job."

Sadly, nearly one out of four daughters in the study had biological fathers who were unsupportive parenting partners and a negative factor in their lives. This obviously increased the stress on mothers who were already challenged in trying to meet the special needs of their gifted offspring and limited their options to pursue self-actualization outside the home. A number of these mothers tried to shield their daughter from their unsupportive father and overcompensated for the father's harmful impact. One mother shared, "This is probably the area where my daughter got the short stick…and it probably influenced all the lessons she had to learn later on about dating."

The situation for the women in the study who experienced single motherhood (most for periods ranging from five to ten years) was extremely challenging at times, although their situations varied. One mother didn't want her alcoholic spouse to have any involvement with their children and required him to live outside the home. Another mother's spouse lived in their home but, as he shared with her, didn't love their children, and as a result, he had minimal involvement with them. Several of the mothers left abusive partners, while another group of sampled mothers were abandoned by their children's fathers when their daughters were very young. Unlike their male partners, these women had little choice (or desire) to just walk away from their families but were forced to scramble to figure out a way to put food on the table, pay the rent, and find childcare, pretty much all on their own. That said, one of the daughters in the study, who herself was a single mother, stressed the positives in her parenting situation, stating that she could follow her own parenting philosophy and style without having to compromise with a partner who may have conflicting beliefs. Additionally, she was free to focus solely on her daughter's needs as well as her own, allowing for a tighter bond between them.

The incredible external and internal pressure to be the best mother, spouse (if relevant), and professional possible at the expense of their own health and sanity is a high-pressure existence for many gifted women. These mothers are increasingly overburdened and strained by the need to meet both earning and care responsibilities. For many, they have been socialized to believe that if they just work hard enough and do everything perfectly, they can "have it all," and nothing will have to be sacrificed. The tasks assigned to gifted mothers as described below underscore the insane level of productivity mothers of neurodiverse offspring are expected to achieve:

- Keep my gifted child mentally and physically healthy, meet her special needs, educate and advocate for her, make sure she's adequately intellectually stimulated, read to her daily, play with her, minimize screen time, and help her find true peers
- Address my social-emotional needs as well as my child's, which requires researching the best

approach to dealing with the complexity of these tender issues and getting the best help, if necessary

- Procure the best healthcare and medications, if required, for all family members
- Seek out enrichment activities for my bright child
- Nurture my partner/support his career (and move, if necessary) to keep our relationship alive
- Volunteer at my daughter's school and in the community
- Keep the house clean and functioning
- Shop and cook healthy meals, prepare school lunches
- Ensure the family has appropriate clothing that's clean and fits
- Keep track of doctor, dentist, and therapy appointments, school and after-school activities, birthdays of family and friends, and social engagements
- Keep track of bills, stay within a budget
- Care for extended family members and friends in need
- Stay fit and exercise daily
- Take care of family pets
- Satisfy my intellectual needs as a lifelong learner (read, have hobbies, take classes), and maintain friendships for my social-emotional needs

- Have a career to maximize my own potential, to give back for my "gifts," and to provide for my family financially
- Be a positive role model
- Monitor my anxiety, depression, anger, and tendency to ruminate (my so-called "bad emotions"), "Don't worry, be happy!" "Smile!
- Be flexible, prioritize family needs, and be prepared to adapt to change and effectively handle emergencies as they arise

THE ENORMITY OF THESE RESPONSIBILITIES MAY REPRESENT one reason why many sampled mothers chose careers in teaching, because teaching, despite being very demanding, offers some flexibility in terms of vacation and sick days and a work schedule that mirrors their children's daily schedules. (However, the sampling approach may have influenced the high number of interviewed women in this profession.) Unfortunately, because teaching, like nursing and childcare, emphasizes caring as opposed to generating revenue for corporate America, these gifted women found themselves in jobs that, for the most part, offered low status and compensation.

Another explanation for the high number of gifted mothers in education may be related to their inherent love of learning and the joy they experience in sharing this with others. In her article "You Could Be Doing Brain Surgery: Gifted Girls Becoming Teachers," Colleen Willard-Holt shares Kerr's finding that the message to many gifted young people is that teaching is a waste of their gifts. Willard-Holt states that gifted students are often encouraged to pursue high-status, prestigious careers, and teaching does not qualify. "As women's career options have expanded into traditionally male fields, gifted women are encouraged into high-level, prestigious careers." However, she shares the findings of her research and others' showing that gifted women find teaching to be a challenging and fulfilling career, not to mention the fact that our nation's younger generation could greatly benefit from having gifted individuals as their teachers. These women felt a sense of accomplishment and contentment at pursuing a career that was in alignment with their own values and was meaningful to them, offering both emotional rewards and intellectual benefits.

However, this love of learning and their passion in handing it down to their children was evident in nearly all of the forty-three women, irrespective of their career type. Nurturing neurodiverse children can be incredibly intellectually and emotionally challenging as well as fulfilling, which helps feed a gifted mother's inner "self-actualization" lion. Gifted mother Terry Bradley describes in an article, "Gifted and Talented Women Who Are Moms," how she read voraciously about neurodiversity, went to gifted conferences, returned to school for a master's degree in gifted education, and focused on informing others about the needs and characteristics of gifted. This was true for many women in my study sample as well. Bradley stresses, "For many parents such as myself, who stayed at home with young children, there is a desire and passion to strive for something beyond just 'round the clock childcare....Although not always understood by others, my 'rage to achieve' served my children well. I couldn't be more proud of the people they have become, and I realize that my efforts helped to move them past potential barriers in the education system." Bradly goes on to quote Seiger, saying, "Women channel their desire for knowledge in a variety of directions...They pursue all there is to know about every stage and phase of their children's lives and find fulfillment in doing so."

The interviewed mothers' lives were incredibly dynamic throughout the course of their parenting journey. Successfully adapting to, and at times even welcoming, changes while raising children required developing a growth mindset (according to Dweck in *Mindset*, this means believing that one's abilities and qualities can be improved and cultivated through effort, learning, and persistence) and helping family members do this as well. One of the interviewed women described this circuitous path to self-actualizing as a gifted mother:

> "When my daughter was born...I was home with her until she was about eighteen months old, and then I went back [to teaching] and worked for one year. It took until about October when my husband and I had a discussion about this, and he stated, 'You know if we can swing this, teaching and raising children just isn't going to be a good mix in our house.' So after that one year, I stopped teaching. My son was on his way, and I stayed home with them until my daughter was in the fifth grade and my son was in second. And then I went back to work half time...until my daughter was in the middle of her senior year in high school when I went full time with the anticipation of college tuition...Teaching

is a very flexible career…and I was fortunate that my husband's business, he's been self-employed all these years…was able to support us, and we were willing to make the delayed gratification we needed to so I could be home and spend more time with the kids…I feel really lucky. All my friends have retired before me now, but you know! [Laughter]… At the moment, I'm an elementary mathematics specialist, so I work with kindergartners through fifth graders in all kinds of different ways. I've been at this current position for four years, and every year is different…I always liked math. I'm just a logical thinker type, and I just had some experiences when I was young going through my own education that kind of…if I had been younger, I might not have been a teacher. I might have been an accountant or something, but my background and age was 'Well, you're going to be either a teacher or a nurse, because those careers will let you always support yourself if your husband can't'.…I actually started my career as an elementary classroom teacher and got my master's in reading. So then I was a reading specialist for a while, but there were opportunities that came along for me to…you know, it's kind of Forrest Gumping your way into things. When I was coming back to teach, after I took those years off with the kids, I was going to job share with the woman who actually was the first-grade teacher for both of my children, because she wanted to take a year to work half time to be with her son. She wanted to do the literacy activities in the morning, so I needed to do math in the afternoon. So they sent me to a three-week-long math workshop during the summer. Then I kind of got focused on math, and when that job was over at the end of the year, this other half-time job in math opened at the school where I am now...I enjoyed it...And then I happened to have the opportunity to attend a three-year-long math educators program at the university here, and it got me going even more...I was busy [with this additional workload], but they paid us, and I was given college credit for the classes so I could get an endorsement as a mathematics specialist. When I went back to work full time, I worked at this job at the elementary school half time, and then I was a district-level mathematics specialist, which just let me do all kinds of other things. So there you go."

This mother's description of how her professional life unfolded, which she called "Forrest Gumping," provides a great description for the way many of the sampled mothers managed to creatively combine their need to self-actualize with prioritizing the needs of their family. As de Marneffe so wisely notes, the adaptations required of mothers may at first seem bittersweet because of their family limitations, but as shown in this sample, these adaptations often result in a far richer and more creative life filled with both caring and professional work in which relationships are central. The challenges these gifted mothers faced trying to self-actualize may be a blessing in disguise, forcing these bright females to use their unique talents and skills to create a new paradigm of utility to both males and females. This paradigm provides an innovative approach in our culture for leading a more fulfilling life than the greedy jobs designed by our corporate culture for most professionals. The struggle inherent in a gifted mother's challenge to self-actualize in both the public and private spheres provided the sampled mothers with fertile ground in which to grow and develop new talents, interests, and life strategies. This led to more work-life balance during their caregiving years, resulting in a life that was exciting and fulfilling, and it created the context for personal and professional growth—feeding their souls as well as their lions. It also enabled them to more successfully nurture a future generation of gifted girls who could maximize their potential based on an innovative approach to combining work and motherhood (if they choose to have children) when they venture into the fray. And if males eventually embrace this model as well, this will free them up to experience the joys and fulfillment caregiving as equals with their partners can bring.

TAKING THE LONG VIEW

Most of the forty-three sampled mothers were involved in income-producing work that added up to periods ranging from ten to thirty-six years. This included periods before and after raising children, demonstrating that life, for most of us fortunate souls, is long, and sadly, our offspring's childhoods end too soon—although this realization typically comes to most of us only after it's over! As a result, these years before and after serving as primary caregivers allowed for "unhindered" self-actualization opportunities for many gifted women. This was demonstrated by a number of women in the study who, having raised their children, were able to focus full time on their passions and discover new ones. And because prioritizing family often meant moving in and out of the workforce, this created the context for them to work in different positions that enhanced their awareness of various career options and helped them realize a number of different interests and passions over their lifetime. Having an empty nest meant they also "flew the coop," putting to good use the skills they gained over the years as both caregivers and in the work world to enhance their contribution to society in a new, more valuable way. In many cases, their adult gifted daughters cheered them on and expressed great pride in their mother's pursuits, which included writing musicals and novels, returning to school for a PhD, teaching, and working full time in the corporate world.

One mother got her pilot's license at age sixty, and when she called her daughter to tell her, her daughter shared the news loudly and proudly with her colleagues within earshot on Wall Street. Another mother claimed during the interview that she had had more than ten careers. She started off as a teacher, got a master's degree in counseling, was director of counseling at a small private school, became a professor in educational psychology at a small university, got married, worked for the State Rehabilitation Commission, moved for her husband's career, worked for a nonprofit for eleven years, developing more than five hundred jobs for the blind, served on the President's Committee for Employment of the Handicapped, was the general contractor and interior designer of her family home, started an interior design business, quit to deal with family issues, developed a new recipe and started her own company to sell this product, took marketing classes, worked for a startup for a year that didn't get funding, interviewed for part-time jobs because her daughter was still in school, was hired ("after dyeing my gray hair") as a marketing and PR consultant, worked full-time for a tech company, and decided she was done with the business world. She got a job at a leading university where she's been for more than six years, now serving as chairperson for a committee to improve the effectiveness of the university. As an added bonus, she said, "I don't have to dye my hair anymore."

These cases exemplify that childbearing and childrearing absorb, according to de Marneffe, "but a small portion of women's adult life span and should point us toward prizing this brief period of our lives...and not just on a personal or individual level; as a culture, we need to express our recognition of its value through our laws, our policies concerning work and family, and our theories of psychological development."

A NEW PARADIGM

Golden notes this in *Career and Family:* "Due in part to the entrenched gender norms...even ambitious, talented women have felt the need to slow down their careers for the greater good of their family. *Men are able to have a family and step up because women step back from their careers to provide more time for the family.* Both are deprived: men forgo time with family; women forgo career." However, by changing our perspective on what constitutes "success" in careers and life, the model for self-actualization developed by most women in my study seems like it would prove beneficial for both males and females.

The majority of interviewed mothers, propelled by their intensity, drive, curiosity, and love of learning, figured out a way to successfully adapt as gifted females raising gifted girls. The new prototype they came up with to successfully self-actualize in both realms (home and the world outside) can best be described, as the mother mentioned above put it, as "Forrest Gumping" (if, in this case, Forrest Gump was female and exceptionally bright). Like Forrest, this prototype created the context for these gifted mothers to live their lives to the fullest while focusing on what worked best for them and their families in the present moment.

Most of the mothers in the study rejected society's career script for "success" (based on money, status, and power) and focused on finding purpose and meaning in their lives, discovering, as De Marneffe notes, that mothering is one of many kinds of work perceived as meaningful by its practitioners even when society doesn't reward them handsomely. They redefined what success and giftedness meant outside of patriarchal norms, took risks, prioritized relationships, and developed a growth mindset. They also adapted to and embraced new adventures, including unique job opportunities, that presented themselves over the course of their parenting journeys. This represents an organic, off-road approach rather than a linear, singular-focused one to combining self-actualization in a career and in nurturing neurodiverse offspring. (The details describing how they created this approach will be the focus of Book Two: *Conquering the Storm*.) But generally, these gifted women, when adjusting to their motherhood role, put on a new lens through which to view self-actualization. As Dr. Paula Wilkes shared in one of our discussions,

> "Be willing to let go of your dream to get what you need. We often have blinders on that keep us narrowly focused on 'our goal' and the steps we think we have to take to achieve it…But maybe the universe has something better in mind for you and

wants to help you manifest your gifts in a different way…Take off your blinders, and explore the off-ramps along your path, and you might find yourself at a better place than anything you could have ever imagined."

CONCLUSION

Unfortunately, the Perfect Storm for gifted mothers forces us to repress our true selves and silence our needs (and those of our special needs children) along with our impulse to question why our situation is so limiting. When this occurs, an unseen hardness between us and the world forms to the point that we can't acknowledge who we truly are and what we need, even to ourselves. By responding to the pressure to prioritize others' views and needs, our ability to develop a strong sense of self dissolves. Not surprisingly, we often feel isolated, unsure of ourselves, and just plain weird, living lives others have designed for us. We may then develop internal obstacles, on top of the external ones, that repress our ability to grow and prosper. Consequently, many gifted mothers are left alone to struggle with this stifling challenge to be all they can be. And frequently, they feel like a personal failure for not achieving the impossible.

Squeezing into a cultural straitjacket that mothers have been forced into for centuries hurts us all and minimizes our positive impact on the next generation. We don't authentically show up, we don't contribute, and we stop caring. We become incapable of honest engagement and limit our gifted potential for innovation, creativity, and productivity. We lose our curiosity, compassion, and unique abilities, but most importantly, we lose our souls.

Fortunately, a number of gifted women throughout history have made the extremely difficult choice to move beyond stereotyping and provide us with amazing role models. In *Work Left Undone*, Reis describes such a woman. According to Reis, Mary Hunter Wolf, born in 1904, directed Broadway productions between 1944 and 1955. At the height of her career, a close friend died, and under considerable pressure, Wolf married her friend's widower, moved to a new state, and became a stepmother to three children between the ages of five and eleven. She grew to love the children, who became an integral part of her life. After ten years, her husband fell in love with someone else and ended the marriage, but she remained close to her children. When asked if she had any regrets about leaving Broadway at the peak of her career, she looked surprised and exclaimed, "Regrets? How could I have regrets? If I had not married him, I would not have had my children." Reis comments that the impact of caring for three children and adjusting to a new husband at age fifty, while simultaneously retiring from the theater, presented Mary with many creative options. She dedicated "her talents and energies to the arts in her adopted state" and became an educator and political force for change in urban arts education. At ninety-two, when asked about the creative cycles of her life, according to Reis, Mary held up her gracefully expressive hands and smiled.

> I believe that women's creativity evolves in a different pattern than men's. Women spend their lives moving from one creative act to another…Men, on the other hand, see an end goal and move toward the pursuit of that…That is why men are able to

achieve goals and fame more quickly...But I think that women have a richer creative journey, find joy in the diversity of their creative acts, and, in the end, enjoy the creative process so much more.

Like Mary Hunter Wolf, the heroic women in my study appeared to heartily enjoy their "creative process." They rejected the oppressive role for gifted female parents to be solely focused on being subservient, obedient, polite, and voiceless wives and mothers. They embraced motherhood as their primary focus while being open to opportunities in the public arena that didn't conflict with their parenting responsibilities. They taught themselves how to be more assertive, to ferret out necessary resources, to adapt to change, to strategize, to negotiate, and to be aggressive, when necessary, to meet their needs as well as their daughter's. They also learned to bring their honed social-emotional abilities, empathy, intelligence, high energy, conscientiousness, and leadership traits into their parenting, workplace, and communities. By resisting cultural restraints, these mothers transformed their own lives and the lives of their daughters, freeing them to become more authentic and fulfilled.

Dr. Heidi Feldman, a professor at Stanford School of Medicine, submitted a letter to the editor in 2009 to *The New York Times* regarding an article related to women and happiness. She commented,

> It's so easy to confuse happiness with ease, security, comfort, or effortlessness. But combining work and family life may increase stress. At the same time, nothing we have discovered in our modern

experience prevents confrontations with the big issues—fear, uncertainty, disappointment, and loss. But I don't know too many who, given the option, would cut the kids out of their life in order to be happier. Indeed, I'm not sure how I would answer a survey about happiness. I know that I'm grateful for a life that is full, complex, challenged, and real.

I think all the women in my study would agree wholeheartedly.

BIBLIOGRAPHY

Preface

Degaetano, Gloria. Parenting Coaching Institute. https://www.thepci.org.

de Marneffe, Daphne. *Maternal Desire*. New York: Little, Brown & Co, 2004.

Gifted Development Center. https://gifteddevelopment.org.

hooks, belle. *All About Love: New Visions*. New York: William Morrow, 1999.

Interview with Steve Jobs. Santa Clara Valley Historical Association. https://allaboutstevejobs.com/verbatim/interviews/santa_clara_1994.

Kerr, Barbara. *Smart Girls: A New Psychology of Girls, Women, and Giftedness*. Rev. ed. Tucson, AZ: Great Potential Press, 1997.

Le Guin, Ursula. K. "Commencement address at Bryn Mawr College in 1986." *Dancing at the Edge of the World: Thoughts on Words, Women, Places*. New York: Harper & Row, 1989.

Miller, Karen Maezen. *Momma Zen: Walking the Crooked Path of Motherhood*. Boston: Trumpeter Books, 2006.

Parent Coaching Institute. https://www.thepci.org.

Penley, Janet P. with Diane Elbe. *MotherStyles: Using Personality Type to Discover Your Parenting Strengths*. Boston: Da Capo Press, 2006.

Roeper, Annemarie. *The "I" of the Beholder: A Guided Journey to the Essence of a Child*. Tucson, AZ: Great Potential Press, 2007.

Silverman, Linda K. "*Appendix:* What We Have Learned about Gifted Children, 1979–1997." *Giftedness 101.* New York: Springer Publishing, 2012.

Solomon, Andrew. *Far from the Tree: Parents, Children, and the Search for Identity.* New York: Scribner, 2012.

Steinem, Gloria. *Revolution from Within: A Book of Self-Esteem.* New York: Little Brown & Co., 1991.

Wallace, David Foster. Commencement address at Kenyon College in 2005.

Chapter 1: Historical Perspective on Gender

Bem, Sandra L. *The Lenses of Gender: Transforming the Debate on Sexual Inequality.* New Haven, CT: Yale University Press, 1994.

Cohen, Nancy L. "Why America Never Had Universal Childcare." *New Republic,* April 23, 2013.

Coontz, Stephanie. "The Myth of Male Decline." *New York Times,* September 29, 2012. https://www.nytimes.com/2012/09/30/opinion/sunday/the-myth-of-male-decline.html.

Coontz, Stephanie. *The Way We Never Were: American Families and the Nostalgia Trap.* New York: Basic Books, 1993.

de Tocqueville, Alexis. "How Americans Understand the Equality of the Sexes, 1840." *Democracy in America. Vol. 2.* E-text. Charlottesville, VA: American Studies Program at the University of Virginia, 1997.

England, Paula and Su Li. "Desegregation Stalled: The Changing Gender Composition of College Majors, 1971–2002." https://journals.sagepub.com/doi/10.1177/0891243206290753.

"Equal Rights Amendment (ERA)." Wikipedia. https://www.google.com/search?q=Equal+Rights+Amendment+(ERA)%2FWikipedia&rlz=1C1CHBF_enUS993US993&oq=Equal+Rights+Amendment+(ERA)%2FWikipedia&gs_lcrp=EgZjaHJvbWUyBggAEEUYOTIHCAEQRigATIHCAIQIR

igAdIBCTEwODM0ajBqOagCALACAA&sourceid=chrome&ie=UTF-8.

Freakonomics Radio. "A New Nobel Laureate Explains the Gender Pay Gap." Interview with Claudia Goldin. Episode 232, October 9, 2023. https://freakonomics.com/podcast/a-new-nobel-laureate-explains-the-gender-pay-gap-replay.

Friedan, Betty. *The Feminine Mystique*. New York: Dell Books, 1974.

Goldin, Claudia. *Career and Family: Women's Century-Long Journey toward Equity*. Princeton, NJ: Princeton University Press, 2021.

Peterson, Esther and Winifred Conkling. *Restless: The Memoirs of Labor and Consumer Activist Esther Peterson*. Caring Publishing, 1997.

"Separate Spheres." Wikipedia. https://www.google.com/search?q=%E2%80%9DSeparate+Spheres%E2%80%9D%2FWikipedia&rlz=1C1CHBF_enUS978US978&oq=%E2%80%9DSeparate+Spheres%E2%80%9D%2FWikipedia&gs_lcrp=EgZjaHJvbWUyBggAEEUYOTIHCAEQIRigAdIBCTExMzJqMGoxNagCALACAA&sourceid=chrome&ie=UTF-8.

Williams, John. "Woman's Work and Woman's Sphere: A Study in Social Ethics, Bibliotheca Sacra (1893)." University of Washington Tacoma Digital Commons. https://digitalcommons.tacoma.us.edu.

Chapter 2: The Role of Gender in the Perfect Storm

Bem, Sandra L. *The Lenses of Gender: Transforming the Debate on Sexual Inequality*. New Haven, CT: Yale University Press, 1994.

Chemaly, Soraya. *Rage Becomes Her: The Power of Women's Anger*. New York: Atria Publishing Group, 2018.

de Tocqueville, Alexis. "How Americans Understand the Equality of the Sexes, 1840." *Democracy in America*. Vol. 2. E-text. Charlottesville, VA: American Studies Program at the University of Virginia, 1997.

Doyle, Glennon M. *Untamed.* New York: The Dial Press, 2020.

Irving, Debby. *Waking Up White and Finding Myself in the Story of Race.* Cambridge, MA: Elephant Room Press, 2014.

Kerr, Barbara. *Smart Girls: A New Psychology of Girls, Women, and Giftedness.* Rev. ed. Tucson, AZ: Great Potential Press, 1997.

Milgram, Stanley. "Obedience to Authority: The Small World Experiment (1960–1963)." Harvard University Department of Psychology. https://psychology.fas.harvard.edu/people/stanley-milgram.

Reis, Sally M. *Work Left Undone: Choices & Compromises of Talented Females.* Storrs, CT: Creative Learning Press, 1998.

Sandberg, Sheryl. *Lean In: Women, Work, and the Will to Lead.* New York: Knopf Publishing, 2013.

Stephens-Davidowitz, Seth. "Google, Tell Me. Is My Son a Genius?" *New York Times,* January 18, 2014. https://www.nytimes.com/2014/01/19/opinion/sunday/google-tell-me-is-my-son-a-genius.html.

Tunnicliffe, Ava. "Artist Audrey Wollen on the Power of Sadness." *Nylon Newsletter,* July 20, 2015. https://www.nylon.com/articles/audrey-wollen-sad-girl-theory.

Chapter 3: Historical Overview

Bem, Sandra L. *The Lenses of Gender: Transforming the Debate on Sexual Inequality.* New Haven, CT: Yale University Press, 1994.

Coontz, Stephanie. *The Way We Never Were: American Families and the Nostalgia Trap.* New York: Basic Books, 1993.

Dowd, Maureen. "What's a Modern Girl to Do?" *New York Times,* October 30, 2005. https://www.nytimes.com/2005/10/30/magazine/whats-a-modern-girl-to-do.html.

Goleman, Daniel. "75 Years Later, Study Still Tracking Geniuses." *New York Times,* March 7, 1995. https://www.nytimes.com/1995/03/07/science/75-years-later-study-still-tracking-geniuses.html.

Hewlett, Sylvia Ann. *Creating a Life: Professional Women and the Quest for Children*. New York: Miramax, 2002.

Jolly, Jennifer. "The Woman Question." In *Teaching and Counseling Gifted Girls*. S. K. Johnsen and J. Kendrick, eds. Waco, TX: Prufrock Press. 2005.

Kimura, Doreen. *Sex and Cognition*. Denver, CO: Bradford Books, 2000.

Noer, Michael. "Don't Marry Career Women." *Forbes*, August 22, 2006. https://www.forbes.com/2006/08/21/careers-marriage-dating_cx_mn_0821women/?sh=1999aaac15c7.

Reis, Sally M. *Work Left Undone: Choices & Compromises of Talented Females*. Storrs, CT: Creative Learning Press, 1998.

Roeper, Annemarie. "The Young Gifted Girl: A Contemporary View." In *Selected Writings and Speeches*. Minneapolis, MN: Free Spirit Publishing, 1995.

Shields, Stephanie A. "The Variability Hypothesis: The History of a Biological Model of Sex Differences in Intelligence." *Signs: Journal of Women in Culture and Society* 7, no. 4 (1982).

Chapter 4: The Role of Female Giftedness in the Perfect Storm

Betts, George and Maureen Neihart. "Profiles of the Gifted and Talented." *Gifted Child Quarterly* (1988).

Brooks, Arthur C. "'Success Addicts' Choose Being Special Over Being Happy." *Atlantic*, July 30, 2020.

Brown, Brené. *Daring Greatly: How the Courage to Be Vulnerable Transforms the Way We Live, Love, Parent, and Lead*. New York: Avery, 2015.

Cimpian, Andrei and Sarah-Jane Leslie. "Why Young Girls Don't Think They're Smart Enough." *New York Times*, January 26, 2017. https://www.nytimes.com/2017/01/26/well/family/whyindentyoung-girls-dont-think-they-are-smart-enough.html.

Clance, Pauline Rose and Suzanne Imes. "The Imposter Phenomenon in High Achieving Women: Dynamics and Therapeutic Intervention." *Psychotherapy: Theory, Research & Practice* 15, no. 3 (1978). https://doi.org/10.1037/h0086006.

Dabrowsk, Kazmierz. *Psychoneurosis Is Not an Illness.* London: Gryf Publications, 1972.

Doyle, Glennon M. *Untamed.* New York: Dial Press, 2020.

Dweck, Carol. *Mindset: The New Psychology of Success.* New York: Ballantine Books, 2007.

Dweck, Carol. *Self-Theories: Their Role in Motivation, Personality, and Development.* London: Psychology Press, 2000.

Fiedler. Ellen D. and Noks Nauta. "Bore-out: A Challenge for Unchallenged Gifted (Young) Adults." SENG, March 23, 2020. https://www.sengifted.org/post/bore-out-a-challenge-for-unchallenged-gifted-young-adults.

Fromm, Erich. *Escape from Freedom.* 1st ed. New York: Holt Paperbacks, 1994.

Kerr, Barbara. *Smart Girls: A New Psychology of Girls, Women, and Giftedness.* Rev. ed. Tucson, AZ: Great Potential Press, 1997.

Kochis, Ginny. "Want to Have Your Heart Broken? Take a Look at an Angry Gifted Kid." April 23, 2018. https://notsoformulaic.com/angry-gifted-kid.

Lind, Sharon. "Overexcitability and the Gifted." SENG, September 14, 2011. https://www.sengifted.org/post/overexcitability-and-the-gifted.

Lovecky, Deirdre. "Can You Hear the Flowers Singing? Issues for Gifted Adults." *Journal of Counseling and Development* 64 (May 1986). https://www.positivedisintegration.com/Lovecky1986.pdf.

McGhee, Heather. *The Sum of Us: What Racism Costs Everyone and How We Can Prosper Together.* London: One World, 2021.

Milgram, Stanley. "Obedience to Authority: The Small World Experiment (1960–1963)." Harvard University Department of Psychology. https://psychology.fas.harvard.edu/people/stanley-milgram.

National Association for Gifted Children. "Twice Exceptional Students." https://www.nagc.org/resources-publications/resources-parents/twice-exceptional-students

Norman, Philip. *John Lennon: The Life*. New York: Ecco, 2008.

Olsen, Tillie. "I Stand Here Ironing." (First appeared in *Pacific Spectator* in 1956.) *Tell Me a Riddle*. J. B. Lippincott & Co., 1961.

Piechowski, Michael M. "Giftedness for All Seasons: Inner Peace in a Time of War." Northland College, Ashland Wisconsin. Presented at the Henry B. and Jocelyn Wallace National Research Symposium on Talent Development, The University of Iowa, Iowa City, May 1991.

Post, Gail. "Why Differentiated Instruction Fails Gifted Children." *Gifted Challenges*, April 15, 2015. https://giftedchallenges.blogspot.com/2015/04/why-differentiated-instruction-fails.html.

Prober, Paula. *Journey into Your Rainforest Mind*. Eugene, OR: Luminaire Press, 2019.

Reis, Sally. "Social and Emotional Issues Faced by Gifted Girls in Elementary and Secondary School." SENG Newsletter 2 (no. 3), 1–5. https://www.sengifted.org/post/reis-giftedgirls.

Rich, Judith Harris. *Nurture Assumption: Why Children Turn Out the Way They Do*. Washington, DC: Free Press, 2009.

Roeper, Annemarie. "Asynchrony and Sensitivity." In *Off the Charts: Asynchrony and the Gifted Child*, edited by C.S. Neville, M.M. Piechowski, and S.S. Tolan, Unionville, NY: Royal Fireworks Press, 2013.

Roeper, Annemarie. *The "I" of the Beholder: A Guided Journey to the Essence of a Child*. Tucson, AZ: Great Potential Press, 2007.

Ruf, Deborah. *5 Levels of Gifted: School Issues and Educational Options*. SBC Distributors, 2009.

Ruff, Deborah. "Why It's Sometimes Hard to Find the 'Right' School for Your Gifted Child." *Medium,* June 15, 2022. https://deborahruf.medium.com/why-its-sometimes-hard-to-find-the-right-school-for-your-gifted-child-f95f08454fc6.

Silverman, Linda K. "The Social Development of the Gifted." Gifted Development Center. https://gifteddevelopment.org/musings/socialdevelopment.

Silverman, Linda K. "To Be Gifted or Feminine: The Forced Choice of Adolescence." *Journal of Secondary Gifted Education* 6 (no. 2).

Tolan, Stephanie. "Hollingworth, Dabrowski, Gandhi, Columbus, and Some Others" The History of the Columbus Group." In *Off the Charts: Asynchrony and the Gifted Child,* edited by C.S. Neville, M.M. Piechowski, and S.S. Tolan, Unionville, NY: Royal Fireworks Press, 2013.

Tolan, Stephanie. "Is It a Cheetah?" 1996. https://www.stephanietolan.com/is_it_a_cheetah.htm.

Tolan, Stephanie. *Out of Sync: Essays on Giftedness,* Unionville, NY: Royal Fireworks Press, 2016.

Tolan, Stephanie. "Self-Knowledge, Self-Esteem and the Gifted Adult." *Advanced Development Journal* 8 (1999). https://talentdevelop.com/articles/Self-Knowledge.html.

Tolan, Stephanie, Christine S. Neville, and Michael M. Piechowski, eds. *Off the Charts: Asynchrony and the Gifted Child.* Unionville, NY: Royal Fireworks Press, 2013.

Tolan, Stephanie, Elizabeth A. Meckstroth, and James T. Webb. *Guiding the Gifted Child: A Practical Source for Parents and Teachers.* Gardena, CA: SCB Distributors, 1989

Tucker, Jill. "School Funding Leaves Gifted Students Behind." *San Francisco Chronical/SF Gate Newsletter,* May 2, 2010. https://www.sfgate.com/education/article/School-funding-leaves-gifted-students-behind-3265829.php.

Tulshyan, Ruchika and Jodi-Ann Burey. "Stop Telling Women They Have Imposter Syndrome." *Harvard Business Review,*

February 11, 2021. https://hbr.org/2021/02/stop-telling-women-they-have-imposter-syndrome.

Widawsky, Shulamit. "Experience and Processing: The Funnel and Cylinder Analogy of Giftedness." *Hoagies' Gifted Education Page*. https://www.hoagiesgifted.org/metaphors.htm.

Winterbrook, Christine A. and Abby Noel Winterbrook. *Gifted Women: On Becoming Ourselves*. Lexington, MA: GHF Press, 2022.

Chapter 5: Historical Overview

Berger, Hilary. *Work Like a Mother*. https://www.worklikeamother.com.

Brown, Brené. *Braving the Wilderness: The Quest for True Belonging and the Courage to Stand Alone*. New York: Random House, 2017.

Budig, Michelle. "The Fatherhood Bonus and the Motherhood Penalty: Parenthood and the Gender Gap in Pay." *Third Way*, September 2, 2014. https://www.thirdway.org/report/the-fatherhood-bonus-and-the-motherhood-penalty-parenthood-and-the-gender-gap-in-pay.

Collins, Caitlyn. *Making Motherhood Work: How Women Manage Careers and Caregiving*. Princeton, NJ: Princeton University Press, 2019.

Coontz, Stephanie. *The Way We Never Were: American Families and the Nostalgia Trap*. New York: Basic Books, 1993.

de Marneffe, Daphne. *Maternal Desire*. New York: Little, Brown & Co, 2004.

DeGaetano, Gloria. "Screen-Free Week: And What About Next Week?" May 3, 2017. https://gloriadegaetano.com/screen-free-week-next-week.

Ehrenreich, Barbara and Deirdre English. *For Her Own Good: Two Centuries of Experts' Advice to Women*. Garden City, NY: Anchor Press: 2005.

Ember, Sydney. "What If It Never Gets Easier to Be a Working Parent?" *New York Times*, October 30, 2021. https://www.nytimes.com/2021/10/30/business/paid-family-leave-working-parents.html.

Global Non-Violent Data Base."Feminists Sit-In at Ladies Home Journal to Protest the Magazine's Depiction of Women, 1970." https://nvdatabase.swarthmore.edu/content/feminists-sit-ladies-home-journal-protest-magazine-s-depiction-women-1970.

Grose, Jessica. "Mothers Are the Shock Absorbers of Our Society." *New York Times*, October 14, 2020. https://www.nytimes.com/2020/10/14/parenting/working-moms-job-loss-coronavirus.html

Harris, Judith Rich. *The Nurture Assumption: Why Children Turn Out The Way They Do*. New York: Free Press, 1998.

Hays, Sharon. *The Cultural Contradictions of Motherhood*. New Haven, CT: Yale University Press, 1998.

Hochschild, Arlie. *The Second Shift: Working Parents and the Revolution at Home*. London: Penguin Books, 2012.

Hulbert, Ann. *Raising America: Experts, Parents, and a Century of Advice About Children*. Visalia, CA: Vintage, 2004.

Human Rights Watch. "Failing Its Families: Lack of Paid Leave and Work-Family Supports in the US." February 23, 2011. https://www.hrw.org/report/2011/02/23/failing-its-families/lack-paid-leave-and-work-family-supports-us.

Kashan, Julie, Sarah Jane Glynn, and Amanda Novello. "How COVID-19 Sent Women's Workforce Progress Backward." *American Progress*, October 20, 2020. https://www.americanprogress.org/article/covid-19-sent-womens-workforce-progress-backward.

Kerber, Linda K. "The Republican Mother: Women and the Enlightenment—An American Perspective." Special Issue: An American Enlightenment. *American Quarterly* 28, no. 2 (1976). https://www.jstor.org/stable/2712349?origin=crossref.

Kerber, Linda K. *Women of the Republic: Intellect and Ideology in Revolutionary America*. Chapel Hill, NC: The University of North Carolina Press, 1997.

Koren, Marina. "Why Men Thought Women Weren't Made to Vote." *Atlantic*, July 11, 2019.

Lenz, Lyz. "America Has Been Failing Mothers for a Long Time. The Pandemic Made It Clear What Needs to Happen." *TIME*, August 6, 2020. https://time.com/5876597/motherhood-america.

Lundberg, Ferdinand and Marynia Farnham. *Modern Woman: The Lost Sex*. New York: Harper and Brothers, 1947.

Miller, Claire Cain. "The Pandemic Created a Child-Care Crisis. Mothers Bore the Burden." *New York Times*, May 17, 2021. https://www.nytimes.com/interactive/2021/05/17/upshot/women-workforce-employment-covid.html.

Miller, Claire Cain. "The Relentlessness of Modern Parenting." *New York Times*, December 25, 2018. https://www.nytimes.com/2018/12/25/upshot/the-relentlessness-of-modern-parenting.html.

Nafisi, Azar. *Reading Lolita in Tehran: A Memoir*. New York: Random House, 2008.

Rich, Adrienne. *Of Woman Born: Motherhood as Experience and Institution*. New York: W. W. Norton & Co., 1995.

Ross, Ellen, *Love and Toil: Motherhood in Outcast London 1870–1918*. Oxford: Oxford University Press, 1993.

Santhanam, Laura. "It's Time to Recognize the Damage of Childbirth, Doctors and Mothers Say." *PBS News Hour*, May 7, 2021.

Slaughter, Anne-Marie. "Rosie Could Be a Riveter Only Because of a Care Economy. Where Is Ours?" *New York Times*, April 16, 2021. https://www.nytimes.com/2021/04/16/opinion/care-economy-infrastructure-rosie-the-riveter.html.

Sorman. Joy. *Life Sciences*, Amherst, MA: Restless Books, 2021

Spock, Benjamin. *The Common Sense Book of Baby and Child Care*. New York: Duell, Sloan and Pierce, 1962.

Thorbecke, Catherine. "1 in 4 Women Considering Leaving Workforce or Downshifting Careers Because of COVID-19." ABC News Report, September 29, 2020. https://abcnews.go.com/Business/women-leaving-workforce-downshifting-careers-covid-19-report/story?id=73310740.

Umansky, Lauri. *Motherhood Reconceived: Feminism and the Legacies of the 60s*. New York: New York University Press, 1996.

US Equal Employment Opportunity Commission. "Fact Sheet: Pregnancy Discrimination in the Workplace." https://www.eeoc.gov/laws/guidance/fact-sheet-pregnancy-discrimination.

USAFacts. "How Much Child Support Do Parents Actually Receive?" March 28, 2023. https://usafacts.org/articles/how-much-child-support-do-parents-actually-receive/#:~:text=About%2030%25%20of%20parents%20who,that%20receive%20child%20support%20payments.

Vandenberg-Daves, Jodi. *Modern Motherhood: An American History*. New Brunswick, NJ: Rutgers University Press, 2014.

Wilkerson, Isabel. *Caste: The Origins of Our Discontents*. New York: Random House, 2020.

Wittner, Michael. "As Childcare Costs Soar, Here's What Parents in California Are Paying." *Patch*, January 26, 2024. https://patch.com/california/across-ca/child-care-costs-spiral-here-s-what-parents-ca-are-paying.

Wylie, Philip. *Generation of Vipers*. Champaign, IL: Dalkey Archive Press, 1996.

Zinn, Howard. *The People's History of the United States*. New York: Harper Perennial Modern Classics, 2015.

Chapter 6: Gifted Motherhood's Role in the Perfect Storm

Bem, Sandra L. *The Lenses of Gender: Transforming the Debate on Sexual Inequality.* New Haven, CT: Yale University Press, 1994.

Bridges, William. *Transitions: Making Sense of Life's Changes.* Boston: DaCapo Lifelong Books, 2019.

Doyle, Glennon M. *Untamed.* New York: The Dial Press, 2020.

Hasseldine, Rosijke. *The Mother-Daughter Puzzle: A New Generational Understanding of the Mother-Daughter Relationship.* Bedford, UK: Women's Bookshelf Publishing, 2017.

hooks, belle. *All About Love: New Visions.* New York: William Morrow, 1999.

Joyce, Amy. "Parenting: We Celebrate Growth, and Mourn Little Losses Along the Way." *Washington Post,* June 23, 2022. https://www.washingtonpost.com/parenting/2022/06/23/parenting-little-losses/.

Kerr, Barbara. *Smart Girls: A New Psychology of Girls, Women, and Giftedness.* Rev. ed. Scottsdale, AZ: Gifted Psychology Press, 1997.

Klein, Barbara. *Raising Gifted Kids: Everything You Need to Know to Help Your Exceptional Child Thrive.* New York: AMACOM, 2006.

Kochis, Ginny. "It's Not Just in Your Head: Self-Care for Moms of Gifted Children." February 13, 2008. https://notsoformulaic.com/self-care-moms-gifted-children.

Nin, Anais. Good Reads. https://www.goodreads.com/quotes/64155-we-do-not-grow-absolutely-chronologically-we-grow-sometimes-in#:~:text=Sign%20Up%20Now-,We%20do%20not%20grow%20absolutely%2C%20chronologically.,We%20grow%20partially.

Post, Gail. *The Gifted Parenting Journey: A Guide to Self-Discovery and Support for Families of Gifted Children.* Goshen, KY: Gifted Unlimited, 2022.

Rimlinger, Natalie. "Dwelling on the Right Side of the Curve: An Exploration of the Psychological Wellbeing of Parents of Gifted Children." The Australian National University, 2016. https://openresearchrepository.anu.edu.au/bitstream/1885/110543/1/Rimlinger%20Thesis%202016.pdf.

Roeper, Annemarie. *The "I" of the Beholder: A Guided Journey to the Essence of a Child.* Tucson, AZ: Great Potential Press, 2007.

Strayed, Cheryl. *Tiny Beautiful Things: Advice from Dear Sugar.* New York: Vintage, 2022.

Tolan, Stephanie. "Giftedness as Asynchronous Development." 2007. https://www.stephanietolan.com/gt_as_asynch.htm.

US Census Bureau. January 30, 2018. https://www.census.gov/newsroom/press-releases/2018/cb18-tps03.html.

Widawsky, Shulamit. "Experience and Processing: The Funnel and Cylinder Analogy of Giftedness." *Hoagies' Gifted Education Page.* https://www.hoagiesgifted.org/metaphors.htm.

Zevin, Gabrielle, *Tomorrow, and Tomorrow, and Tomorrow.* New York: Knopf, 2022.

Chapter 7: Challenges Within the Family

Corrigan, Kelly. *The Middle Place.* San Francisco: Hatchette Books, 2009.

Dweck, Carol. *Mindset: The New Psychology of Success.* New York: Ballantine Books, 2007.

Gilligan, Carol. *In a Different Voice: Psychological Theory and Women's Development.* Cambridge, MA: Harvard University Press, 2016.

Hornung, Tonilyn. "I'm a Parenting Perfectionist and It's Going to Be the Death of Me," *SheKnows,* June 21, 2019. https://www.sheknows.com/parenting/articles/2056045/parenting-perfectionism-will-kill-me.

Kochis, Ginny. "It's Not Just in Your Head: Self-Care for Moms of Gifted Children." February 13, 2008. https://notsoformulaic.com/self-care-moms-gifted-children.

Kuipers, William. *Enjoying the Gift of Being Uncommon: Extra Intelligent, Intense, and Effective.* Scotts Valley, CA: CreateSpace Independent Publishing Platform, 2011.

Lovecky, Deirdre. "Can You Hear the Flowers Singing? Issues for Gifted Adults." *Journal of Counseling and Development* 64 (May 1986). https://www.positivedisintegration.com/Lovecky1986.pdf.

Miller, Alice. *The Drama of the Gifted Child: The Search for the True Self.* New York: Basic Books, 1997.

Papadopoulos, Dimitrios. "Parenting the Exceptional Social-Emotional Needs of Gifted and Talented Children: What Do We Know?" Multidisciplinary Digital Publishing Institute, November 8, 2021. https://www.ncbi.nlm.nih.gov/pmc/articles/PMC8624036.

Roeper, Annemarie. *The "I" of the Beholder: A Guided Journey to the Essence of a Child.* Tucson, AZ: Great Potential Press, 2007.

Silverman, Linda and Kathi Kearney. "Parents of the Extraordinarily Gifted." *Hoagies' Gifted Page.* https://www.hoagiesgifted.org/parents_of_eg.htm.

Smith, Emilie. "When I Replaced Strength with Vulnerability, I Grew Closer to My Daughters." *Vermont Moms,* April 23, 2018. https://vermontmoms.com/vulnerability-strength-in-parenting/#:~:text=At%20that%20moment%20where%20my,connect%20on%20a%20different%20level.

Strout, Elizabeth. *The Burgess Boys: A Novel.* New York: Random House: 2014.

Waldman, Ayelet. *Bad Mother: A Chronicle of Maternal Crimes, Minor Calamities, and Occasional Moments of Grace.* New York: Anchor, 2010.

Whippman, Ruth. "Can We Really Love Our Children Unconditionally?" *New York Times,* November 29, 2022. https://www.nytimes.com/2022/11/29/opinion/children-unconditional-love.html.

Chapter 8: Challenges Outside the Family

Clark, Barbara. *Growing Up Gifted: Developing the Potential of Children at School and at Home.* 8th ed. Saddle River, NJ: Pearson Education, 2012.

Fiedler, Ellen D. and Noks Nauta. "Bore-out: A Challenge for Unchallenged Gifted (Young) Adults." SENG Resources, March 23, 2020. https://www.sengifted.org/post/bore-out-a-challenge-for-unchallenged-gifted-young-adults.

Gross, Miraca U. M. "Play Partner, or Sure Shelter: What Gifted Children Look for in Friendship." SENG, May 2, 2002. https://www.sengifted.org/post/play-partner-or-sure-shelter-what-gifted-children-look-for-in-friendship.

Gross, Miraca. "Tips for Parents: Gifted Children's Friendships." Seminar hosted by Gross, 2006. Posted on the Davidson Institute website, June 24, 2021.

Halsted, Judith Wynn. *Some of My Best friends Are Books: Guiding Gifted Readers.* 3rd ed. Gardena, CA: SCB Distributors, 2009.

Hildenbrand, Kim. "My Son Is A 'Gifted Child'. Here's Why Raising Him Has Been Anything But Easy." *Huffington Post,* 2021. https://www.huffpost.com/entry/gifted-child-parenting-is-hard_n_5c0808d8e4b069028dc5ef79.

Kerr, Barbara and Robyn McKay. *Smart Girls in the 21st Century.* Gardena, CA: SCB Distributors, 2014.

Kochis, Ginny. Facebook post, Not So Formulaic, February 3, 2021.

Marshall, Stephanie. *The Power to Transform: Leadership that Brings Learning and Schooling to Life.* San Francisco: Jossey Bass, 2006.

Miller, Karen Maezen, keynote speaker, Palo Alto Mothers' Symposium, Stanford University, March 7, 2009.

Neihart, Maureen. "Finding True Peers." *Gifted Today*, October 2, 2003. https://blogs.tip.duke.edu/giftedtoday/2003/10/02/finding-true-peers.

Post, Gail. "Is It All Right to Feel Proud of Your Gifted Child?" Gifted Challenges, May 1, 2019. https://giftedchallenges.blogspot.com/2019/05/is-it-all-right-to-feel-proud-of-your.html.

Post, Gail. "Welcome to Gifted Parenting: A checklist of Emotions." Gifted Challenges, July 16, 2018.

Post, Gail. "Why Differentiated Instruction Fails Gifted Children." Gifted Challenges. April 15, 2015. https://giftedchallenges.blogspot.com/2015/04/why-differentiated-instruction-fails.html.

Ruf, Deborah. "A Reflective Conversation with Deborah Ruf, President, Talentigniter, USA." Interview with Michael F. Shaughnessy. January 2013. https://journals.sagepub.com/doi/10.1177/0261429413487400.

Silverman, Linda K. *Counselling the Gifted and Talented*. Denver, CO: Love Publishing Co., 2000.

Tannen, Deborah. *You Just Don't Understand: Women and Men in Conversation*. New York: William Morrow Paperbacks, 2007.

Webb, James, Janet L. Gore, Edward R. Amend, and Arlene R. DeVries. *A Parent's Guide to Gifted Children*. Gardena, CA: SCB Distributors, 2007.

Winterbrook, Christine A. and Abby Noel Winterbrook. *Gifted Women: On Becoming Ourselves*. Lexington, MA: GHF Press, 2022.

Wurman, Jill Williford. "Beyond Playdates: Finding Gifted Friends." Grayson School Gifted blog. https://thegraysonschool.org/our-gifted-blog.

Wurman, Jill Williford. "Warning: Parenting a Gifted Child May be Hazardous to Your (Mental) Health?" Grayson School blog. https://thegraysonschool.org/coming-soon-gifted-blog.

Chapter 9: Challenges Finding Professional Support

Amend, Edward and Richard Clouse. "The Role of Physicians in the Lives of Gifted Children." *Parenting Gifted Children: The Authoritative Guide from the National Association of Gifted Children*, chapter 31. New York: Rutledge, 2010.

Azpeitia, Lynne and Mary Rocamora. "Misdiagnosis of the Gifted." *Mensa Bulletin*. Talent Development Resources, November 1994. https://talentdevelop.com/articles/Page10.html.

Azpeitia, Lynne. "Successful Coaching and Psychotherapy with Multi-Talented Gifted and Creative Adults" Gifted, Talented and Creative Adults. https://gifted-adults.com/therapy-coaching-with-gifted-adults.

Bader, Michael. "Are Parents Always to Blame? A Therapist Answers." *Medium*, April 1, 2016. https://medium.com/@michaelbader/are-parents-always-to-blame-a-therapist-answers-c0894aaa6457.

Kuzujanakis, Marianne. "The Misunderstood Face of Giftedness." *Huffington Post*, 2005. https://www.huffpost.com/entry/gifted-children_b_2948258.

Piechowski, Michael. *Mellow Out, They Say. If I Only Could: Intensities and Sensitivities of the Young and Bright*. Yunasa Books, 2006.

Webb, James, Janet L. Gore, Edward R. Amend, and Arlene R. DeVries. *A Parent's Guide to Gifted Children*. Gardena, CA: SCB Distributors, 2007.

Webb, James. "Dabrowski's Theory and Existential Depression in Gifted Children and Adults." Davidson Institute, July 9, 2020. https://www.davidsongifted.org/gifted-blog/dabrowskis-theory-and-existential-depression-in-gifted-children-and-adults.

Yermish, Aimee. "Clues on Finding a Therapist for a Gifted Client." da Vinci Learning Center, August 20, 2010. https://davincilearning.wordpress.com/2010/08/20/clues-on-finding-a-therapifor-a-gifted-client.

Chapter 10: Self-Actualizing for Gifted Mothers in the Perfect Storm

Bradley, Terry. "Gifted and Talented Women who are Moms." July 30, 2015. https://www.terrybradleygifted.com/_files/ugd/9db903_e54e1dd9e96341ba9456826563ba0e91.pdf.

Caro, Jane. *Accidental Feminists*. Carlton VIC 3053, AUS: Melbourne University Publishing, 2019.

Carter, Allison B. "A Stay-At-Home-Parent Is Not a Luxury." *New York Times*, March 12, 2015. https://archive.nytimes.com/parenting.blogs.nytimes.com/2015/03/12/stay-at-home-parent-is-not-a-luxury.

Catton, Eleanor. *Birnam Wood: A Novel*. New York: Farrar, Straus and Giroux, 2023.

David, Susan. "The Gift and Power of Emotional Courage." TED Talk, November 2017. https://www.ted.com/talks/susan_david_the_gift_and_power_of_emotional_courage?language=en.

de Marneffe, Daphne. *Maternal Desire*. New York: Little, Brown & Co, 2004.

Dweck, Carol. *Mindset: The New Psychology of Success*. New York: Ballantine Books, 2007.

Goldin, Claudia. *Career and Family: Women's Century-Long Journey toward Equity*. Princeton, NJ: Princeton University Press, 2021.

Levine, Madeline. *Price of Privilege: How Parental Pressure and Material Advantage Are Creating a Generation of Disconnected and Unhappy Kids*. San Francisco: Harper Perennial, 2008.

Reis, Sally M. *Work Left Undone: Choices & Compromises of Talented Females*. Storrs, CT: Creative Learning Press, 1998.

Rumi (Jalal ad-Din Muhammad ar-Rumi). https://www.goodreads.com/quotes/812358-sell-your-cleverness-and-buy-bewilderment-cleverness-is-mere-opinion.

Seiger, Belinda. "The Special Challenges of Highly Intelligent and Talented Women Who Are Moms." High Ability blog. https://highability.org/the-special-challenges-of-highly-intelligent-and-talented-women-who-are-moms.

Silverman, Linda K. and Nancy B. Miller. "A Feminine Perspective of Giftedness." *International Handbook on Giftedness.* New York: Springer, 2009. https://link.springer.com/chapter/10.1007/978-1-4020-6162-2_5.

Slaughter, Anne-Marie. "Why Women Still Can't Have It All." *Atlantic,* July/August 2012. https://www.theatlantic.com/magazine/archive/2012/07/why-women-still-cant-have-it-all/309020.

Tolan, Stephanie. "Is It a Cheetah?" 1996. https://www.stephanietolan.com/is_it_a_cheetah.htm.

Willard-Holt, Colleen. "You Could Be Doing Brain Surgery." *Gifted Child Quarterly* 52, no. 4 (2008).

Conclusion

Feldman, Heidi. Letter to the editor (September 20, 2009) regarding *New York Times* article by Maureen Dowd, "Women and the Pursuit of Happiness." https://www.nytimes.com/2009/09/22/opinion/l22dowd.html.

Reis, Sally M. *Work Left Undone: Choices & Compromises of Talented Females.* Storrs, CT: Creative Learning Press, 1998.

ACKNOWLEDGMENTS

Caring and bright females made this book possible. The origin of this study was sparked by my two daughters. The great adventure I experienced raising them triggered my curiosity and growing awareness of giftedness, both personally and professionally.

I am also most grateful to the mothers and daughters who so openly shared their innermost thoughts and deeply personal experiences about growing up gifted and nurturing female giftedness. The assistance given so generously to me by two experts in the field of giftedness, Dr. Carol Dweck, an internationally renowned professor of psychology at Stanford University, and Dr. Paula Wilkes, a specialist with Summit Center-Los Angeles, was invaluable. The help in publicizing a request for study participants by the women I contacted at SENG, NAGC, and Gifted Homeschoolers Forum was critical in developing the study sample. And the predominantly female staff at Luminaire Press was incredibly skilled and supportive in guiding me as a novice in the publishing world.

And then there's my husband (the token male in this effort) whose ongoing support was key as he never fails to demonstrate what "love as a verb" looks like in real life for both our family as well as anyone lucky enough to cross his path.

To all these very special individuals, thank you, thank you.

www.ingramcontent.com/pod-product-compliance
Lightning Source LLC
LaVergne TN
LVHW021220080526
838199LV00084B/4291